NUMBER 123

Yale French Studies

Rethinking Claude Lévi-Strauss (1908–2009)

Yale French Studies

Robert Doran, *Special editor for this issue*

Alyson Waters, *Managing editor*

Editorial board: Alice Kaplan (Chair), R. Howard
   Bloch, Edwin Duval, Thomas Kavanagh,
   Christopher L. Miller, Maurice Samuels, Christopher
   Semk, Edwige Tamalet-Talbayev, Yue Zhuo

Editorial assistant: Elizabeth K. Hebbard

Editorial office: 82-90 Wall Street, Room 308

Mailing address: P.O. Box 208251, New Haven,
   Connecticut 06520-8251

Sales and subscription office:

Yale University Press, P.O. Box 209040

New Haven, Connecticut 06520-0940

Designed by James J. Johnson and set in Trump
   Medieval Roman by Newgen North America.
   Printed in the United States of America by Sheridan
   Books, Ann Arbor, Michigan.

ISSN 044-0078

ISBN for this issue 978-0-300-19020-5

ROBERT DORAN

Editor's Preface: Rethinking
Claude Lévi-Strauss (1908–2009)

This issue of *Yale French Studies* commemorates, reassesses, develops, and debates the work of Claude Lévi-Strauss, who died on October 30, 2009, at the age of 100. One of the most celebrated, original, and influential writers and thinkers of the twentieth century, Lévi-Strauss casts a long shadow over many areas of inquiry, including ethnology, cultural anthropology, literary studies, linguistics, philosophy, Marxist theory, feminism, psychoanalysis, and religious studies. Though most famous for his role in the mid-twentieth-century movement of structuralism, Lévi-Strauss's work has of late experienced a kind of renaissance. The publication, in 2008, of a large selection of his works (chosen by Lévi-Strauss himself) in the prestigious "Pléiade" edition,[1] in addition to the recent spate of monographs and collective works devoted to his oeuvre—most notably, the *Cambridge Companion to Lévi-Strauss* (2008), edited by Boris Wiseman (a contributor to this volume) and the massive (482-page) special issue of the *Cahiers de l'Herne* (2004), edited by Michel Izard—announce a new chapter in the development and reception of Lévi-Strauss's thought.[2]

1. Claude Lévi-Strauss, *Œuvres*, ed. Vincent Debaene *et al* (Paris: Gallimard, Bibliothèque de la Pléiade, 2008). The prestige of this edition consecrated Lévi-Strauss as a classical writer in the French intellectual tradition. It was also quite popular: it has sold nearly 30,000 copies since its publication and was reviewed in a 2008 issue of the *Times Literary Supplement*, whose cover read "Lévi-Strauss at 100."

2. Monographs on Lévi-Strauss published just during in the past five years include: Patrick Wilcken, *Claude Lévi-Strauss: The Poet in the Laboratory* (London: Bloomsbury, 2011); Anton Fischer, *Natur und Kultur in der Literatur nach Claude Lévi-Strauss* (Leipzig: Leipziger Universitätsverlag, 2011); Vincent Debaene and Frédéric Keck, *Claude Lévi-Strauss: l'homme au regard éloigné* (Paris: Gallimard, 2009); Camilla Pagani, *Genealogia del primitivo: il Musée du quai Branly, Lévi-Strauss e la scrittura etnografica* (Castel d'Ario: Negretto, 2009); Marcus Dick Welt, *Struktur, Denken. Philosophische Untersuchungen zu Claude Lévi-Strauss* (Würzburg: Königs-

YFS 123, *Rethinking Claude Lévi-Strauss (1908–2009)*, ed. Doran, © 2013 by Yale University.

"Rethinking Claude Lévi-Strauss" is certainly part of this revival of or reengagement with Lévi-Strauss, but it differs from the above-mentioned publications in that it does not strive to offer a panoramic or a specialist's view of Lévi-Strauss's oeuvre. It endeavors, on the one hand, to show how Lévi-Strauss's thought can be considered from a multiplicity of perspectives, most of which lie outside the narrow precincts of "anthropology," and, on the other, to illustrate how an engagement with Lévi-Strauss can be productive for today's leading intellectuals, for many of this volume's contributors are influential thinkers in their own right. The essays in this collection thus portray Lévi-Strauss as a vibrant presence in a wide variety of contemporary discussions.

In 1966, *Yale French Studies* published a double issue entitled "Structuralism." The volume covered the rise and influence of this new movement in the areas of linguistics, anthropology, art, psycho-analysis (the section was actually called "psychiatry"), and literature, and included essays by Lévi-Strauss, Jacques Lacan, Geoffrey Hartman, and Michael Riffaterre. The issue featured some older material (Lacan's "The Insistence of the Letter in the Unconscious," 1957), but also broke new ground by publishing the first English translation of Lévi-Strauss's "overture" to *Le cru et le cuit* (1964), a book that appeared in English translation in 1969.[3] In his introduction to the 1966 volume, Jacques Ehrmann commented on the "enthusiasm" for this new intellectual movement:

> We shall not speculate at any length on the reasons behind the French enthusiasm for this new "ism." It may result from a combination of various factors such as the centralization of French intellectual life in Paris, the tendency of French intellectual milieus to think in terms of schools of thought and follow in the steps of eminent figures, the fairly homogeneous tradition of Hegeliano-Marxist theory around which issues crystallize, the end of the French colonial wars which, given the semi-failure of engagement theories, allowed this new kind of formalism to gain ground.[4]

---

hausen & Neumann, 2008); Emmanuel Désveaux, *Au-delà du structuralisme: six méditations sur Claude Lévi-Strauss* (Paris: Éditions Complexe, 2008); Claude Imbert, *Lévi-Strauss, le passage du nord-ouest: précédé d'un texte de Claude Lévi-Strauss, Indian cosmetics* (Paris: Herne, 2008).

3. Lévi-Strauss, *The Raw and the Cooked* (New York: Harper & Row, 1969).

4. *Structuralism*, ed. and intro. Jacques Ehrmann (New York: Anchor Books, 1970), viii; originally published as *Yale French Studies* 36/37 (1966).

Ehrmann further advises the reader to be cognizant of the "fashion-able" aspect of structuralism and of the importance of not accepting it "uncritically."[5]

As it turned out, 1966 proved to be the high-water mark of struc-turalism in the United States. In the same year, a symposium was convened at The Johns Hopkins University, boldly entitled "The Languages of Criticism and the Sciences of Man: The Structuralist Controversy" (organized by Eugene Donato, Richard Macksey, and René Girard, and later published in book form),[6] where an obscure figure named Jacques Derrida delivered a scathing assessment of Lévi-Strauss's work, which would become the siren call for a new current of thought.[7] This current crystallized ten years later with the English translation of Derrida's *Of Grammotology* (1976), a polemical tome that brought together German phenomenology with a critique of Rousseau and Lévi-Strauss. With the ascendancy of Derrida and "de-construction" in the United States, structuralism quickly receded into the background. Though it would still continue to exert considerable influence in France, particularly in the literary sphere (in the works of Roland Barthes, Gérard Genette, and Tzvetan Todorov), where it was seen as a kind of formalism, the vibrancy that had characterized the movement had largely been lost by the end of the 1970s. In fact, as the popularity of "French Theory" grew in the United States, particularly in the field of literary studies, the first contact with structuralism, and with Lévi-Strauss, most often came via its "poststructuralist" cri-tique. Thus, at least with regard to its reception in American depart-ments of literature, structuralism was in many respects dead on ar-rival; Lévi-Strauss became famous as a figure who was already passé.

However, the situation was quite different among American an-thropologists, who saw Lévi-Strauss as an important ethnologist even before he became known in France. Lévi-Strauss spent the years 1941–48 living in the United States, mostly in New York, where he taught at the New School for Social Research and became acquainted with the founder of American anthropology, Franz Boas, before his death in

5. Ibid.

6. *The Structuralist Controversy: The Languages of Criticism and the Sciences of Man*, ed. Richard Macksey and Eugene Donato (Baltimore: Johns Hopkins University Press, 2007 [40th Anniversary Edition]).

7. See Jacques Derrida, "Structure, Sign, and Play in the Discourse of the Human Sciences," in *The Structuralist Controversy*, 247–72. This essay was also published in Derrida, *Writing and Difference*, trans. Alan Bass (London: Routledge, 1978), 278–94.

1942.[8] He also frequented Boas's American students, including Margaret Mead and Robert Lowie, and, drawing on his fieldwork in Brazil in 1935–39, contributed articles to the *Handbook of South-American Indians* (1940–47), edited by Lowie's student Julian Steward. These exchanges greatly facilitated the later reception of Lévi-Strauss in American anthropology departments, where he has always been regarded with esteem, though sometimes criticized for his fieldwork.[9]

The thorny issue of Lévi-Strauss's reception is taken up by Vincent Debaene in his contribution to this volume. Debaene wonders if it might be too soon or even improper to pose the question of "Lévi-Strauss's legacy"; for, on the one hand, it presupposes and reinforces the "poststructuralist" narrative (inscribed in the term itself) that structuralism, and thus implicitly Lévi-Strauss, has been superseded; and, on the other, it allows anthropologists to ignore Lévi-Strauss's continuing influence on their practice as well as the recent revival of Lévi-Strauss's thought in various parts of the world. Coming from the opposite temporal perspective, Boris Wiseman takes us on a tour of Lévi-Strauss's early field notes from his second Brazilian expedition (1938–39), describing how they prefigure—quite literally—Lévi-Strauss's later thought and offer new insights into "a structural understanding of the human relationship to the sensorium."

The essays by Jonathan Culler and Thomas Pavel offer contrasting views on the value of Lévi-Strauss's methodology as it relates to literary criticism. Culler, the author of one of the earliest and most influential works on structuralism, *Structuralist Poetics: Structuralism, Linguistics and the Study of Literature* (1975),[10] describes how Lévi-Strauss's thought was formative for his own, in particular Lévi-Strauss's attempt to discover a general language of myth, which, Culler argues, can be taken as a theory of reading itself. Thomas Pavel contends, however, that if such is the case, the level of generality at which Lévi-Strauss operates in his analyses should not be considered as fundamental or basic but rather as simply the level of analysis at which his anthropological insights have meaning; hence

8. According to legend, Franz Boas died "in Lévi-Strauss's arms" at a dinner held at the Faculty House of Columbia University in 1942.

9. A second wave of the reception of Lévi-Strauss in American anthropology can be said to begin with the work of anthropologist Marshall Sahlins, who studied with Lévi-Strauss in Paris in the late 1960s.

10. This book was awarded the James Russell Prize from the Modern Language Association.

Lévi-Strauss's famous reading of the Oedipus myth, which Pavel carefully reconsiders alongside his own, should be seen as more hermeneutic than structural.

The essays by Marcel Hénaff and Camille Robcis address the much neglected questions of ethics and politics in Lévi-Strauss's work: Hénaff shows how the ethical implications of alterity are crucial to Lévi-Strauss's cardinal notion of reciprocity; and Robcis argues that, despite Lévi-Strauss's famous aversion to politics, a certain concept of the political, namely social contract theory, can be seen as integral to an understanding of *The Elementary Structures of Kinship*.

The remaining essays relate Lévi-Strauss to one or more major figures of twentieth-century thought. One of the most important of these relations is certainly that between Lévi-Strauss and Jacques Lacan. Through an analysis of Lacan's two readings of Freud's Dora case (in 1951 and 1957), Jean-Michel Rabaté shows how Lacan's thought evolved from an early dependence on Lévi-Strauss's theories of myth and symbolic structures to a more "poststructuralist" view of structure, namely the "structurality of structure." Eleanor Kaufman, using Lévi-Strauss's 1956 essay "Do Dual Organizations Exist?" as a starting point, explores what she calls the "structural-ontological synthesis" that defined a short period of "high structuralism" in the thought of Lévi-Strauss, Lacan, and Giles Deleuze. Two essays explore the relation between Jean-Paul Sartre and Lévi-Strauss, which, though less studied than the relation with Lacan, is no less important. Robert Doran challenges the commonplace that Sartrean existentialism and Lévi-Straussean structuralism are simple antipodes, by examining their efforts to appropriate each other's vocabulary in works published in the early 1960s. Françoise Lionnet also examines the debate between Sartre and Lévi-Strauss, but takes it as a basis for the interrogation of a larger set of issues, namely the postcolonial and global aspects of intersubjectivity, which she analyzes via the notion of "relationality" in the philosophies of Simone de Beauvoir and Édouard Glissant.

Lastly, I would like to thank the managing editor of *Yale French Studies*, Alyson Waters, for her support, encouragement, and insight during the preparation of this volume, one that I hope will reopen the debate about Lévi-Strauss's thought and significance in the American academy.[11]

11. I would also like to thank Vincent Debaene for his comments on this preface, which improved it substantially.

JONATHAN CULLER

Lévi-Strauss: Good to Think With

The opportunity to write about Claude Lévi-Strauss, whose work was very important for me, invites me to go back forty-four years to 1968, when as a young graduate student at Oxford I was casting around for a dissertation topic. I had been very interested in Maurice Merleau-Ponty and phenomenology, but found the Geneva School criticism that was associated with phenomenology something of a regression from the more rigorous formalism to which I had been exposed, and Merleau-Ponty's late work, *Le visible et l'invisible* (1964) seemed to me to be moving toward a kind of infrastructural analysis, an account of conditions of possibilities of experience, with affinities to the latest development in French thought, structuralism.

At that point, there was not a lot of structuralist literary criticism. Barthes had written *Sur Racine* (1963), which became the target of conservative attacks on *la nouvelle critique*, but its psychoanalytic approach to "Racinian man" and his universe did not seem a solid methodological model. Some of the essays in Barthes's *Essais critiques* (1964) were much more suggestive but again did not really provide a framework, and they already displayed a rather dilettantish approach to linguistics. Gérard Genette had published the first volume of *Figures* (1966), with a number of promising essays; and Tzvetan Todorov had written *Littérature et signification* (1967) and a handful of articles, but really, things were just getting underway.

I needed above all a methodological guide, someone with real intellectual heft, and Lévi-Strauss became indispensible, since I needed to think through the relation of structural linguistics to the study of cultural phenomena. Lévi-Strauss's path-breaking article, "Structural Analysis in Linguistics and Anthropology," from 1945, argued that other disciplines, such as anthropology, could revolutionize them-

YFS 123, *Rethinking Claude Lévi-Strauss (1908–2009)*, ed. Doran, © 2013 by Yale University.

selves by following the example of structural linguistics, particularly that of phonology. "Phonology cannot help but play for the social sciences the same renovating role that nuclear physics played for all the exact sciences."[1] Since that renovation involved the focus on underlying systems that make meaning possible, it would seem pertinent to any discipline that studies social and cultural meanings, not just the social sciences; in his inaugural lecture at the Collège de France, of 1960, translated as *The Scope of Anthropology*, Lévi-Strauss defined anthropology as "the bona-fide occupant of the domain of semiology which linguistics has not already claimed for its own."[2] Ferdinand de Saussure, of course, had imagined semiology as a broad science of signs that would study social and cultural phenomena. Claiming for anthropology everything in this domain except the study of linguistic signs, Lévi-Strauss certainly declares the relevance of a linguistically-renovated anthropology to a wide range of disciplines. Why would this not apply to the study of literature, which would become a matter of working out the underlying system of conventional oppositions that make possible the rich cultural meanings that occur in this realm?

The phonological revolution that Lévi-Strauss described consists of moving from conscious linguistic phenomena to their unconscious infrastructure, refusing to treat terms as independent entities but analyzing relations between terms, and introducing the notion of a system (collective and at least partially unconscious).[3] In his seminal "Introduction à l'œuvre de Marcel Mauss" (1950), he writes, "particular actions of individuals are never symbolic in themselves; they are the elements out of which is constructed a symbolic system, which must be collective."[4] The idea that linguistics might provide a model for studying cultural phenomena other than language itself is based on two fundamental (now obvious) insights, which Lévi-Strauss repeatedly affirms: first, that social and cultural phenomena are not simply material objects or events but objects or events with meaning and hence signs; and, second, that they do not have essences but are defined by a network of relations, both internal and external. To

1. Claude Lévi-Strauss, "Structural Analysis in Linguistics and Anthropology," *Word* 1/2 (1945), reprinted in *Structural Anthropology*, trans. Claire Jacobson and Brooke Schoepf (New York: Basic Books, 1963), 33 (translation modified).

2. Lévi-Strauss, *The Scope of Anthropology*, trans. Sherry Ortner Paul and Robert Paul (London: Cape, 1967), 17.

3. Lévi-Strauss, *Structural Anthropology*, 33.

4. Lévi-Strauss, "Introduction à l'œuvre de Marcel Mauss," in Mauss, *Sociologie et anthropologie* (Paris: PUF, 1950), xvi.

analyze social and cultural phenomena by identifying the underlying system of oppositions that makes them possible is to undertake a distinctive kind of explanation, not causal explanation, not historical explanation, and especially not piecemeal explanation that focuses on some phenomenon in isolation.

In the 1960s, Lévi-Strauss was the foremost proponent of this methodological orientation, and his usefulness as methodological stimulus was reinforced, certainly for me, by two things: first, his success in his own discipline—as his election to the Collège de France in 1959 indicated. Lévi-Strauss was not a struggling, marginal figure, as for instance Roland Barthes was at that time in the field of literary studies, but someone whose method had led to real contributions to his field and could thus be studied, evaluated, argued with. Second, except for a brief foray into literary analysis in his famous article with Roman Jakobson on Baudelaire's "Les Chats,"[5] Lévi-Strauss was not promoting a specific approach to literary studies, and this gave his thought an independence that was particularly useful. If his way of conceiving and approaching cultural phenomena turned out to work for literature, this seemed to serve as an independent confirmation of its validity. More important, because he did not work on literature, his was not a model that one would adopt, as a disciple, or that came freighted with particular conclusions about literature. Because of its independence from literature, his methodological model asked to be evaluated at a certain level of abstraction: one needed to understand the logic and see how such logic would work in the case of literature. It was not simply a matter of judging, as often happened in those days with formulations in the realm of literary theory, whether this orientation led to new and better interpretations of individual literary works.

Setting out to study structuralism, I thus began with Lévi-Strauss, and with his first great systematic project, *The Elementary Structures of Kinship* (1949), since the article on structural analysis in linguistics and anthropology took kinship terms as the example of why we need to look to relations and analyze the underlying system. Focus on this huge book turned out to be a mistake; it led into recondite and controversial matters that I was not competent to adjudicate and that were not very pertinent to the analysis of literature, though my at-

5. Roman Jakobson and Claude Lévi-Strauss, "'Les Chats' de Charles Baudelaire," *L'homme* 2/1 (1962): 5–21.

tempt to write about it may have helped me think through the problems of comparing cultures. Much more important for me, at this early stage, was the Lévi-Strauss of *La pensée sauvage* (1962) and *Le totémisme aujourd'hui* (1962). My title, "Good to Think With," alludes to a passage in *Totemism* where, after reviewing an extensive literature on tribes' use of various natural objects as identifiers for human groups and arguing against various functionalist and piecemeal explanations, Lévi-Strauss concludes, "natural species are not chosen because they are 'good to eat' [*bonnes à manger*] but because they are 'good to think' [*bonnes à penser*]."[6] For example: "To say that Clan A is 'descended' from the bear and Clan B is 'descended' from the eagle is only a concrete and abbreviated way of stating the relationship between A and B as analogous to the relationship between the two species."[7] Thus: "it is not the resemblances but the differences which resemble one another."[8] In initiating this wonderfully concrete example of structuralist thought—not piecemeal explanation, nor causal nor functionalist explanation, but the reconstruction of a system— Lévi-Strauss cites the example of Freud, whose discoveries were based on the fundamental insight that there was no essential difference between the mentally ill and supposedly normal human beings; in the same way, Lévi-Strauss proceeds by recognizing that the allegedly exotic totemic practices of primitive tribes are a logic of the concrete, not fundamentally different from the logics civilized peoples develop. The more general lesson is one Lévi-Strauss describes explicitly as something he learned from geology, from Freud, and from Marx: to account for experience one must construct a model of the system that underwrites it, a model that will be abstract. "I had learned from my three sources of inspiration that the transition between one order and the other is discontinuous, that to reach reality one has first to reject *experience* [*le vécu*] and *then* subsequently to reintegrate it into an objective synthesis devoid of any sentimentality."[9]

This logic of the concrete operates through binary oppositions— raw/cooked, sun/moon—lately much derided as an approach to the world. We are all now inclined to suspicions of binary oppositions

6. Lévi-Strauss, *Le totemisme aujourdhui* (Paris: PUF, 1962), 132; *Totemism*, trans. Rodney Needham (Harmondsworth: Penguin, 1969), 162.

7. Lévi-Strauss, *Totemism*, 100.

8. Ibid., 149.

9. Lévi-Strauss, *Tristes tropiques* (Paris: Plon, 1955), 50; *Tristes tropiques*, trans. John and Doreen Weightman (Harmondsworth: Penguin, 1976), 71.

and interested in how they are subverted or undone, but Lévi-Strauss explains that simplification at one level leads to complication at another. He shows how oppositions can be projected onto another level: so at one level there is an opposition between nature and culture, and then at the next level *within* culture terms are again opposed as natural versus cultural. Thus, starting with *raw* versus *cooked* (the culinary instantiation of *natural* versus *cultural*) there is then within *cooked*, as a projection of the opposition *raw/cooked*, the opposition between *roasted* and *boiled*. These structures are obviously very relevant to the logics of literary symbol and theme.

Lévi-Strauss's work on myth was very important for me, not just because of the elucidation of a logic of the concrete, but because of the lessons its difficulties offered concerning the application of the linguistic model. Phonology studies the system of a given language: which oppositions are functional for that language. Thus, the distinction between what we would call two different "u" sounds in French—*dessous/dessus*—is not distinctive in English: variation does not produce change in meaning for speakers of English, whereas it is meaningful in French. The task is to identify the distinctions that are functional within a given system. In his study of myth, however, Lévi-Strauss puts himself in a different situation from that of the linguist. He is not analyzing the system of myths of a particular culture but that of the North and South American continents. In *Mythologiques*, he is trying to show that the myths from various cultures *do* go together, but the linguist does not have to prove that the sentences of English should be treated as a group, that there is a grammar of English. The linguist can discover which formal differences are correlated with and responsible for differences of meaning by comparing and analyzing sequences, because he or she has available information about judgments of speakers and meanings of sentences. But the difference between a myth in one culture and that in another is not used to communicate anything. Lévi-Strauss can compare structures, but without evidence about meaning it is difficult to show that these patterns or structures are more relevant than others. Is there, in the case of myth, anything comparable to linguistic competence to be elucidated?

This is the key question. It is important to stress here that Lévi-Strauss's difficulties are not, like Barthes's, due to inadvertence or methodological confusion. His is a deliberate methodological choice. He could have set out to elucidate the system of myths of a particular society but chose to posit a general language of myths. As he wrote at the beginning of *Le cru et le cuit* (1964), "I therefore claim to show not how men think in myths but how myths think [*se pensent*] in men, without them being aware of the fact."[10] Here the analogy with literature is instructive. A critic analyzing a Renaissance sonnet is not interested only in what it might have meant to its original readers but how it functions within the system of literature as a whole, within the institution of literature that has been greatly enriched and expanded since this poem was written. The critic is in effect interested in how literature *thinks itself*. The difference between the case of literature and that of myth is that the institution of literature has been fostered and maintained by considerable cultural effort and has many experienced readers aware of the range of its possibilities and whose judgments can serve as data in a project of analysis; whereas the institution of mythology, especially the mythology of North and South American Indians, leads a very uncertain existence, few besides Lévi-Strauss having a sense of it. To put it crudely, we know how to read literature but not how to read myths. Lévi-Strauss is asking, in effect, what the conventions and procedures of reading are that would enable us to read and understand myths as we do literature. He is trying to teach himself and his readers a broad language of myth, which has no native speakers, postulating various codes and operations that will enable us to read one myth in relation to another. Taken as a theory of reading, Lévi-Strauss's account of myth offers the student of literature the rare spectacle of an attempt to invent and test conventions for the reading of fictional discourse. Since myth and literature share, at the very least, a logic of the concrete, one can consider his analyses as hypotheses about semiotic operations that may be performed intuitively in the reading of literature. At any rate, his example was extraordinarily instructive for someone venturing into the domain of poetics: he was, in a word, good to think with.

But what of Lévi-Strauss today? It is an interesting question, since he so much outlived structuralism. In 2008 he was consecrated with a volume entitled simply *Œuvres* in the Bibliothèque de la Pléiade. Apparently he himself selected what should be included, and the result is surprising. The volume includes the autobiographical *Tristes tropiques* (1955) and the structuralist *Le totemisme aujourd'hui* and

10. Lévi-Strauss, *The Raw and the Cooked*, trans. John and Doreen Weightman (New York: Harpers, 1969), 12.

La pensée sauvage, both from 1962, but, as the editor, Vincent Debaene, notes, it otherwise consecrates a "late historical moment,
1975–93, not the period of a triumphant structuralism but rather that
of the retreat of a mature and consecrated anthropologist."[11] It is not
surprising that the huge book on kinship or the four volumes of *Mythologiques* were not included, but it is surprising to have omitted
key, historic methodological essays, such as "Structural Analysis in
Linguistics and Anthropology," or the introduction to Mauss, very
important for Gilles Deleuze, Jacques Lacan, Barthes, and Jacques
Derrida, or "The Sorcerer and His Magic" (1949), also influential
for Barthes, and the short book *Race et Histoire* (1952), an important study debunking racism commissioned by UNESCO. Debaene
detects both a refusal on Lévi-Strauss's part to situate himself in a
particular intellectual history and a refusal to focus on the critical
function of anthropology, which he had previously espoused. But Debaene also draws the to-me-absurd conclusion that structuralism was
not essential to Lévi-Strauss: "La mode du structuralisme était ines-
sentielle à son œuvre."[12] Of course, no one wants to treat someone
he admires as fashion's slave, but Lévi-Strauss was a fashion-setter, a
different matter, and he needs to be recognized as such. While there
are many late studies that are not of a programmatic structuralist
character, he would not have been Lévi-Strauss or occupied the place
he did without the range of studies based on a revised conception of
anthropology that was explicitly structuralist rather than functionalist and on a methodological program that he to a considerable extent
pioneered.

I am pleased that the Lévi-Strauss who is preserved in the Pléiade
has not been entirely appropriated as a humanist—as risks happening with Barthes, who is now celebrated as a great writer who loved
his mother and wrote about photography and the loss of the past.
The Lévi-Strauss who insisted that the task of the human sciences is
"not to constitute but to dissolve man"[13] is still here in the Pléiade,
and the conclusion of *Tristes tropiques* remains a desolate requisitory
against the idea of a humanist individual subject. Taking up the tradition of the French moralists, Lévi-Strauss writes: "The ego is not only
hateful; it has no place between a *we* and a *nothing* ("Le moi n'est pas

11. Lévi-Strauss, *Œuvres*, ed. Vincent Debaene *et al* (Paris : Gallimard, 2008), xii.
12. Ibid., xx.
13. Lévi-Strauss, *The Savage Mind* (Chicago: University of Chicago Press,
1966), 247.

seulement haissable; il n'a pas de place entre un nous et un rien").[14]
He not only treats the ego as an even more dubious fiction than the
"we"; he denies it any place at all—a move that can scarcely be sustained but whose radical impulse one can appreciate. He concludes
this early work with a remarkable passage, maintaining that the only
hope for the human *we*, as we busy ourselves in the exploitation of
the universe, lies in the possibility of "disengagement"—the attempt
to *se déprendre*—in the contemplation of a mineral, in the smell of
a lily, or most remarkably, "in the brief glance, heavy with patience,
serenity and mutual forgiveness, that, through some involuntary understanding, one can sometimes exchange with a cat."[15] With this
remark ends *Tristes tropiques*. As one who has never experienced the
mutual forgiveness that Lévi-Strauss claims sometimes to find in the
exchange of a gaze with a cat, I can admire the stimulus to surprise
of this concluding image and even concede that this remarkable conclusion might be good to think; but I would maintain, in the face
of this arresting claim, that Lévi-Strauss is above all good to think
with when he imagines a non-hermeneutic method for *les sciences
humaines* that does not kowtow to history but maintains the importance of the lessons he drew from geology, Freud, and Marx for reconstructing the underlying systems that make our experience possible.

14. Lévi-Strauss, *Tristes tropiques*, 448; English, 543.
15. Ibid., 449; English, 544.

VINCENT DEBAENE

Lévi-Strauss: What Legacy?

More than fifty years after the first edition of *Structural Anthropology* and forty years after the last volume of *Mythologiques*, it is time, it would seem, to address the question of Lévi-Strauss's legacy. After four decades of poststructuralist, postmodernist, and postcolonial critique, it would appear that Lévi-Strauss's stock has been permanently delisted from American academia's fashion-driven marketplace of ideas. If the word "poststructuralism" itself, with its barbarous consonance, its prefix and ending, already appears outmoded, so "twentieth century," what about structuralism itself? When the death of Lévi-Strauss was announced in November of 2009, how many discretely remarked: "Was he indeed still alive"? Thus, the question "What is Lévi-Strauss's legacy today?" is one whose accompanying shrug already constitutes an answer, as if it were the ultimate concession to an important episode of twentieth-century thought, to which one must pay pious homage before moving on to something else.

However, it is possible that this question—whether it is purely rhetorical or whether it testifies to a sincere desire to "save" a part of Lévi-Strauss's œuvre—might not be the one we should be asking. It is based on a set of postulates concerning the progress of knowledge in the social sciences, as well as on the status of anthropological works and of anthropological knowledge itself. As soon as we begin to unpack these postulates and make them explicit, it becomes clear that they are far from self-evident. Rather than considering the question of Lévi-Strauss's legacy, it might perhaps be better to ask whether we can do anything with Lévi-Strauss today. Indeed, there is a simple factual response to this question. As it happens, more than a quarter-century of relative silence, there has been, since the mid-1990s, a

YFS 123, *Rethinking Claude Lévi-Strauss (1908–2009)*, ed. Doran, © 2013 by Yale University.

resurgence of interest in Lévi-Strauss's texts, particularly in France, England, and Brazil, which has given rise to numerous interpretations and analyses across a variety of disciplines. This return is quite meaningful in itself: Michel Foucault used to say that physicists do not reread Galileo and Newton, since such a reexamination "could alter our knowledge of the history, but not the science, of mechanics."[1] That Lévi-Strauss is being reread both within anthropology and outside it, however, surely indicates that his œuvre is not truly outdated like that of Newton. Perhaps the famous "paradigm shift" that made the structuralist project appear as exotic and as baroque as the Phlogiston theory of chemistry never actually occurred; perhaps we have only begun to grasp the true implications of this project.

These new readings of Lévi-Strauss are multifaceted, multivalent, and, as one might expect, heterogeneous. While it is impossible to synthesize them all, I will attempt to draw out the principal orientations.

*   *   *

The question of Lévi-Strauss's legacy can be considered from two perspectives: that of the history of the discipline of anthropology and that of the history of "theory," of which structuralism is considered an episode. The first perspective thinks in terms of disciplinary knowledge, the second in terms of supersession and radicalization. The first questions whether Lévi-Strauss's sources were reliable and whether or not recent discoveries invalidate past conclusions; it defines the present through its difference from the past and situates itself "after Lévi-Strauss." The second conceives of Lévi-Strauss as the initiator of a movement that has since been superseded; it speaks of poststructuralism or situates itself "beyond structuralism." These two approaches are legitimate as far as they go, and they still form the basis of many works on Lévi-Strauss today. Let us be clear: they appear to me to be the two methods for considering Lévi-Strauss in the United States; and this explains to a great extent why contemporary re-readings of structural anthropology have so little impact in the U.S., as well as why these re-readings circulate in exchange networks that skirt North America and are thus deprived of the

---

1. Michel Foucault, "Qu'est-ce qu'un auteur?" in *Language, Counter-Memory, Practice: Selected Essays and Interviews*, trans. Donald F. Bouchard and Sherry Simon (Ithaca, NY: Cornell University Press, 1980), 135–36.

immense sounding board that is the American university system and its publishing industry.

Let us first consider the perspective of disciplinary history. There is, without a doubt, a Lévi-Straussian legacy in anthropology. It is not that of a type of practice, such as that of Bronisław Malinowski, who provided ethnography with its foundational charter (at least in the Anglophone world), *Argonauts of the Western Pacific*, as well as with a distinct method, namely participant observation. It has, however, bequeathed a number of conceptions and perspectives that have been integrated into the discipline's common set of principles and methods. For example, even the ethnographer the most assiduously concerned with establishing the concrete conditions of enunciation of Native American myths (which Lévi-Strauss was sometimes accused of neglecting in *Mythologiques*) knows that a myth can be considered as the combinatory variant of another in the context of a regional whole—a major component of Lévi-Strauss's structural anthropology. On another point, *The Savage Mind* bequeathed to the discipline the idea that observable differences in the sensible world can serve as sources for a logic of the concrete, enabling it to "tinker" [*bricoler*] with meanings, without the need to postulate a mental, collective, or individual subject that imposes its formal constraints on the content. Philippe Descola has noted that this idea was "such an obvious one" for "all of those who have worked on representations of the environment" that one no longer "mentions one's debt" to Lévi-Strauss on this point, which is now part of the public domain of contemporary anthropology.[2] One could adduce many other such examples.

In a more general and deeper sense, Lévi-Strauss has bequeathed to anthropology a type of approach that has been routinized (even to the point of being shopworn), which consists in studying the relevant differential features, allowing for the revelation of "necessary relations [that organize] certain sectors of social life": i.e., mythical narrations, culinary techniques, clothing customs, the exchange and circulation of marriage partners, etc. In its most stripped-down version, structural analysis thus consists in "an extremely efficient method for detecting and ordering regularities in utterances and practices."[3] It is

---

2. Philippe Descola, "Sur Lévi-Strauss, le structuralisme et l'anthropologie de la nature," *Philosophie* 98 (2008): 24. (All non-attributed translations in this essay are by the translator.)

3. Ibid., 9–10.

this method that was adopted and applied to all sorts of cultural and textual objects in the course of the ephemeral "structuralist" vogue in the 1960s and 1970s in France, all while obscuring two of its essential dimensions. First, structural analysis has no *a priori* generalizing potential. It is not some global "analysis-grid" that one can simply "apply" to any object; it is very effective when it is brought to bear on certain aspects of social life, less effective in other cases, and utterly useless in still others; if it is found to be fruitful, it is the very process of investigation that allows one to determine these domains *a posteriori*. Secondly, structural analysis only possesses explanatory power if the system of differences it highlights is compared and connected to other systems—in other words, there is no "structure of the work," for example, nor is there a "structure of the text"; every structure presupposes a plurality of objects that can be designated as "structured" only because they are in a relationship of variation, one from the other.[4]

Finally, one can recognize a Lévi-Straussian legacy that does not affect anthropology in its entirety, but that is nevertheless foundational to a large part of the discipline. Indeed, even if they distance themselves from Lévi-Strauss and refuse to be labeled "structuralists," a great number of anthropologists work according to principles that Lévi-Strauss's œuvre has consolidated and strengthened. Philippe Descola summarizes this tendency thus: "the conviction that the task of anthropology is to elucidate the apparent variability of social and cultural phenomena by shedding light on minimal invariants [. . .] whose function most often follows unconscious rules"; "the hypothesis that these invariants are founded on material determinations" of an external order (environmental constraints) or internal order (sensory-motor equipment), as well as "on certain transhistorical imperatives of social life"; "the precedence accorded to synchronic over diachronic analysis, not because of a rejection of the historical dimension, but because of the rejection of the empiricist position, which

---

4. See Patrice Maniglier, "Des us et des signes. Lévi-Strauss, philosophie pratique," *Revue de métaphysique et de morale* 1 (2005): 101–102. In this sense, despite his critiques of Lévi-Strauss, Pierre Bourdieu was able to qualify his own approach as "structural anthropology" (see for example, *Ce que parler veut dire. L'économie des échanges linguistiques* [Paris : Fayard, 1982], 41–42). See also Bourdieu's tribute to Lévi-Strauss in the preface to his *The Logic of Practice* (Stanford, CA: Stanford University Press, 1990).

consists in accounting for the genesis of a system prior to defining its structure."[5]

Nevertheless, we must recognize that, unless one is oneself an anthropologist, it is difficult to determine with any greater precision the specifically disciplinary legacy of Lévi-Strauss. This is something we need to keep in mind when we seek to draw out the implications of the question of Lévi-Strauss's legacy. Indeed, any attempt at superseding structural anthropology requires first that we determine and circumscribe, once and for all, its domain of validity. Yet this condition is, on the one hand, very difficult to satisfy in practice, and relies, on the other, and above all, on an erroneous view of the progress of knowledge in anthropology.

This condition is difficult to satisfy in practice because anthropology is *de facto* a specialized field, about which only the specially trained can speak with authority. It is certainly legitimate to ask about the legacy of *The Elementary Structures of Kinship*; there are indeed numerous contestable and contested assertions in this work that are of a variable degree of generality: from the ethnographic "data" and facts marshaled by Lévi-Strauss to the universality of the incest prohibition, via the opposition between prescriptive and preferential marriages or the fact that women are the ones exchanged.[6] However, the sheer fact that *The Elementary Structures* is still an object of discussion today suffices to forestall any final verdict on its obsolescence or relevance: the jury is still out; and taking part in the debate presupposes an entry fee, namely the integration of the considerable body of theoretical and technical knowledge that has been accumulated in the anthropology of kinship over the past century. One can apply the same reasoning to the structural analysis of myths, which also continues to be the object of interdisciplinary discussions that are quite technical,[7] as well as to the more properly ethnographic

5. Descola, "Anthropologie structurale et ethnologie structuraliste," in *Une école pour les sciences sociales. De la VIe Section à l'École des Hautes Études en Sciences Sociales*, ed. Jacques Revel and Nathan Wachtel (Paris: Éditions du Cerf, 1994), 140.

6. For an assessment and classification of the objections to *The Elementary Structures of Kinship*, see Françoise Héritier, "La citadelle imprenable," *Critique* 620–21 (1999): 61–83.

7. See in particular: Lucien Scubla, *Lire Lévi-Strausss. Le déploiement d'une intuition* (Paris: Odile Jacob, 1998); *The Double Twist: From Ethnography to Morphodynamics*, ed. Pierre Maranda (Toronto: University of Toronto Press, 2001); Emmanuel Désveaux, *Quadratura americana: essai d'anthropologie lévi-straussienne* (Genève: Georg Editor, 2001).

observations in Lévi-Strauss's work: unless one is a specialist of the history of exchanges between tribes of the West coast of Canada, it is difficult to assess Lévi-Strauss's hypotheses in *The Way of the Masks* regarding the meaning and allocation of the swaihwé and xwéxwé masks of the Salish and Kwakiutl; unless one is a specialist in the social organization of native tribes in the Brazilian plateau, it is difficult to speak authoritatively about the interpretation of the structure of the Bororo or Kayapo villages and its relation to indigenous cosmology. It can be noted in passing that the ability to make such observations has nothing at all to do with the question of whether the anthropological discipline is "truly scientific"; it is a fact that anthropology *progresses*—not because it mercilessly sheds its blinding light on some of the most neglected aspects of human societies, but simply because its practice is cumulative and because anthropologists read one another's work.

But this progress is not linear. Behind the question of Lévi-Strauss's legacy often lies the idea of a rectilinear and unidirectional development of knowledge, such that what was relevant at one time ceases automatically to be so as soon as new work on the same objects emerges. Such a model is no more valid for anthropology than for the other sciences; unpredictable phenomena of return and rehabilitation can be observed in, for instance, biology. For example, Marcela Coelho de Souza has demonstrated that if one deemphasizes the opposition between nature and culture in the introduction to *The Elementary Structures of Kinship*, which does not in fact have any substantive value in Lévi-Strauss, it is susceptible to a reassessment that gives the work a new relevance—this despite the objections, first from British "descent theory," but especially from three decades of "fire of critics from culturalist, practice theory, and feminist perspectives, among other tendencies that entered the anthropological scene from the seventies onwards." We thought we had seen "the demise of kinship itself as an anthropological concept," but "the news of its passing had been premature."[8]

8. Marcela Coelho de Souza, "The Future of the Structural Theory of Kinship," in *The Cambridge Companion to Claude Lévi-Strauss*, ed. Boris Wiseman (Cambridge: Cambridge University Press, 2004), 80. Descola and others have often noted the extreme privilege given to the first pages of *The Elementary Structures* and to what appears (but only appears) to be a reification of the opposition between nature and culture. See for instance, Descola, "Sur Lévi-Strauss, le structuralisme et l'anthropologie de la nature," 14–16.

Moreover, one could also observe that, with the notable exception of the anthropology of kinship, the critiques of structural anthropology coming from within anthropology itself have rarely been based on the supersession of assertions rendered obsolete by the progress of knowledge or by the gathering of new empirical data. On the contrary, it is almost always with regard to the fundamental, philosophical questions of epistemology or of disciplinary definition, sometimes even of ethics, that Lévi-Strauss has been criticized; and one could add to this the charge, most often made in the American academy, that Lévi-Strauss's field practice was neither extensive nor sufficiently rigorous. With a few rare exceptions, Lévi-Strauss did not respond to these criticisms. One of the most famous polemics in which he did take part—a debate with Marvin Harris after the Gildersleeve conference of 1972—reveals, on the contrary, that he addressed a controversy only when it involved the very specific realm of ethnographic facts: the discussion was not at all centered on the definition of structure, nor even on the relations between environmental constraints and social organization (all of which are abstract questions of social theory that only philosophers seek to resolve *a priori*), but on the identity of bivalves (clams or horse clams) mentioned in the bella bella versions of the Kawaka myth and on the question of the dietary use of these clams' siphons by the natives of that region.[9]

In other words, the reception of structural anthropology is marked by an essential paradox: from the outset it has almost always been read as a "school of thought," which made it imperative to understand its initial axioms (sometimes before deducing its fundamental biases: logocentrism, rigid dualism, universalist rationalism, surreptitious metaphysics, etc.). And yet, when we look at the facts, structural anthropology was conceived—both theoretically by Lévi-Strauss himself, but also and first of all, historically, during structuralism's gestation period in New York in the 1940s—not as an explanatory schema (which would have followed evolutionism, functionalism, etc.) but as an original *method* aimed at solving specific problems that arose in the practice of anthropologists: it is because he wanted to provide the anthropology of kinship with a way out of the endless quarrels about classification that Lévi-Strauss sought to consider

9. Marvin Harris, "Lévi-Strauss et la palourde," *L'homme* 16 (1976): 5–22. Claude Lévi-Strauss, "Structuralism and Empiricism" [1976], in Lévi-Strauss, *The View from Afar*, trans. Joachim Neugroschel and Phoebe Hoss (Chicago: Chicago University Press, 1985/1992), 121–37.

kinship terms through an analogy with phonemes; it is because he wanted to resolve the "totemic problem" (that is, the recurrence in a considerable number of societies of the idea of a relation between men and animals, a recurrence that anthropologists were unable to account for in any satisfactory manner) that he borrowed from structural linguistics the idea that "it is not resemblances, but differences which resemble each other";[10] it was because he wanted to respond to the "crisis of anthropological knowledge" (anthropology was at one time threatened by a rift between the accumulation of ethnographic data that was increasingly dispersed and comparative syntheses that were increasingly fragile) that Lévi-Strauss introduced structural analysis as a new tool of intercultural comparison.[11]

There is therefore something surprising in Clifford Geertz's critique of Lévi-Strauss. Geertz speaks of an "intraprofessional suspicion that what is presented as High Science may really be an ingenious and somewhat roundabout attempt to defend a metaphysical position, advance an ideological argument, and serve a moral cause."[12] The polemical advantage of such a description is clear: it allows Geertz to play the (responsible) role of the pragmatic, matter-of-fact practitioner who refuses to be intimidated by theoretical elaborations. Yet, it is paradoxical to present such suspicion as *professional*, given that the "philosophical" affirmations that one finds in the work of Lévi-Strauss (in which Geertz claims to recognize the "universal rationalism of the French Enlightenment")[13] are really peripheral to a body of work that is primarily grounded in a disciplinary tradition and that dedicates itself to the resolution of problems—which are often quite technical—inherited from past anthropological inquiry. Despite its "high theory" reputation, in practice structural anthropology relies upon a scrupulous attention to ethnographic content and the problems it poses, as well as upon an "almost maniacal deference for the facts."[14]

10. Lévi-Strauss, *Totemism*, trans. Rodney Needham (Boston: Beacon Press, 1963), 77. Lévi-Strauss, *Le totémisme aujourd'hui* [1962], in *Œuvres* (Paris: Gallimard, Bibliothèque de la Pléiade, 2008), 522. See Frédéric Keck, *Lévi-Strauss et la pensée sauvage* (Paris: PUF, Philosophies, 2004), 34–37.

11. See Gildas Salmon, *Les structures de l'esprit: Lévi-Strauss et les mythes* (Paris: PUF, 2013).

12. Clifford Geertz, "The Cerebral Savage" [1967], in Geertz, *The Interpretation of Cultures: Selected Essays* (New York: Basic Books 1973), 347.

13. Ibid., 356.

14. Lévi-Strauss, *The Way of the Masks*, trans. Sylvia Modelski (Vancouver: Douglas & McIntyre, 1982), 145.

*   *   *

The other perspective from which Lévi-Strauss's legacy—as well as his supersession—has been viewed is that of the grand narrative of postmodernism. I shall not dwell on this perspective, which one mostly finds in literature departments, and which conceives of structuralism as an avant-garde movement that followed existentialism before being swiftly superseded in turn. According to this narrative, after the structuralism of Lévi-Strauss, Lacan, Althusser, the "first" Foucault (*The Order of Things*) and the "first" Barthes (*The Fashion System*), came the poststructuralism of Derrida, Lyotard, Deleuze, the "second" Foucault (*The History of Sexuality*) and the "second" Barthes (*The Pleasure of the Text*). After a philosophy of structure came a philosophy of the event and of difference. After the rationalist faith in systems and grammars came the resistance of texts and the subversive work of writing. Many authors have noted the flawed character of this presentation, given that, for instance, on either side of this supposed rupture, we find the very same thinkers. As Jonathan Culler astutely remarks: "When so many of yesterday's structuralists are today's poststructuralists, doubts arise about the distinction."[15] One can indeed go even further: as Patrice Maniglier observes, the fact that the same authors "embraced the 'structuralist' cause and led the polemic against it [. . .] often for the same reasons" is an index of structuralist identity: structuralism is not defined by a set of theses, nor by a shared method or common program, but rather as a problematic site. In other words, one must adopt a structuralist perspective in order to grasp the unity of structuralism: structuralism does not position itself beyond or above "the dispersion and distribution of works and authors"; it consists "not in a common trait, but in the matrix of their divergences" and in the reconfiguration of the "pertinent divides" around which "the essential alternatives are distributed."[16] Thus, it is not a matter of a historical sequence leading from the subjective freedom of existentialism to the objective necessity of structures, followed by a return of the subject and its agency. Rather, it consists in a subterranean displacement in the manner of

15. Jonathan Culler, *On Deconstruction: Theory and Criticism after Structuralism* (New York: Routledge, 1982), 25.
16. Maniglier, "Les années 1960 aujourd'hui," in *Le moment philosophique des années 1960 en France*, ed. Maniglier (Paris: PUF, 2011), 16–18.

thinking such abstract notions as causality, comparison, or the sign—
a displacement in which the theses of numerous authors as well as
various moments of their work are situated.

In any event, the structural anthropology of Lévi-Strauss was associated in the academic imaginary with a kind of "hard" or scientistic
sort of structuralism, that of Saussurean linguistics and the phonolo-
gism of Jakobson and Troubetskoï. It was conceived as an ambitious
attempt to extract the "codes" determining human actions and discourse. Beyond their "early" twentieth-century odor and the image of
good old-fashioned science they evoked, the common element shared
by these thinkers supposedly consisted in the privileging of *langue*
over *parole*, system over its elements, structure over the subject,
and synchrony over diachrony. In the works of these scholars, these
contrasted pairs (which, in certain cases, they had conceptualized
themselves, and which, it must be said, are in no way superimpos-
able) have an instrumental value; yet, curiously, they were accused
of excessively privileging the first terms, which for a run-of-the-mill
history of ideas, could only provoke dialectically the "revolt" of
the second terms: the subject against the structure, history against
the system, meaning (interpretation) against science, performance
against grammar, and so on. Structuralism was thus quickly blamed
for being "incapable of dealing with heteroglossia, plurivocality, ambiguity" and for having "reduced the task of interpretation to the act
of decoding."[17] But that is a flawed understanding of its project. Structuralism never tried to determine "what makes people do what they
do" or "what makes people say what they say," but to determine under what conditions their actions and words can have meaning. There
is no need, therefore, to accuse structural analysis of reductionism
and of neglecting ambiguous acts and utterances, since its concern
is to precisely determine what makes them appear ambiguous in the
first place. The genealogical link between Saussure, Jakobson, and
Lévi-Strauss is incontestable, but it is not at all based on the priority
of the "system" to the detriment of history or the subject; rather, it
seeks to shed light on a "liminal problem common to all 'sciences
of culture,'" namely the difficulty of identifying what constitutes an

17. E. Valentine Daniel, "Culture/Contexture: an Introduction," in *Culture and Contexture: Readings in Anthropology and Literary Study*, ed. E. Valentine Daniel and Jeffrey M. Peck (Berkeley: The University of California Press, 1996), 9.

observable fact (respectively, a sign, a phoneme, a usage). The structural method resolves this difficulty when it highlights the correlated variation of two series of differences.[18]

It is nonetheless useless to try to clear up such confusions or to rectify such a narrative, if only because of its performative efficacy: the creation of an imaginary "structuralism"—that is, in the words of Edward Said, "formalist, authoritative, claiming to domesticate the moving force of life and behavior" in its "system"[19]—allowed for the development of many fruitful reflections on the production of meaning within political and cultural power structures. This historical narrative is one effect among others in the circulation and relocation of concepts and reflections within varied intellectual traditions and academic environments: from positive knowledge (linguistic and anthropological) developed within the European tradition, to French philosophy, to the American academy, which has adapted these reflections according to its own theoretical and political preoccupations.[20] Thus structuralism appeared almost immediately in American literature departments (and as a result, of course, in other university contexts where English is the dominant language of "theory") as a synonym for the authoritarian violence of systematic science, which ultimately essentializes and naturalizes the historical and political constraints on thought and on the production of discourse. It was perceived as the ultimate incarnation of Western, logocentrist science, and was accused of seeking to establish a relation of "mastery" over its objects, that is, of constructing an imaginary overarching or external perspective relative to an object that it seeks immediately to dominate by separating it from itself.[21]

Among the factors contributing to these misunderstandings, one can note a particular contingency of dates: in the area of literary studies (the case of anthropology is different, given that Lévi-Strauss had interlocutors in American anthropology since the 1940s), Lévi-Strauss was imported to the United States through Jacques Derrida's

18. Maniglier, "Des us et des signes," 93. See Gilles Deleuze, *How Do We Recognize Structuralism?* trans. Melissa McMahon and Charles Stivale, in Stivale, *The Two-Fold Thought of Deleuze and Guattari* (London: Guilford, 1998).

19. Edward Said, *Beginnings: Invention and Method* (New York: Columbia University Press, 1985), 379–80.

20. See François Cusset, *French Theory: How Foucault, Derrida, Deleuze, & Co. Transformed the Intellectual Life of the United States*, trans. Jeff Fort (Minneapolis: University of Minnesota Press, 2008).

21. Culler, *On Deconstruction*, 222–25.

conference paper "Structure, Sign and Play in the Discourse of the Human Sciences" given in 1966 at the famous colloquium held at Johns Hopkins University entitled "The Language of Criticism and the Sciences of Man." This paper has since been considered as embodying the advent of poststructuralism. Yet, at that time, the only works of Lévi-Strauss that had been translated into English were *Tristes Tropiques* (in an incomplete version) (1955, tr. 1961), the first volume of *Structural Anthropology* (1958, tr. 1963), and *Totemism* (1962, tr. 1964). The translation of *The Savage Mind* appeared the year of the colloquium. In other words, before even being read, Lévi-Strauss is presented in the United States as a precursor, whose œuvre has already been glossed and superseded. This would have paradoxical consequences for the reception of both authors. With regard to Lévi-Strauss, as Derrida had well perceived, one can consider that true structuralism only began with a radical desubstantivation of the nature-culture opposition; this was in fact already present in *The Elementary Structures* but was only made explicit in *The Savage Mind*; for many commentators today, it is the latter book, along with the "large" and "small" volumes of *Mythologiques*, that best illustrate the analytical power of structuralism.[22] With respect to Derrida, his 1966 paper (which further develops his earlier critique of Lévi-Strauss's "Rousseauism," in the journal *Cahiers pour l'analyse*, later included in *Of Grammatology* (1967) was less about denouncing the putative logocentrism of anthropology than about *siding with* Lévi-Strauss against the Althusserian structuralists and their pretense of founding a science that was untouched by both the ambiguities of writing and violence.[23]

In any case, it is largely a shared conviction that, since the advent of poststructuralism, we have now been cured of "the great illusion— the modern phantasm—of theory" once embodied by Lévi-Strauss:

22. See Viveiros de Castro, "Xamanismo Transversal: Lévi-Strauss e a Cosmopolítica Amazônica" in *Lévi-Strauss: Leituras Brasileiras*, ed. R.C. de Queiroz & R.F. Nobre (Belo Horizonte: UFMG, 2008), 79–124. Also see the readings of Maniglier and Salmon, the latter of whom prefers to talk about "structural functionalism" in reference to *The Elementary Structures of Kinship*. The phrase "small *Mythologiques*" is used by Lévi-Strauss to designate his late analyses of Native American myths (*The Way of the Masks, The Jealous Potter, The Story of Lynx*).

23. See the excellent study by Edward Baring, "Derrida and the Cercle d'Épistémologie: How to be a Good Structuralist," in *Concept and Form, Vol. II: The Cahiers pour l'Analyse and Contemporary French Thought*, ed. Peter Hallward and Knox Peden (London: Verso 2012).

"the assumption that theory faithfully represents the real." Structuralism tried "to convince us that the only existing reality is the one that theory claims to provide through its interpretive grid, outside of which no other reality can exist," but its ultimate goal was to avoid "the confrontation with reality": "in order for the model to function, one must eliminate anything that draws attention to the empirical character of facts."[24] Two things can be pointed out regarding this grand narrative: on the one hand, it reestablishes the schematic dualism between empirical reality and theoretical model, form and content, which all of the structuralists, from Lévi-Strauss to Deleuze, via Foucault and Barthes, had set out to overcome; on the other hand, it surreptitiously reintroduces the teleology of philosophies of consciousness. It no longer consists, as in the positivist narrative, in a linear progression of knowledge that leaves structuralism behind, but rather in the implacable—albeit unexplained—progress of postmodern lucidity.

*   *   *

Though its presuppositions are not always addressed, the question of legacy is thus the underlying question that determines for the most part, even today, the reception of Lévi-Strauss. However, in the last fifteen years, particularly in France, England, and Brazil, one can observe what one could call a return to structuralism in the flowering of a group of texts and analyses that have resurrected the work of Lévi-Strauss, without thereby posing the question of legacy.

If one had to assign a historical origin to what Eduardo Viveiros de Castro has called the "second spring" of the literature on Lévi-Strauss,"[25] one could certainly point to two series of events. First, there was the successive publication of the last two works of Lévi-Strauss, *The Story of Lynx* (1991) and *Look, Listen, Read* (1993). In a certain way, these two short books, written by a man more than 80 years old and signed "Claude Lévi-Strauss, of the Académie française," could have appeared as somewhat outdated, the final sparks of an anthropological reflection from an earlier age and nearing extinction. Yet in another way, they revealed astonishing contemporane-

24. Josué V. Harari, *Scenarios of the Imaginary: Theorizing the French Enlightenment* (Ithaca, NY: Cornell University Press, 1987), 25, 20, 218.
25. Viveiros de Castro, "Claude Lévi-Strauss, Œuvres," *Gradhiva* 8 (2008): 131.

ity: on the five-hundredth anniversary of the conquest of the American continent, *The Story of Lynx* combined the structural analysis of mythical Native American material with an ethical reflection on alterity and violence; the work presented itself both as an extension of *Mythologiques* and as an expiatory homage to the systems of thought of the North American natives. *Look, Listen, Read* not only brought together considerations on art that had hitherto been scattered in isolated digressions and articles; this short book also completed the work of Lévi-Strauss through an aesthetic theory that is as organically linked to his anthropological reflection as the *Critique of the Power of Judgment* is to Kant's Critical Philosophy.[26] Calling on Rameau, Diderot, Batteux, and Kant, this book offered a kind of "Lévi-Strauss in the eighteenth century" (as in the title of the famous issue of the 1966 *Cahiers pour l'analyse*, which contained, among other texts, Derrida's reflection on the lesson of writing), allowing Lévi-Strauss this time to distance himself from Rousseau. It inscribed structuralism in a long history, giving it some unexpected interlocutors, all while clarifying, through examples, the connection between perception and the structural activity of the human spirit. Finally, without breaking with the ethnographic grounding of structural anthropology (*Look, Listen, Read* ends with reflections on sculpture in the Tsimshian and Tlingit populations), the book established new entryways into the work of Lévi-Strauss through a dialogue with figures well known to the general public: Proust, Ingres, Rimbaud . . . In fact, the two works were unexpectedly successful, appearing as they did in the wake of the first general synthesis of Lévi-Strauss's œuvre, by Marcel Hénaff.[27]

Around the same time, in anthropology, an important current of Americanist ethnology was being developed (which was in fact closely related to the reflections on Native American dualism in *The Story of Lynx*) that revisited the Lévi-Straussian opposition between consanguinity and the marriage alliance (which itself represents a particular expression, in the realm of kinship, of the nature/culture opposition). Basing their conclusions on Native American cosmology—for which the nature/culture dichotomy has no privileged status, nor indeed even any relevance—these studies aimed to create a

26. I am borrowing this analogy from Martin Rueff, "Notice de *Regarder écouter lire*," in Lévi-Strauss, *Œuvres*, 1919, 1931–1937.

27. Marcel Hénaff, *Claude Lévi-Strauss and the Making of Structural Anthropology*, trans. Mary Baker (Minneapolis: University of Minnesota Press, 1998 [Fr. 1991]).

kind of radical structuralism, one that was entirely "relationist" and desubstantivized.[28] In the wake of these studies, there have been recent reflections on animism and perspectivism—no doubt one of the most remarkable developments that anthropology has seen in the past few years, not only because they respect the tension in the discipline between theoretical ambitions and a grounding in ethnography, but also because these debates are, strictly speaking, *anthropological*, after many years during which anthropology seemed to be caught between two fates: postmodern narcissism, on the one hand, and the threat of its absorption by other disciplines (cognitive science or history), on the other. [29]

This return to structuralism was inaugurated by another, specifically French event, that is, the special issue of the journal *Critique* devoted to Lévi-Strauss (1999), in honor of his 90th birthday.[30] It was the first time that one could perceive a change in the cultural status of Lévi-Strauss's work—a change that was confirmed nine years later by the publication of a volume of his work in the prestigious Bibliothèque de la Pléiade, a collection that had previously welcomed only writers and philosophers. In addition to several contributions that offered a historical reevaluation of Lévi-Strauss's work, this special issue of *Critique* also contained reflections by historians and musicologists, writers and essayists (Jacques Deguy, Pascal Quignard), who had little interest in "applying" structuralism to their respective domains. From this point forward, Lévi-Strauss emerged as a "classic": it suddenly became clear that his œuvre—read and re-read, distilled and solidified in scattered citations—forms the mental accompaniment of numerous authors and lends itself to myriad uses in a variety of fields unconcerned by the hackneyed debates on structure and the subject. During this period, Lévi-Strauss made a short and famous speech, in which he compared himself to a "broken hologram,"[31] thus

28. Viveiros de Castro, "The Gift and the Given: Three Nano-Essays on Kinship and Magic," in *Kinship and Beyond: The Genealogical Model Reconsidered*, ed. Sandra C. Bamford and James Leach (New York: Berghahn Books, 2009), 237–67.

29. See among others: Viveiros de Castro, *From the Enemy's Point of View: Humanity and Divinity in an Amazonian Society*, trans. Catherine V. Howard (Chicago: University of Chicago Press, 1992); Viveiros de Castro, "Cosmological Deixis and Ameridian Perspectivism," *Journal of the Royal Anthropological Institute* 4 (1998): 469–88; Descola, *Par-delà nature et culture* (Paris: Gallimard, 2005); Bruno Latour, "Perspectivism: 'type' or 'bomb,'" *Anthropology Today* 25/2 (2009): 1–2.

30. *Critique* 620–621 (1999).

31. Notes from Roger-Pol Droit, *Le monde*, January 29, 1999.

inaugurating a ten-year period, during which, under the specter of an aging Lévi-Strauss, the number of studies dedicated to his work steadily increased.

While it would be impossible to enumerate them all, we can highlight three collective endeavors that contributed to this reevaluation: the publication of the voluminous *Cahier de l'Herne Lévi-Strauss*, edited by Michel Izard (2004), the *Cambridge Companion to Lévi-Strauss*, edited by Boris Wiseman (2009), and, one year earlier, the aforementioned 2000-page volume, entitled *Œuvres*, which appeared in the Bibliothèque de la Pléiade series. The success of the Pléiade book was quite unexpected, when one considers the difficulty of most of the texts included. It also has a special authorial status. In a certain sense, one can legitimately regard it as Lévi-Strauss's last work, since he himself selected the contents and,[32] most of all, because he annotated and modified certain passages of his works, particularly the end of *The Savage Mind*.[33] In another sense, by proposing a critical edition based on the study of his manuscripts and accompanied by an abundance of historical annotations and annexes, this collection confirmed Lévi-Strauss's change of status; Lévi-Strauss no longer appeared merely as a professional anthropologist or as the leader of structuralism, but rather as an "author," and more specifically, as a "founder of discursivity," according to Foucault's famous formula, which referred to figures such as Marx and Freud.[34]

To these three collective enterprises, one could add the innumerable monographs and special journal issues that were published in three successive waves: those published around 2000; those published at the time of the Lévi-Strauss's 100th birthday; and the tributes that followed his death in 2009: la *Revista de Antropología* in 1999; *Archives de Philosophie* in 2003; *Les temps modernes* in 2004; *Esprit* in 2004 and 2011; *Philosophie* in 2008 . . .

A cultural sociologist would have noted a generational effect. It is incontestable that these works reflect, in some respects, a "post-

32. The selection surprised commentators because it did not include many of Lévi-Strauss's most famous texts and because it was centered on a later period of his work (post 1975). For an interpretation of this choice, see Vincent Debaene, "Préface," in Lévi-Strauss, *Œuvres*, xii-xviii.

33. See Frédéric Keck, "Notice du *Totémisme aujourd'hui* et de *La pensée sauvage*," in Lévi-Strauss, *Œuvres*, 1804–1810, and Keck, "*La pensée sauvage* aujourd'hui. D'Auguste Comte à Claude Lévi-Strauss," in *Le moment philosophique des années 1960 en France*, 113–24.

34. On this point, see Debaene, "Préface," in Lévi-Strauss, *Œuvres*, xxii–xxxi.

poststructuralism," in both senses of the term. On the one hand, these are the product of researchers who are part of an intellectual landscape that is no longer polarized by structuralism (whether by an opposition to structuralism or by a concern for its supersession by poststructuralism). In any case, whether we are speaking of a renewal, a re-reading, or a return, this "second spring" presupposes the end of structuralism, that is, a theoretical discontinuity between then and now. It will be interesting to someday trace the history of this rapprochement between our time and this "philosophical moment of the 1960s."[35] This generational effect appears, on the other hand, through the fact that these works almost always historicize Lévi-Strauss. Notwithstanding the specifically biographical studies, the general aim was to better read and understand Lévi-Strauss by reconstructing the contexts in which his work developed and the problems it endeavored to address: his œuvre has been resituated within the French intellectual tradition and university system;[36] the study of totemism and the savage mind has been reinscribed within the history of the question, which is both philosophical and sociological, of the relationship between logic and affectivity;[37] his theory of symbolism has been redefined as a response to the crisis of philosophical transcendentalism that was latent in the 1930s and became manifest after 1945;[38] *Tristes tropiques* has been resituated within the history of French ethnographic writing and within the internal development of Lévi-Strauss's œuvre;[39] new light was shed on the foundational links between structuralism and the ethnography of the South-American lowlands—Lévi-Strauss's initial area of specialization;[40] the connections between structural anthropology and the symbolist aesthetic tradition, previously ana-

35. For an initial diagnosis, see Maniglier, "Les années 1960 aujourd'hui," and "The Structuralist Legacy," in *The History of Continental Philosophy, Volume 7: After Poststructuralism: Transitions and Transformations*, ed. Rosi Braidotti (Durham: Acumen, 2010), 55–82.

36. Christopher Johnson, *Claude Lévi-Strauss: The Formative Years* (Cambridge: Cambridge University Press, 2003).

37. Keck, *Lévi-Strauss et la pensée sauvage.*

38. Claude Imbert, *Lévi-Strauss, le passage du Nord-Ouest* (Paris: L'Herne, 2008).

39. Debaene, *L'adieu au voyage. L'ethnologie française entre science et littérature* (Paris: Gallimard, 2010).

40. Anne Christine Taylor, "Don Quichotte en Amérique. Claude Lévi-Strauss et l'anthropologie américaniste," in *Cahier de L'Herne Lévi-Strauss*, ed. Michel Izard (2004), 92–98. Carlos Fausto et Coelho de Souza, "Reconquistando o campo perdido: o que Lévi-Strauss deve aos ameríndios," *Revista de Antropologia* 47/1 (2004): 87–131.

lyzed by James Boon, have been newly illuminated;[41] the role of Lévi-Strauss's American exile within the genealogy of structuralism has been redefined;[42] the (seemingly simplistic) anti-racism and relativism of the two lectures, *Race and History* (1952) and *Race and Culture* (1971) have been reinterpreted in light of the political education of the young Lévi-Strauss and of the ideological shifts of Unesco;[43] new perspective has been given to the 1960s debates among structuralism, phenomenology, and hermeneutics around the question of meaning and symbolism;[44] the method of transformation, first used in *The Savage Mind* and later in *Mythologiques*, has been thoroughly reinterpreted as a way out of the crisis of anthropological comparativism, brought on by American ethnology at the beginning of the twentieth century;[45] structural anthropology has been resituated within a genealogy of structuralism, as a response to an ontological problem, that of the identity of the sign.[46]

Some anthropologists regretted this historicization of Lévi-Strauss's œuvre; they perceived it as an "embalming" and a "fossilization" that would eclipse or neglect the still vibrant theoretical power of Lévi-Straussian thought.[47] Not every attempt at historicization is conservative, however; it does not necessarily signify a patrimonialization or a salvage operation. On the contrary, by varying the contexts and by increasing the number of narratives in which the œuvre of Lévi-Strauss is inscribed, these recent works have revitalized structuralism in two ways. First, they have introduced an internal difference. Indeed, many of these analyses have revealed that structural

41. Boris Wiseman, *Lévi-Strauss, Anthropology and Aesthetics* (Cambridge: Cambridge University Press, 2007).

42. Laurent Jeanpierre, "Les structures d'une pensée d'exil: la formation du structuralisme de Claude Lévi-Strauss," *French Politics, Culture, and Society* 28/1 (2010): 58–76. Debaene, "'Like Alice through the Looking Glass.' Claude Lévi-Strauss in New York," *French Politics, Culture, and Society*, 28, number 1 (2010), 46–57.

43. Wiktor Stoczkowski, *Anthropologies rédemptrices. Le monde selon Lévi-Strauss*, (Paris: Hermann, 2008).

44. Hénaff, *Claude Lévi-Strauss, le passeur de sens* (Paris: Perrin, 2008).

45. Salmon, "Du système à la structure," in *Le moment philosophique des années 1960 en France*, 159–76.

46. Maniglier, *La vie énigmatique des signes. Saussure et la naissance du structuralisme* (Paris: Leo Scheer, 2006); Maniglier, "Des us et des signes."

47. Emmanuel Désveaux, "Claude Lévi-Strauss, *Œuvres*," *L'homme* 190 (2009): 199–201. See my response to his objections: Vincent Debaene, "La Pléiade en débat. Réponse à Emmanuel Désveaux," *L'homme* 193 (2010): 45–50.

anthropology is not a coherent and monolithic doctrine whose principles are to be accepted, rejected or overcome. Rather, it is a discursive
space riddled with tensions: for example, there are tensions between
two uses of the nature/culture opposition;[48] between two forms of
moral and epistemological skepticism that do not overlap;[49] between,
on the one hand, an "irenic" definition of the social as a system of
signs, and, on the other, the repeated affirmation that symbolic systems are still only partially convertible into each other—that is to
say that far from reducing social life to the simple implementation
of a "grammar" determined from the beginning of time and whose
rules the anthropologist is supposed to elucidate, structural anthropology integrates the double possibility of freedom and violence.[50]
Furthermore, several of these studies reveal the fecundity of Lévi-
Strauss's thought for anthropological, philosophical, and aesthetic reflection, as well as for contemporary politics. In that case, it is no longer a question of revealing an internal tension within Lévi-Strauss's
thought, but rather of using it to think new problems, to rethink the
old ones in a new way, or to question some of our received categories.
A single example will suffice: if the aesthetic thought of Lévi-Strauss
seems to hesitate between modernism and anti-modernism, it might
not be the symptom of an internal incoherence so much as the sign
of the insufficiency of these notions—however conventional—whose
descriptive capacity is in fact quite limited.[51] The resurgence of Lévi-

48. Descola, "The two natures of Lévi-Strauss," in *The Cambridge Companion to Claude Lévi-Strauss*, 103–117.

49. Stoczkowski, *Anthropologies rédemptrices*, 305–326.

50. Maniglier, "La condition symbolique," *Philosophie* 98 (2008): 37–53.

51. One could make the same remark about the recent readings that oppose a "poetic" tendency to a "scientific" one in Lévi-Strauss and that believe to have unmasked
his true character by describing him as a "failed artist": his isolation in the discipline
would prove that he is not a true "social scientist," and in reality, his most rationalistic
claims would mask a more fundamental "aesthetic impulse," as his field notes would
also seem to show, notes that, we are told, reveal more of an "artist trawling for ideas
rather than an academic at work" (Patrick Wilcken, *Claude Lévi-Strauss: The Poet in
the Laboratory*, New York: Penguin, 2010, 95). One could, of course, consider these
apparent contradictions as insurmountable, but one can also see this as an occasion to
revisit our conventional distinction—which seems obvious, though in reality it is local
and historical—between "science" and "poetry," as well as our preconceived image of
what constitutes the normal behavior of an "academic at work." On these questions,
see Debaene, "Claude Lévi-Strauss, 2008: What Anniversary?" in *My Favorite Lévi-
Strauss*, ed. Dipankar Gupta (New Delhi: Yoda Press, 2011), 61–75.

Strauss can thus be found in contemporary reflections on biopolitics, architecture, forms of art appraisal, and animal illness.

★   ★   ★

While it is impossible to synthesize every return to structuralism, two aspects of Lévi-Strauss's œuvre reflect this move—aspects that were explicit from the beginning, but that have frequently been overlooked or neglected in the past. First, these recent works provide a deliberately anti-formalist reading of Lévi-Strauss, by opposing any reduction of structure to form; structuralism is conceived as a means of exploring content: "*form* is defined by opposition to material other than itself. But *structure* does not have any distinct content: it is content itself, apprehended in a logical organization conceived as a property of the real."[52] As Lévi-Strauss further observes in *The Savage Mind* "the principle underlying a classification can never be postulated in advance";[53] in other words, structural analysis does not attempt to extract the modes of organization of the given through an intellectual process of abstraction that would unveil a system of constraints "behind" empirical appearances; on the contrary, these modes of organization gradually emerge through local variation. Contrary to the image of the anthropologist who seeks to "isolate" formal systems before comparing them in the abstract, these studies employ—and follow, step by step—the gradual and centrifugal method of structural analysis whose point of departure is always empirical. A canonical example is the volumes of *Mythologiques*, which do not propose any *a priori* theory of myth but which unfold their analyses by using a specific Bororo myth as a starting point; the local variations of this myth are progressively apprehended, gradually encompassing the entirety of the American continent.

This priority given to content—that is, to ethnographic data, social organization, environmental constraints, kinship systems, mythical variants, and so on—very clearly distinguishes these new readings of Lévi-Strauss from the more traditional ways of approaching

52. Lévi-Strauss, "Structure and Form: Reflections on a Work by Vladimir Propp," *Structural Anthropology*, Vol. 2, trans. Monique Layton (Chicago: University of Chicago Press, 1983), 115.

53. Lévi-Strauss, *The Savage Mind* (Chicago: University of Chicago Press, 1966), 58 (*La Pensée sauvage* [1962], in Lévi-Strauss, *Œuvres*, 620–621).

his œuvre: Lévi-Strauss is now reread *as a scholar/researcher* and no longer from the perspective of the philosophical propositions sprinkled throughout his texts. On the other hand, the inability to perceive this practical and applied dimension of structural anthropology explains the failure of the attempts to decipher structuralism historically, which claim to uncover the presuppositions or latent ideology of what is wrongly understood as a "school of thought."[54] The real difficulty of Lévi-Strauss's reflections resides less in understanding their principles than in assimilating an enormous mass of facts, unpronounceable words, tribes, languages, usages, plant and fish varieties, all of which are quite foreign to the Western reader.

The other aspect that these new readings highlight (and this is directly linked to the preceding point) is the notion of transformation. In his inaugural lecture at the Collège de France, Lévi-Strauss remarked:

> An arrangement is structured which meets but two conditions: that it be a system ruled by an internal cohesiveness; and that this cohesiveness, inaccessible to observation in an isolated system, be revealed in the study of transformations, through which similar properties are recognized in apparently different systems.[55]

It is this second part of the definition that many recent works have focused on. It has consequences on two levels. First, it allows a re-evaluation of structuralism in its entirety. This aspect is based on the fundamental idea that one "cannot prejudge the nature of a practice [of a usage, or of any cultural fact] by relying solely on relations of resemblance that [the observer is] inclined to find in them."[56] As Patrice Maniglier acutely argues, the first task of the anthropologist is not to explain the difference between cultural usages, but rather to *identify* what constitutes a usage—that is, to delimit what "is done" before asking the question "why does one do it?" (in response to which the anthropologist is invariably told "one does it because it is done").[57] As

---

54. See for example Adam Shatz's perplexity mixed with annoyance in "Jottings, Scraps and Doodles," *London Review of Books* 33/21 (November 3, 2011): 3–7.

55. Lévi-Strauss, "The Scope of Anthropology," in *Structural Anthropology*, Vol. 2, 18.

56. Maniglier, "Des us et des signes," 105.

57. Ibid., 95–105. See the following remark by Lévi-Strauss: "Lowie's work seems to consist entirely in an exacting endeavor to meet the question (which was acknowledged as a prerequisite for any study in social structure): *What are the facts?*" (Lévi-Strauss, *Structural Anthropology*, 307–308). The English translation of this passage is

we know, structural anthropology answers this question by analyzing possible variations and substitutions. The only way to determine the pertinent features of a myth, for example, is to describe the qualitative variations it presents in relation to other versions, and to grasp the rules that account for the correlation of these variations. The concept of "transformation" allows one to grasp this essential idea: a structure is a "'group of transformations' through which one can determine content by means of variants." "If the content is thus 'structured,' it is not because it is subject to (external) determination by an abstract form, but because it can only be defined in relation to other content."[58] In other words, these re-readings show that structuralism *is not* a new anthropological theory aimed at "explaining" cultural and social facts (to be paired alongside evolutionism, functionalism, and so on) but rather consists in a new way of *determining* them.

This insistence on the notion of transformation thereby affects the very conception of anthropological knowledge. Against the image of a static structuralism that rigidly compares fixed systems (an image supported by some passages in Lévi-Strauss),[59] the recent re-readings give serious weight to the idea that anthropological reflection can be situated in a relation of immanence to its object. This object is not situated in some abstract frame of reference created by Western rationality. This is what one should understand when Lévi-Strauss states (in *The Raw and the Cooked*) that "a reader would not be wrong if he took the book itself as a myth: the myth of mythology":[60] i.e., anthropology has no privileged principle for the forms of thought it studies. Its task is not to translate (and thus betray) the Other's thought in Western terms, but to create interconnections between conceptual fields. To the schoolteacher who suggested that a native Piro (Peruvian Amazon) woman boil water in order to avoid infantile diarrhea, the latter retorted: "our bodies are different from yours." Faced with

---

more of a paraphrase. A more literal rendition of what appears in parentheses would read: "Even for the structuralist, the first question one must answer is *What are the facts?* This question controls all others" (Lévi-Strauss, *Anthropologie structural* [Paris: Plon, 1958], 340).

58. Manglier, "Des us et des signes," 101–102.

59. In particular, the analogy between the typology of customs and the periodic table of elements—which horrified Clifford Geertz and which can be found in *Tristes tropiques*—is a nice analogy, but it is also an unfortunate one due to the confusion it introduces between structure and system or between structure and repertory.

60. Lévi-Strauss, "Overture to *le Cru et le cuit*," trans. Joseph H. McMahon, *Yale French Studies* 36–37 "Structuralism" (1966): 56.

such a response, the work of the anthropologist is not to try to "understand"—with a vaguely condescending benevolence—a "worldview" different from our own, which should be respected despite its obvious insufficiencies. Rather, it is about understanding that the Piro natives do not have a different "view" of the same "world" but different concepts of corporeality and humanity that are spread across different axes and networks of opposition: "The problem is not that the Amazonians and Euro-Americans give different names to (or have different representations of) the same things; the problem is that we and they are not talking about the same things. What we call 'body' is not what they call 'body.'"[61] One must therefore invent a domain and concepts—such as multi-naturalism—which can allow for connections and conversions between different systems of thought, thereby bringing the Western division between body and spirit in line with the way in which the Piro natives determine identity and alterity.

The priority given to the immanent logic of transformation thus invalidates the type of critique that is characteristic of "poststructural" re-readings, which condemned structural anthropology for claiming excessive authority and for the position of "mastery" it appeared to adopt in relation to its object. Oddly, through these rereadings of Lévi-Strauss, one can thus witness a rapprochement between the most abstract reflections on notions of transformation and the most detailed works on Amazonian ethnography. Indeed, many of them study native American cosmology, whose framework of relations extends to the entire universe. As just one example among hundreds, the Makuna natives of the high-Amazon believe that animal communities are rigorously organized in a way that is akin to human communities (they possess their own culture, customs, commodities, and so on), such that their relationship to the animals they hunt is conceived precisely as a relation of exchange and reciprocity with married kin.[62] One could see here (one more) sign that the distinction between consanguinity and kinship, which is essential to the structural anthropology of kinship, is a Western conception artificially projected onto a world that is fundamentally "other." Yet, rather than lamenting the discipline's confinement within its own

---

61. Viveiros de Castro, "The Gift and the Given: Three Nano-Essays on Kinship and Magic," 241.

62. Kaj Arhem, "The Cosmic Food Web: Human-Nature Relatedness in the Northwest Amazon," in *Nature and Society: Anthropological Perspectives*, ed. Descola and Gilsi Palsson (London: Routledge, 1996), 185–204.

categories, several recent anthropological works have proposed rather to follow the natives' conception of how living beings should be organized and have proposed to extend the notion of kinship to the non-human world:

> first considered as an internal mechanism for the constitution of local groups, kinship then [appeared] as a relational system organizing extra-local relationships, connecting persons or groups beyond the kinship relation, and finally, as a language and a relational schema between the Same and the Other, identity and difference.[63]

These ethnographic works reveal quite consciously an intuition that Lévi-Strauss expressed in his works of the 1940s on the Nambikwara, where, for the first time, he affirmed that a system of reciprocity does not necessarily demand an extrinsic determination of classes to define desirable or prohibited partners, but simply the formal determination of a series of relations independently of the nature of the elements that these series bring together.

And yet, without even considering the results, such a raising of "kinship" to the level of a "politico-ritual phenomenon, exterior and superior to the encompassed aspect of kinship"[64] modifies the status of structural anthropology; for it is no longer seen as a set of conceptual tools that are heterogeneous to its object, but as the translation of the shock inflicted on the categories of Western thought by Amerindian socio-cosmologies. By desubstantivizing the difference between nature and culture (which, starting with *The Savage Mind*, appears as only one expression among other possible contrasts between opposed qualities), structural anthropology can rediscover one of the organizing principles of Amazonian thought and thus be seen as a mediation that allows one to go from an animistic ontological framework (in which natural beings are endowed with "human" and "social" dispositions) to a naturalistic ontological framework (which divides beings between a singular nature and varied cultures).[65] The recent debates surrounding the notions of animism and perspectivism thus shed new light on structural anthropology: by highlighting "the Amazonian underpinnings of structuralism," these debates invert the perspective, showing not that Lévi-Strauss understood

63. Fausto and Coelho de Souza, "Reconquistando o campo perdido," 98–99.
64. Fausto and Viveiros de Castro, "La puissance et l'acte: la parenté dans les basses terres de l'Amérique du Sud," *L'homme* 126–128 (1993): 150.
65. See Descola, *Par-delà nature et culture*.

the natives, but, on the contrary, what his thought *owes to them*.[66] "Through a striking reversal"—according to one of Lévi-Strauss's own formulas glossed by Viveiros de Castro[67]—structuralism is no longer conceived of as an instrument for analyzing social organizations or systems of thought, but as the reverberation of Amazonian ontologies in Western thought. It would have thrilled Lévi-Strauss to see structural anthropology considered as a "simple transformation" of forms of thought it had taken as its object of study.

*   *   *

These re-readings of Lévi-Strauss have indeed revived the anthropological project against the two rejections of which structural anthropology was the collateral victim. The first depicted anthropology as a knowledge that does violence to otherness. By returning to the essential notion of transformation and by internalizing it in some way within disciplinary practice, these returns to structuralism situate the work of anthropology not as being aloof and above but "in a strict structural continuity with the intellectual practices of the collectives that find themselves historically in the 'position of object' of the discipline."[68]

The second objection relates to the question of generalization. This is an essential point in the misunderstanding of the reception of structural anthropology in the Anglophone world and particularly in the United States. Very early on, within the anthropological discipline itself, Lévi-Strauss was criticized for having "constructed" his theory "out of" obsolete, insufficient—even erroneous—data. Why, then, would Lévi-Strauss have *The Elementary Structures of Kinship* republished (in 1967) with no alterations, when ethnographic knowledge had evolved, revealing some errors and confusions? Why try to maintain this edifice at all costs when the very "foundations" are receding? In addition, one could cite the radical postmodern critique, which sees the very notion of fact, proof, or empirical verification as modernistic constructions inherited from the universal rationalism of the Enlightenment. The only solution is to reconceptualize

66. Respectively: Taylor, "Don Quichotte en Amérique. Claude Lévi-Strauss et l'anthropologie américaniste," 97; Fausto and Coelho de Souza, "Reconquistando o campo perdido," 87.
67. Viveiros de Castro, *Métaphysiques cannibales* (Paris: PUF, 2009), 6–12.
68. Ibid., 6.

the very idea of generalization. One must abandon the idea that anthropological generality "rises" through a progressive distancing from ethnographic reality (thus betraying it). As Patrice Maniglier and Gildas Salmon have recently demonstrated, the radical newness of structural anthropology resides not in its having proposed a new interpretation of ethnographic facts, but in its having rethought, in a single gesture, the determination of these facts and the relation between ethnography and anthropology: the object of anthropological knowledge is organized, through local variations, into a cultural continuum; consequently, ethnography does not precede anthropological comparison; rather, it is conditioned by the comparative anthropological project. This is a difficult idea to accept, since it goes against the commonsense anthropological view, which says that one ought first to know the facts before comparing them; but, in another sense, this is the only way to respond to the objection that "facts are facts," for the researcher is always suspected of warping reality to make it conform to his/her own categories. One must thus admit that (like the principle of a classification) the delimitation of an ethnographic fact can never be postulated *a priori*; it emerges only through its differentiation from what surrounds it, and for this reason, Lévi-Strauss used to say that differential gaps are the proper object of anthropological inquiry. This is undoubtedly the reason why the reception of structuralism has encountered such difficulties in the American culturalist tradition, for which anthropology is only legitimate (if at all . . .) as a comparison between cultures that have themselves been determined inductively. By founding anthropological comparison not on inventories of resemblances, but on the systematicity of differences between "cultures" (which are never given, but are provisionally inferred through analysis), structural anthropology has modified "the very manner of constructing comparables."[69]

In 1963, Susan Sontag introduced Lévi-Strauss to the American public (that is, beyond departments of anthropology, where he was already well known) through a somewhat unfortunate phrase: "the anthropologist as hero." Fifty years later, a very different portrait has emerged from these re-readings of structural anthropology. On the one hand, Lévi-Strauss appears in retrospect as the one who rescued anthropology from its simple status as a discipline, an essentially colonial discipline, for that matter, less because of its relation to its

69. Salmon, *Les structures de l'esprit*, 4. See also, Maniglier, "Des us et des signes."

"objects" than because it was once believed that anthropology could develop within a restricted domain, without affecting other areas of Western thought. If one can still speak of heroism, it has nothing to do with a "hard-won impassivity"[70] but rather with the fact that, in the wake of Lévi-Strauss, the shock of ethnography unsettles Western thought *in toto*—which explains his recently acquired status as "classical."[71] On the other hand, these re-readings, which give a great deal of attention to the properly scholarly work of Lévi-Strauss, and which are centered on the notion of transformation rather than structure, make Lévi-Strauss the precursor of a new anthropology—an anthropology that is neither modern or postmodern, colonial or postcolonial, but one that can be qualified as "a-modern" and "de-colonial," and which replaces the Great Divide between Us and the Others with the multiplicity of variations.

—Translated by Caroline Vial

70. Susan Sontag, "The anthropologist as hero" [1963], in Sontag, *Against Interpretation and Other Essays* (New York: Picador, 2001), 72.
71. See Debaene, "Préface," in Lévi-Strauss, *Œuvres*, xiv–xxii.

ROBERT DORAN

Sartre's *Critique of Dialectical Reason* and the Debate with Lévi-Strauss

> It is precisely because all these aspects of the savage mind can be found in Sartre's philosophy, that the latter is in my view unqualified to pass judgment on it: he is prevented from doing so by the very fact of furnishing its equivalent. To the anthropologist, on the contrary, this philosophy (like all others) affords a first-class ethnographic document, the study of which is essential to an understanding of the mythology of our own time.
>
> —Claude Lévi-Strauss[1]

It is almost an article of faith that the existentialism of Jean-Paul Sartre and the structuralism of Claude Lévi-Strauss are antipodes and that the displacement of the former by the latter represented the triumph of unconscious structures over a philosophy of consciousness and freedom. And yet, in works published at the beginning of the 1960s, there was an attempt on the part of both thinkers to synthesize aspects of their respective systems. In 1960, Sartre published his massive *Critique of Dialectical Reason* (*Critique de la raison dialectique*), which extends his existential phenomenology into the domains of social ontology and the philosophy of history. But Sartre also situates his work with respect to the contemporary debate over structuralism: "it could be said that the aim of the critical investigation is to establish a structural and historical anthropology."[2] This claim, coupled with Sartre's substantial discussion of Lévi-Strauss's

---

1. Claude Lévi-Strauss, *The Savage Mind* (Chicago: University of Chicago Press, 1966), n. 249.

2. Jean-Paul Sartre, *Critique of Dialectical Reason, Volume One*, trans. Alan Sheridan-Smith (London: Verso, 2004), 69.

YFS 123, *Rethinking Claude Lévi-Strauss (1908–2009)*, ed. Doran, © 2013 by Yale University.

The Elementary Structures of Kinship (*Les structures élémentaires de la parenté*) (1949), inspired Lévi-Strauss to devote the final chapter of *The Savage Mind* (*La pensée sauvage*, 1962), entitled "History and Dialectic," to an examination of Sartre's *Critique*. Though Lévi-Strauss therein expresses his "disagreement with Sartre regarding the points which bear on the philosophical fundaments of anthropology,"[3] he also considers *The Savage Mind* (and not merely the final chapter) as a kind of tribute to Sartre: "a homage of admiration and respect,"[4] as he writes in his preface to this work.

Sartre's engagement with Lévi-Strauss and structuralism in his *Critique* can certainly be seen as opportunistic. Lévi-Strauss was named to the Collège de France in 1959 and was on the verge of becoming an international sensation, much like Sartre himself had been a decade earlier.[5] The publication of Lévi-Strauss's *The Elementary Structures of Kinship* in 1949 had generated a great deal of attention; it was reviewed favorably by Simone de Beauvoir, and was considered by many to be a seminal work.[6] The essays written in the 1940s and 1950s and collected in *Structural Anthropology* (1958) had laid out a bold intellectual agenda that was quickly growing into a movement. It was, however, the highly literary travelogue *Tristes tropiques* (1955, English translation, 1961) that made Lévi-Strauss famous outside his discipline, in some sense replicating Sartre's success in generating popular interest in his thought through his plays and his novel *Nausea* (1938). Thus Sartre, in his most important philosophical work since *Being and Nothingness* (1943), no doubt wished to show his philosophy's pertinence by co-opting an ascendant current of French thought. It should also be noted that Lévi-Strauss was only three years younger than Sartre, and though Sartre's intellectual career had climaxed in France in the late 1930s and 1940s, while Lévi-Strauss was living abroad, Sartre could still view Lévi-Strauss as a contemporary—in contrast to the studied indifference that would later characterize Sartre's attitude to younger philosophers such as Michel Foucault and Jacques Derrida.

---

3. Lévi-Strauss, *The Savage Mind*, xii.
4. Ibid.
5. Though the bulk of Sartre's *Critique* had been written by 1957, one could certainly see where Lévi-Strauss's career was heading by that time.
6. See the essay by Françoise Lionnet in this volume, for a detailed discussion of the relation between Beauvoir, Sartre, and Lévi-Strauss.

For his part, Lévi-Strauss immediately recognized the importance of Sartre's *Critique*, assigning it in his seminar at the École des Hautes Études during the 1960–61 academic year and recommending it to colleagues. As a Sartre biographer recounts:

> In the spring of 1960, Claude Lévi-Strauss asks Jean Pouillon to talk about [the *Critique of Dialectical Reason*] in his [Pouillon's] seminar at the École Pratique des Hautes Études. This happened three months after its publication. Pouillon remembers. "At first I refused, thinking that nobody as yet had the time to read the entire text. But then I changed my mind and proposed to divide my reading of the *Critique* into three two-hour seminars. Generally, my courses in anthropology drew about thirty people . . . but this one drew a real crowd. I recognized a few faces, such as, for instance Lucien Goldmann's."[7]

Due to its formidable stylistic difficulties, Sartre's *Critique* is little read today;[8] but, as this passage suggests, it made a rather large splash among the Parisian intelligentsia at the time of its publication, particularly among those interested in structuralism.

SARTRE'S *CRITIQUE* AND LÉVI-STRAUSS'S *THE ELEMENTARY STRUCTURES*

The *Critique of Dialectical Reason* is the first of a projected multi-volume work laying out Sartre's philosophy of history (volume two

7. Annie Cohen-Solal, *Sartre: A Life*, trans. Anna Cancogni, ed. Norman Macafee (New York: Pantheon Books, 1987), 389. These course offerings were evidently much more successful than Sartre's public reading of parts of his *Critique*, which preceded its publication. According to Annie Cohen-Solal: "The lecture took place at 44 Rue de Rennes, exactly opposite his own apartment. [Sartre] entered the packed room around six in the evening, carrying a huge folder under his arm. 'I am going to tell you what I am doing now,' he started in a mechanical, hurried tone of voice. And he continued to speak without ever raising his eyes from the text, as if still absorbed in his writing. 'He spoke for three quarters of an hour,' Jean Pouillon remembers, 'one hour, an hour and a quarter, an hour and a half, an hour and three quarters, without ever raising his head. All those who were standing, half of the audience, were exhausted. Some had already crumpled to the floor. [. . .] It was as if Sartre had completely forgotten about time.' At last Jean Wahl signaled him to stop, and the philosopher picked up his papers and walked to his study as abruptly as he had come" (ibid., 388–89).

8. The English translation was published in 1976, and the corrected edition, based on the revised French version of 1985, was published in 1991. Needless to say, by 1976 the intellectual world had left both existentialism and structuralism far behind, and thus, apart from a few Marxist organs such as *New Left Review*, Sartre's great work was met with virtual silence in the English-speaking world.

appeared posthumously and will not be discussed in this essay).[9] However, this volume of the *Critique* is not philosophy of history in the traditional sense, that is, in the speculative sense of Hegel and Marx. It does not seek to determine the meaning and direction of history-in-general but aims rather to elucidate the tools of analysis from which any meaning or directionality of history might be deduced or constructed. Though the *Critique* is often seen as a "Marxist turn" in Sartre's thought,[10] it represents less a break with the individualistic existentialism of *Being and Nothingness* than a reformulation and extension of its major concepts into the analysis of social being. The fundamental dichotomy distinction of Sartre's *Being and Nothingness*—that between bad faith and authenticity—is revived in the central dialectic of the *Critique*: that between an inauthentic "seriality" and an authentic "group praxis." But Sartre's vocabulary also shows signs of being influenced by Lévi-Strauss, with concepts such as "structure" and "reciprocity" playing a major role.

Sartre believes that the great error of social science, including Marxist social science, lies in the inability to distinguish between two types of social structure, which he calls "groups" and "collectives." According to Sartre, groups are the true motor of history, whereas collectives, which resemble groups only superficially, possess no intrinsic historical force. Groups are defined by a common *purpose*, collectives by a common *interest*. Groups *actively* seek to achieve consciously conceived goals through concerted, committed action; in a group, my goal is the other's goal, and the other's goal is my goal. This is what Sartre calls group *praxis* (*praxis* thus corresponds to Sartre's existentialist concept of the "project"). But Sartre rejects the idea of collective consciousness (à la Durkheim) or "group mind" (à la Hegel's *Geist*). The group is rather a special coincidence of individual and group praxis, which Sartre terms "mediated reciprocity" or reciprocity mediated by a "third party" (*le tiers*), which can also be the group itself: "this newcomer joins a group of 100 *through me* insofar as the group which I join will have 100 *through him*. [. . .]

9. Sartre, *Critique de la raison dialectique II* (Paris: Gallimard, 1985); *Critique of Dialectical Reason, Volume 2*, trans. Alan Sheridan-Smith (London: Verso, 2006).

10. Sartre's relationship with Marxism is complex. The *Critique*, as Sartre himself insists, is a "Marxist work" written "against the communists" (see Emmanuel Barot, "Le marxisme, philosophie vivante: La leçon de Sartre," in *Lectures de Sartre*, ed. Philippe Cabestan and Jean-Peirre Zarader [Paris: Ellipses, 2011], 165).

Each of us is the 100th of the other."[11] Collectives, on the other hand, are composed of atomistic individuals who are incapable of acting in concert; even in a panic or riot, it is "every man for himself." This is because the interest that unites members of a collective is purely external: it does not emanate from the gathering itself but arises contingently from an amalgam of discrete, uncoordinated actions. Collectives are thus what Sartre calls a *series*: neither purely random (like a clustering of individuals at an intersection waiting for the light to change), nor purposeful (a group). Serial gatherings are *passive* social structures; they are figures of social and political impotence.

A close corollary of Sartre's notion of seriality is the concept of the "practico-inert," his term for the material remains of past praxis, insofar as they persist as inertia and no longer respond to or resist the needs of the group. The practico-inert is found most readily in language, institutions, rituals, and norms; it is the functional equivalent of the more familiar (Marxist) notion of objectification, except that it retains a more explicit dialectical relation to praxis. Sartre's location of language in the practico-inert recalls the structuralist binary of signifying system versus speech-act (though Lévi-Strauss's version is significantly more complex than the basic Saussurian schema).[12] As Thomas Flynn observes, "[Sartre] translates Saussure's *langue/parole* distinction into his own practico-inert/praxis scheme. But unlike the structuralists, Sartre places the emphasis on praxis-parole."[13] As we shall shortly see, Sartre effectively defines Lévi-Strauss's structural anthropology as a discipline that seeks to reveal the structures of the practico-inert; because it remains at this level, it is incapable of accounting for human *praxis* (freedom) or the dialectic (history).

What Sartre calls the "practico-inert field" is the domain of the *passive activity* of seriality, that is, an activity permeated by impo-

11. Sartre, *Critique*, 375 (original emphasis).

12. For a discussion of this, see Vincent Debaene's contribution to this issue: "Lévi-Strauss: What Legacy?" Marcel Hénaff observes in his essay "L'adieu à la structure" (*Esprit*, août-septembre, 2011) that, particularly after 1962, Lévi-Strauss's concept of "structure" evolves away from the traditional structuralist conception of Saussure and Jakobson toward a notion of "transformation." Could this shift have been a response to Sartre's critique?

13. Thomas Flynn, *Sartre and Marxist Existentialism* (Chicago: Chicago University Press, 1984), 100. Thus praxis-parole / practico-inert language form a dialectic of their own: "there can be no doubt that language is *in one sense* an inert totality. But this materiality is *also* a constantly developing organic totalization" (Sartre, *Critique*, 98, original emphasis).

tence, indifference, and unfreedom. To the extent that the practico-inert inhibits or cancels out group praxis, it shows itself to be "anti-praxis" or even "anti-dialectical": the repository of the non-volitional effects (unintended consequences) of human praxis (e.g., the invention of the automobile is designed to increase mobility but often results in the traffic that restricts it). However, the practico-inert field is not an ethically neutral inertia, for in this condition individuals are constantly subject to *scarcity* (*rareté*), that is, the impossibility of satisfying the needs of a social ensemble, which Sartre sees as the most basic, untranscended condition of humanity. Only the cooperation of group praxis—the affirmation of freedom on the level of the social ensemble—can transcend the rivalry and competition (social conflict and violence) that inevitably arises among serial, atomized individuals in the practico-inert field.

Sartre's famous everyday examples of seriality—waiting in line for the bus and listening to the radio—are vivid descriptions of the *alterity* (a degraded form of sociality) that Sartre sees as the essence of serial existence. In the bus queue no organic relations subsist among the bus riders; I am as indifferent to my fellow bus rider as he is to me. The common interest in transportation is extrinsic to the gathering itself; it has no unifying potential, even if it unites individuals in a *shared* (but not a *common*) activity: "the acts of waiting are not a communal fact, but are lived separately as identical instances of the same act."[14] Though this being-together is a relation of sorts, it is nevertheless based on a fundamental alterity, a kind of pseudo- or counter-reciprocity that is diametrically opposed to the reciprocity of true groups. Moreover, the seriality of the bus queue is conditioned by the practico-inert field of the bus transportation system itself: the insufficient number of seats (scarcity), the density and interchangeability of people (massification),[15] the rigidity of the time schedule (standardization), etc., all of which augment the alienation and isolation of the individual.[16] The other bus riders are seen as either superfluous (their addition is unimportant) or an obstacle (taking my seat). Serial individuals relate to one another *as others*: "The Other is me in

14. Sartre, *Critique*, 262.
15. "The intensity of isolation, as a relation of exteriority between the members of a temporary and contingent gathering, expresses *the degree of massification* of the social ensemble" (ibid., 257, original emphasis).
16. Sartre also speaks of the "interpenetration" of individuals and their environment. See ibid., 253–56.

every Other and every Other in me and everyone as Other in all the Others."[17] The self-alienation I experience in situations such as the bus queue is the result of an "interiorization" of alterity: "everyone's interiorization of his common-being-outside-himself in the unifying object can be conceived as the unity of all in the form of common-being-outside-oneself-in-the-other."[18] In other words, the "unity" of a serial gathering does nothing to diminish my social alienation, for I can, in fact, only be "isolated" with others.[19] Seriality thus defines a whole mode of social being: "there are serial behavior, serial feelings and serial thoughts" (i.e., received or unexamined opinion, social imitation).[20]

According to Sartre, there are different levels of serial alterity, as evidenced in the more extreme example of "indirect gatherings," such as the radio broadcast, which is also defined by *absence*: I am united through the disembodied voice to listeners who lie outside my perceptual field; however, there is nothing that I as an individual can do to effectively respond to the Voice; the very form of the radio audience—the lack of two-way communication—inhibits group formation and engenders feelings of extreme impotence and passivity (much more so than in the example of the queue, in which at least a riot could erupt in response to some sudden scarcity). Particularly in this example, Sartre's *Critique* can be seen as a contribution to the study of mass media culture, an emerging field in the 1960s. Fredric Jameson avers that Sartre's account of seriality is "the only genuine philosophy of the media that anyone has proposed to date" and that its power derives from its avoidance of the "conceptual traps of collective consciousness on the one hand, and of behaviorism or manipulation on the other."[21] Sartre's analysis of seriality has also been important to feminist thought, most notably in Iris Marion Young's essay "Gender as Seriality: Thinking about Women as a

17. Ibid., 267.

18. Ibid., 268.

19. "Isolation does not remove one from the visual and practical field of the Other" (ibid., 258).

20. Thus there must be a minimal reciprocity, even at the level of seriality: "the ensemble of isolated behavior . . . presupposes a structure of reciprocity at every level. [. . .] For otherwise the social models in currency (clothes, hair style, bearing, etc.) would not be adopted by everyone" (ibid., 258). Seriality thus suggests René Girard's notion of "mimetic desire." See René Girard, *Deceit, Desire, and the Novel* (Baltimore: Johns Hopkins University Press, 1965).

21. Fredric Jameson, "Foreword," in Sartre, *Critique*, xxviii.

Social Collective."[22] Both Jameson and Young see Sartre's notion of seriality as a superior way of conceiving of social ensembles that have been traditionally thought of as groups.

Indeed, the ultimate aim of Sartre's discussion of seriality is to criticize the Marxist tendency to treat classes as if they were true groups, as organic forces that motivate historical change.[23] According to Sartre, socioeconomic classes are in fact collectives; they are characterized by seriality and impotence. The class system is simply the differentiated effect of the practico-inert field as modified by scarcity: membership in a class is not freely chosen; it is an external determination based on the unequal allocation of resources. Responsible group praxis thus involves transcending the entire practico-inert structure of serial class being (the negation of scarcity), towards the creation of a classless society of abundance: "*it is seriality* which must be overcome in order to achieve the smallest common result."[24]

Sartre's characterization of groups and collectives should not, however, be seen as static or essentializing: groups ceaselessly arise out of and devolve back into collectives, in the "totalizing" movement of history.[25] "Totalization" (in contradistinction to Georg Lukács's static notion of "totality") is Sartre's term for the constantly developing, dynamic relations between part and whole—e.g., agent and environment, past and present—insofar as these make up synthetic entities (e.g., the farmer and his/her field, the historian and the history he/she writes). Sartre contrasts the dynamic structures revealed in the dialectic of totalization with the fixed structures studied by the analytical reason of the sciences (including anthropology)—a contrast Lévi-Strauss will reject, as we shall shortly see.

It is important to note that seriality recalls what Martin Heidegger outlined in *Being in Time* under the concept of "the they" (*das Man*),

22. Iris Marion Young, "Gender as Seriality: Thinking about Women as a Social Collective," *Signs* 19/ 3 (1994): 713–38.

23. This goes as well for ethnic groups, such as Jews, which for Sartre are also defined by seriality. See Sartre, *Critique*, 267–68.

24. Ibid., 687 (original emphasis). As Thomas Flynn notes, "the true 'subject' of history is the closely knit group, in the sense that only in the group does one overcome the passiveness and exteriority of the practico-inert and achieve a degree of mutual recognition among freedoms that Sartre visualizes as the 'reign of man'" (Flynn, *Sartre, Foucault and Historical Reason: Toward an Existentialist Theory of History, Volume One* [Chicago: Chicago University Press, 1997], 126).

25. However, there is no ontological priority for series or group in terms of one being more fundamental or temporally prior; any such foundationalism would be inimical to Sartre's dialectical method.

which, though ostensibly an onto-existential concept is also a histori-cal one, insofar as it describes the effects of mass urbanized society that arose in the West in the late nineteenth and early twentieth cen-turies. Heidegger similarly uses the examples of mass transportation and mass media in his evocation of "the they":

> In utilizing public transportation, in the use of information services such as the newspaper, every other is like the next. This being-with-one-another dissolves one's own Da-sein completely into the kind of being of "the others" in such a way that the others, as distinguishable and explicit, disappear more and more.[26]

Sartre shares Heidegger's antipathy toward mass culture, which both see as the apogee of inauthentic social relations. However, Heidegger's *mitsein* (being-with-others), the inauthentic crowd, lacks the sense of conflict or violence that permeates Sartre's (Marxist) conception of serial scarcity.[27]

The fact that seriality is designed to describe modern or at least urbanized social forms would appear to exclude from the dialectic and thus from history the types of societies that anthropologists such as Lévi-Strauss typically study. Lévi-Strauss thus objects that

> indeed what can one make of peoples "without history" when one has defined man in terms of dialectic and dialectic in terms of history? Sometimes Sartre seems tempted to distinguish two dialectics: the "true" one which is supposed to be that of historical societies, and a repetitive, short-term dialectic, which he grants to so-called primitive societies whilst at the same time placing it very near biology.[28]

Given anthropology's own roots in colonialism, Lévi-Strauss neces-sarily approaches the question of history as an ethical as well as a theoretical problem. Indeed, Lévi-Strauss's entire career is predicated on erasing the difference between the "savage mind" and the mod-ern (Western) mind, so as to declare them equal in their humanity. Thus for Lévi-Strauss, Sartre's "dialectical reason" is simply another example of Western ethnocentrism masquerading as "philosophy of history." From Sartre's perspective, however, it is Lévi-Strauss who is

26. Martin Heidegger, *Being and Time: A Translation of* Sein und Zeit, trans. Joan Stambaugh (Albany: State University of New York Press, 1996), 119.
27. In Sartre's *Critique* the contrast between the authentic individual and the (se-rial) crowd is replaced by that between the authentic group and the crowd.
28. Lévi-Strauss, *The Savage Mind*, 248.

denying archaic societies (and all others) their full humanity by refusing to consider them dialectically, i.e., in terms of free praxis.[29]

I will return to Lévi-Strauss's perspective later in this essay; but
let us first examine how Sartre proposes to "save" Lévi-Strauss's analyses of kinship by integrating them into the dialectical framework of
the *Critique*. Sartre discusses Lévi-Strauss in the part of the *Critique*
devoted to groups, thus placing "primitive" societies on the side of
authentic praxis, which, given what was said above, may seem coun-
terintuitive. Indeed, Sartre introduces the section on Lévi-Strauss
by asking if there is not a paradox in the fact that organized praxis
can be analyzed as an objective structure by social science (such as
structural anthropology) and yet at the same time be an expression of
group freedom:

> [I]f it really is possible to devise a theory of reciprocal multiplicities in
> organized groups, independently of all concrete, historical ends and of
> any particular circumstances, do we not immediately collapse in the
> face of an inert ossature of the organization? And do we not abandon
> the terrain of liberating *praxis* and the dialectic and revert to some
> kind of inorganic necessity?[30]

Prima facie it would appear that the kind of unconscious necessity
Lévi-Strauss seemingly posits in his concept of structure (which, for
Sartre, is simply the intelligibility of a group's organization) would
inhibit the possibility of authentic praxis (spontaneous, conscious
construction of social forms) on the part of organized groups. Indeed,
highly structured groups appear to be ossified in their very organization, namely in the resistance of this organization to change (its
seeming permanence). Sartre remarks that "function as lived *praxis*
appears in the study of the group *as objectivity* in the *objectified*
form of structure."[31] But if this were the whole story, then organized
groups, and, in particular, "primitive" groups, would simply be reducible to the practico-inert and would therefore lose their status

---

29. In a sense, however, Sartre is also saying that primitive societies lack history
"insofar as the relationship between purposeful action and the universe of material and
man-made limitations has reached such a state of equilibrium that men simply live out
their existence in a sort of ritualistic myth. Only when events pose a contradiction is
history made" (Lawrence Rosen, "Language, History, and the Logic of Inquiry in Lévi-
Strauss and Sartre," *History and Theory* 10/3 [1971]: 283).

30. Sartre, *Critique*, 479 (original emphasis).

31. Ibid., 480 (original emphasis).

as "groups" in Sartre's terminology. The dialectical analysis of such organized groups thus presents more hurdles than the other group types that Sartre sketches, which are spontaneous and evanescent: the "group-in-fusion" (*groupe en fusion*) (e.g., the group of citizens that stormed the Bastille in 1789); and the "pledged group" (e.g., the Tennis Court Oath by members of the Third Estate).

Sartre seeks to resolve the dilemma by arguing—contra Lévi-Strauss—that it is not structure that conditions praxis but rather praxis that conditions structure. Though the rules of kinship that Lévi-Strauss observes in *The Elementary Structures of Kinship* appear, on the structural-analytical level, to restrict possibilities and choice, on the structural-dialectical level they reveal themselves as a transcendence; for the "rules" are a mode of group praxis, which, precisely because of its inertia, the inertia of praxis-structure, enables it to resist the inertia of the practico-inert that the group would otherwise fall into. Sartre thus sees the relation between structure and the practio-inert as the relation between two inertias: "active passivity" and "passive activity" respectively.[32] The passivity of structure reveals itself as a kind of activity insofar as it resists the ruinous passivity of the practico-inert, namely the threat of scarcity: "the exchange of women [is] organized in such a way as to combat, *as far as possible*, scarcity and its consequences for the human ensemble."[33] Far from being inimical to freedom, the structure actually realizes it (albeit in a way that Lévi-Strauss finds unconvincing when compared to Sartre's "higher" dialectic of seriality-group praxis). Joseph Catalano observes that "freedom is the act by which we interiorize exterior structure, actualizing and transcending it to accomplish our purpose. The organized group . . . protects the individual from the unconscious structure of the practico-inert and provides consciously chosen structures."[34] Lawrence Rosen similarly remarks that, in Sartre's analysis, structure is not a "supra-individual constraint" but rather "a construction of human intelligence."[35] Needless to say,

32. Ibid., 489.

33. Ibid., 483.

34. Joseph S. Catalano, *A Commentary on Jean-Paul Sartre's* Critique of Dialectical Reason (Chicago: University of Chicago Press, 1986), 194.

35. Rosen continues: "[structure] is that pattern of freedoms and constraints which men have chosen in concert as their own solution to the problems of scarcity and the needs with which they are necessarily confronted" (Rosen, "Language, History," 282). Similarly, Richard Harvey Brown observes that Sartre sees individuals

Lévi-Strauss would find the idea of being "protected" from the "constraints" of unconscious structures anathema to his theory (as if one needed to be "protected" from grammar). In Sartre's view, however, to the extent that Lévi-Strauss refuses to recognize the praxis of structure, its conscious and creative aspect (active passivity), he in effect reduces structure to the practico-inert.

Lévi-Strauss clearly felt the sting of Sartre's critique, as when he laments (in *The Savage Mind*):

> I must now confess to having myself unintentionally and unwittingly lent support to these erroneous ideas, by having seemed all too often in *Les structures élémentaires de la parenté* as if I were seeking out an unconscious genesis of matrimonial exchange. I should have made more distinction between exchange as it is expressed spontaneously and forcefully in the *praxis* of groups and the conscious and deliberate rules by which these same groups . . . spend their time in codifying and controlling it. [. . .] Thus we must, as Sartre advocates, apply dialectical reason to the knowledge of our own and other societies. But we must not lose sight of the fact that analytical reason occupies a considerable place in all of them.[36]

Lévi-Strauss sounds much more Sartrean in this passage than he perhaps intends, but we should not be led to think that Lévi-Strauss has thereby embraced a philosophy of consciousness and freedom. For the supposedly "conscious and deliberate rules" are still expressions of the universal structures of the mind. Even if the mere assertion of universality does not ipso facto make human beings into automatons, Lévi-Strauss is nonetheless resistant to determining the scope of freedom according to observable praxis; most often, in fact, he describes such "freedom" as an illusion. For example, Lévi-Strauss notes that the goal of "ethnographic research" is to reach "a level where necessity reveals itself as immanent in the illusions of freedom."[37] For his part, Sartre, in an essay from 1969, sums up his differences with Lévi-

"as conscious, intentional actors, whose projects, meanings, and moral decisions are not merely epiphenomena of deeper unconscious structures that somehow possess a superior ontological status" (Brown, "Dialectic and Structure in Jean-Paul Sartre and Claude Lévi-Strauss," *Human Studies* 2 [1979]: 16).

36. Lévi-Strauss, *The Savage Mind*, 253.

37. Lévi-Strauss, "Overture to *le Cru et le cuit*," trans. Joseph H. McMahon, *Yale French Studies* 36–37 "Structuralism" (1966): 53. And in *Tristes tropiques* (trans. John Russell [New York: Atheneum 1964], 160), Lévi-Strauss remarks: "I am convinced that the number of these systems is not unlimited and that human societies, like individual

Strauss thus: "I am in complete agreement that social facts have their own structure and laws that dominate individuals, but I see in this the reply of worked matter [i.e., the practico-inert] to the agents who work it. . . . Structures are created by activity which has no structure, but suffers its results as structure."[38]

We will return to Lévi-Strauss's response to Sartre in the second part of this essay. But let us briefly consider how Sartre himself might have benefitted from Lévi-Strauss's analyses. In a footnote to the section we have just been discussing, Sartre offers a very personal example of the dynamic he observes in Lévi-Strauss's analyses of kinship. Whereas Sartre had previously held that atheism, since it is supposedly unstructured, is more conducive to individual freedom than indoctrination into a specific belief system, he now acknowledges that baptism may in fact lead to greater freedom, because it opens the possibility of a richer structure, *in the context of the group to which the individual belongs*:

> As someone who had been baptized, but who had no real links with the Catholic group, it seemed to me that baptism was a mortgage of future freedom . . . I thought that total indeterminacy was the true basis of choice. But from the point of view of the group . . . the opposite is true: baptism is a way of creating freedom in the common individual at the same time as qualifying him by his function and his reciprocal relation to everyone; he interiorizes common freedom as the true power of his individual freedom.[39]

The idea of individual freedom being conditioned by "common freedom" (i.e., reciprocal relations in the group), particularly in this very personal example, shows just how far Sartre has evolved since *Being and Nothingness*. While it is impossible to locate precisely the inspiration for Sartre's change of position, one could speculate that, whatever his differences with Lévi-Strauss, it was *The Elementary Structures* that taught Sartre to see that an understanding of human groups was essential to any conception of human reality and that the "scandal of the existence of others" in *Being and Nothingness* (or "hell is other people," from *No Exit*) was perhaps overblown, leading

---

human beings . . . never create absolutely: all they do is to choose certain combinations from a repertory of ideas which it should be possible to reconstitute."

38. Sartre, "Itinerary of a Thought," *New Left Review* 58 (1969): 57.

39. Sartre, *Critique*, 486.

him to neglect the positive meaning of reciprocity.[40] Sartre surely took note of the famous last paragraph of *The Elementary Structures*, wherein Lévi-Strauss writes (perhaps thinking of Sartre): "to this very day, mankind has always dreamed of seizing and fixing that fleeting moment when it was permissible to believe that the law of exchange could be evaded, that one could gain without losing, enjoy without sharing."[41] One could perhaps read Sartre's entire *Critique* as a response to this passage: the elucidation of the "law of exchange"—reciprocity—as freedom.

LÉVI-STRAUSS'S *THE SAVAGE MIND* AND SARTRE'S *CRITIQUE*

Lévi-Strauss's professional concern with the question of history certainly predates the debate with Sartre in *The Savage Mind*. In 1949, the same year as *The Elementary Structures*, Lévi-Strauss published an article entitled "History and Anthropology" ("Histoire et Ethnologie");[42] nine years later the essay would serve as the "Introduction" to his *Structural Anthropology* (1958).

What is most striking in this essay is its rhetoric of complementarity. Lévi-Strauss chastises those (like Boas and Malinowski) who tend to regard the discipline of history with suspicion and seek to distance themselves from it. Though each discipline has certain advantages over the other—the anthropologist speaks about a society he/she has "experienced as a living reality,"[43] whereas the historian has extensive written records to work with, documents that seemingly provide a higher level of objectivity—Lévi-Strauss does not see this distinction as crucial. He argues first (*pace* Malinowski) that "the best ethnographic study will never make the reader a native,"[44] for the perspective of the ethnographer is no closer to "objective reality" than

40. I am adapting Fredric Jameson's remark in his "Foreword" to Sartre's *Critique* that "the scandal of the existence of other people [is] surely Sartre's central philosophical motif and the most original and durable element of his various systems" (xxii).

41. Lévi-Strauss, *The Elementary Structures of Kinship*, trans. James Harle Bell, John Richard von Sturmer, and Rodney Needham (Boston: Beacon Press, 1969), 497.

42. Lévi-Strauss, "Histoire et ethnologie," *Revue de métaphysique et de morale* 54/3–4 (1949): 363–91.

43. Lévi-Strauss, *Structural Anthropology*, trans. Claire Jacobson and Brooke Schoepf (New York: Basic Books, 1963), 18.

44. Ibid., 16.

that of the historian;[45] and second, the idea that "the critical study of documents by numerous observers" (history) is methodologically superior to "the observations of a single individual" (anthropology) is not an indictment of anthropology; it simply highlights the need "to increase the number of ethnographers."[46] Moreover, the cherished documents that the historian cites as evidence are, after all, simply "the testimony of amateur ethnographers."[47] Thus history and anthropology share a method. But this method differs in one crucial respect: "history organizes its data in relation to conscious expressions of social life, while anthropology proceeds by examining its unconscious foundations."[48] In this distinction, Lévi-Strauss introduces his structural theory of anthropology as the making explicit of patterns or invariants that underlie conscious actions and thoughts. The anthropologist's task is to uncover these implicit structures, whereas the historian is interested in motivations and desires—i.e., the self-understanding—of historical actors as they manifest themselves in the evidence adduced. The dichotomy in this early essay between conscious expression (praxis, history) and unconscious structures already sets the stage for Sartre's dialectical critique of Lévi-Strauss.

However, it must be stressed that Lévi-Strauss is speaking in this essay about the *discipline* of history, not history as a philosophical concept. As Michael Harkin notes, one of the principal motivations for this essay was to establish "the institutional identity of anthropology, which in France lagged far behind its status in the United States and Great Britain."[49] Franz Boas and Bronisław Malinowski had founded national traditions of ethnological study in the United States and Great Britain respectively, but France had no comparable figure. While Émile Durkheim and Marcel Mauss had established the French tradition of sociology (even if Mauss is more remembered today for his contributions to anthropology), Lévi-Strauss felt that sociology could not be used as a model, given its tendency to study its own

45. "The French Revolution of 1789 lived through by an aristocrat is not the same phenomenon as the Revolution of 1789 lived through by a *sans-culotte*, and neither would correspond to the Revolution of 1789 as conceived by Michelet or Taine" (ibid., 16–17). Lévi-Strauss repeats this idea in *The Savage Mind*, 258.
46. Ibid., 17.
47. Ibid.
48. Ibid., 18.
49. Michael E. Harkin, "Lévi-Strauss and History," in *The Cambridge Companion to Lévi-Strauss*, ed. Boris Wiseman (Cambridge: Cambridge University Press, 2009), 40.

society rather than that of the Other. Lévi-Strauss instead saw history as the more complimentary discipline to anthropology, due to the above-described similarity in method. Though, as Harkin argues, this alignment with history was perhaps more immediately motivated by a desire to associate anthropology with the prestige of an established discipline,[50] Lévi-Strauss appears to have continued to believe in a natural affinity between the disciplines of history and anthropology throughout his career. In a 2001 interview with Marcello Massenzio, Lévi-Strauss affirmed that "now I would say that history and ethnology are the same thing, with the slight difference that we study societies spread out in space whereas history studies societies spread out in time."[51] Lévi-Strauss had written the almost identical phrase in *The Savage Mind*—"[the anthropologist] conceives [of history] as a study complementary to his own: one of them unfurls the range of human societies in time, the other in space"[52]—except that in this work Lévi-Strauss is quite critical of history, both as a discipline and as a philosophical concept. Nevertheless, the proximity Lévi-Strauss posits between the disciplines of history and anthropology seemingly supports Sartre's attempt in his *Critique* to bring the two disciplines together as a "structural and historical anthropology."

In 1967, a year after the English translation of *The Savage Mind*, Lévi-Strauss published a new edition of *The Elementary Structures*. Though this new edition contains no substantive changes,[53] Lévi-Strauss nevertheless adds a footnote in which he briefly responds to Sartre:

> In *Critique de la raison dialectique* (p. 744), Sartre has called attention to this formula, in which he sees a confusion between dialectical and analytical reasoning. But we do not conceive of dialectical reasoning in the same way as Sartre. As we see it, the dichotomous approach

---

50. "Rather than make the difficult argument that anthropology was *sui generis*, being able to align it with an established prestigious discipline [such as history] was helpful" (ibid.).

51. Quoted in ibid., 41 (Marcello Massenzio, "An Interview with Claude Lévi-Strauss," *Current Anthropology* 42 [2001]: 420).

52. Lévi-Strauss, *The Savage Mind*, 256.

53. Vincent Debaene notes in his essay for this volume that Lévi-Strauss republished *The Elementary Structures* with "no alterations," even though "ethnographic knowledge had evolved, revealing some errors and confusions" ("Lévi-Strauss: What Legacy?").

is in no way incompatible with dialectical thought, but clearly the contrary. See on this subject, Lévi-Strauss, 1966, ch IX.[54]

Indeed, in the chapter of *The Savage Mind* to which Lévi-Strauss refers, he will take great pains to reject Sartre's dichotomy between analytical and dialectical reason. Lévi-Strauss's objections are threefold: 1) inconsistency: Sartre both opposes dialectical and analytical reason and sees them as complimentary; therefore, the distinction is either "contradictory" or "superfluous";[55] 2) ethnocentrism: dialectical reason is used to establish the superiority and singularity of Western historical humanity over peoples that "refuse history" (Lévi-Strauss's term);[56] 3) lack of foundation or legitimacy: "dialectical reason can account neither for itself nor for analytical reason."[57] I shall address these objections in turn.

With regard to the first, Lévi-Strauss is keen on extricating himself from Sartre's prison-house of analytical reason and the limiting concept of scientific rationality it denotes. In effect, Sartre, like Heidegger before him, is reasserting through this dichotomy the primacy and encompassing nature of philosophy in the face of the ever increasing prestige accorded to techno-scientific inquiry (hence the bifurcation—still prevalent today—between a Continental approach that defines itself in contradistinction to scientific rationality and an Anglo-Analytic approach that embraces it). Sartre's distinction between dialectical and analytical reason thus recalls Heidegger's famous "ontological difference" between *being* (phenomenological ontology, hermeneutics) and *beings* (objective science, metaphysics, epistemology). By reinterpreting philosophy as the search for being and thus as the more encompassing form of inquiry, Heidegger carves out an autonomous and imperious space for philosophy, thereby reasserting its preeminence vis-à-vis science.

For his part, Lévi-Strauss seeks to turn the tables on philosophy: in his view, structural anthropology, as the *human* science *par excellence*, should be considered the more encompassing discipline, for it alone reveals the fundamental structures that condition philosophical

54. Lévi-Strauss, *The Elementary Structures*, 108, n. 3.
55. Lévi-Strauss, *The Savage Mind*, 246.
56. "Sartre resigns himself to putting 'a stunted and deformed' humanity on man's side, but not without implying that its place in humanity does not belong to it in its own right" (ibid., 248). The phrase "refuse history" is referred to below.
57. Ibid., 253.

thought itself (including dialectical thought); philosophical works such as Sartre's should thus be treated like ethnographic documents.[58] This intellectual jujitsu allows Lévi-Strauss to disarm Sartrean concepts by noting their proximity to "savage thought": "[Sartre's] analysis of the practico-inert quite simply revives the language of animism";[59] "it is possible that the requirement of 'totalization' is a great novelty to some historians, sociologists, and psychologists. It has been taken for granted by anthropologists ever since they learned it from Malinowski."[60] Given its encompassing nature, structural anthropology cannot, in Lévi-Strauss's view, be reducible to Sartre's analytical reason; nor can it be opposed to it without relinquishing the mantle of science. Lévi-Strauss thus concludes that there is one type of rationality with two aspects: "I do not regard dialectical reason as *something other than* analytical reason . . . but as something *additional in* analytical reason."[61]

In making this move, Lévi-Strauss neglects two points. One concerns Lévi-Strauss's complaint that "sometimes [Sartre] opposes dialectical and analytical reason as truth and error, if not as God and the devil, while at other times these two kinds of reason are apparently complimentary,"[62] which fails to recognize the fact that, for Sartre, analytical reason is not ethically neutral. Catalano notes that "Lévi-Strauss has . . . missed this important distinction in methodology. [. . .] As a 'tool' the analytic reason of science can be a source of benefit or harm."[63] The other point is that Sartre sees the dialectical unity of human praxis as irreducible. Thus, Rosen points out that "if for Lévi-Strauss the constituent elements of man's existence and works are to be reintegrated through the dialectic, Sartre denies the possibility of their original analytic dissolution and argues that man is at base a unity of dialectical forces."[64] In other words, there is no bridge between the ahistorical (the universal, the totality) and the historical (the dialectic, totalization) that would preserve their difference, hence Sartre's separation between the two types of reason. Since this separation is, moreover, the basis for the divide between Continental

58. Ibid., 249, note.
59. Ibid., 249.
60. Ibid.
61. Ibid., 246 (original emphasis).
62. Ibid., 245.
63. Catalano, *A Commentary*, 75, note.
64. Rosen, "Language, History," 274.

and Analytic philosophy, one better understands why "poststructuralism," which reaffirms the Heideggarian position, could so easily
displace structuralism. Thus, ultimately, Lévi-Strauss's attempted
appropriation of Sartrean terms is much less effective than Sartre's
appropriation of terms such as structure and reciprocity.

With regard to the second point, the charge of ethnocentrism,
Lévi-Strauss appears to be on firmer ground. As was discussed above,
the idea that the dialectic applies most fully to modern, capitalistic
societies and only in a more limited way to non-historical, archaic
societies, does suggest that Sartre sees the latter as embryonic. As
Marcel Hénaff writes, in his book on Lévi-Strauss:

> They ["primitive" societies] would thus be waiting for their true tem-
> porality: that in which we are already immersed. In short they are in
> the "not yet." The historical dimension is supposed to provide them
> with the meaning they are lacking. Such is the general—implicit
> or explicit—conception of historical thought respecting traditional
> societies.[65]

In other words, all historical thought contains an inherent bias
against unhistorical societies; and thus it is not on the basis of historical thought that any legitimate understanding of the latter can be
sought. Hénaff summarizes Lévi-Strauss's structural approach as the
elucidation of an alternative form of meaning to the historical—an
alternative temporal meaning—which is no less rich or less human
and that manifests itself as a *necessary refusal* of historical temporality, in favor of a mythical temporality of continuity and permanence.

Thus, on one level, structural anthropology itself must also "refuse
history"—not history as a discipline but as a concept conditioned by a
specific philosophical conception, such as the dialectic—to maintain
its encompassing ambition and to show that the same mental structures subsist in historical and non-historical humanity. Lévi-Strauss
thus seeks to delegitimize the notion that "some special prestige
seems to attach to the temporal dimension, as if diachrony were to
establish a kind of intelligibility not merely superior to that provided
by synchrony, but above all more specifically human."[66] Lévi-Strauss
has perhaps obscured his own point in this passage, by making it appear as if the diachrony/synchrony dyad can simply be grafted onto

65. Marcel Hénaff, *Claude Lévi-Strauss and the Making of Structural Anthropology*, trans. Mary Baker (Minneapolis: University of Minnesota Press, 1998), 235.
    66. Lévi-Strauss, *The Savage Mind*, 256.

the temporal/non-temporal opposition.[67] In fact, this dyad is a matter of two temporalities—succession and simultaneity—and thus not one that supports a simple equation between diachrony and history. Though chronology and succession are most often associated with history, if one takes a sufficiently long period of time—the *longue durée*, as the *Annalistes* historians demonstrated—it is possible to see how history might also be subjected to synchronic analysis.[68]

Lévi-Strauss addresses the relation between time and history with greater clarity (and more powerfully, in my view) in an essay, published around the same time as *The Savage Mind*, entitled "Cultural Discontinuity and Economic and Social Development" (1963):

> The question is not knowing whether societies called "primitive" have or do not have a history in the sense that we give this term. These societies exist in time like all others, and with the same title to it, but unlike us, they refuse to belong to history and they try very hard to inhibit, within themselves, whatever would constitute the faint promise of a historical development. [. . .] Our Western societies are made for change; it is the principal of their structure and their organization.[69]

Here Lévi-Strauss separates the question of time from the question of history. One cannot assume that just because a society does not see itself or show itself as historical that is static or incapable of history. The idea that such societies *actively refuse* history, that they "try very hard to inhibit" historical change, is another way of saying that they essentially *choose* to be non-historical and affirm their freedom thereby. This quasi-existentialist manner of expressing the matter may have been unintended, but the Sartrean resonances are clear. In Sartrean terms, this is their *praxis-structure*: "primitive" societies transcend history by consciously and actively *refusing the dia-*

67. Hénaff notes that "for [Lévi-Strauss] the diachronic is not to be confused with the historical perspective" (Hénaff, *Claude Lévi-Strauss*, 230); this may be true in general; however, in these pages Lévi-Strauss seems to unnecessarily confuse the issue.

68. Fernand Braudel's article "Histoire et sciences sociales: La longue durée" was published in 1958, and Braudel's most famous work, *The Mediterranean and the Mediterranean World in the Age of Philip II*, had appeared in 1949.

69. Lévi-Strauss, *Structural Anthropology*, vol. 2, trans. Monique Layton (Chicago: University of Chicago Press, 1983), 321–22. Original source: Lévi-Strauss, "Les discontinuités culturelles et le développement économique et social," *Information sur les sciences sociales* 2/2 (1963): 7–15. Hénaff also quotes part of this passage in his analysis. See Hénaff, *Claude Lévi-Strauss*, 225–27.

lectic. Western societies, on the other hand, are "made for change," i.e., *for the dialectic;* thus any refusal on their part appears as stagnation (the fall into the practico-inert). Lévi-Strauss might therefore be seen as more Sartrean than Sartre in this instance, since he appears to have unwittingly uncovered a new layer of the dialectic (a dialectical anti-dialectic).

With regard to the final point, concerning the foundation, or lack thereof, of dialectical reason, Lévi-Strauss is no doubt reacting to passages such as the following: "Volume I of the *Critique of Dialectical Reason* stops as soon as we reach the 'locus of history'; it is solely concerned with finding the intelligible foundations of a structural anthropology."[70] Though Sartre here employs the language of foundationalism, he in fact stakes out a more nuanced position, which Catalano helpfully summarizes as follows:

> The dialectic must accept the idealist goal that reason founds itself, but it must reject the foundationalism of this view. There is no wider, nondialectical perspective from which the dialectic can be justified. Nevertheless, the dialectic does not validate itself in one stroke as an abstract schema that is then imposed on the facts. If the dialectic is true, it is so because material conditions are such that it must be true. From this perspective, the dialectic is a nominalism; that is, what exists are individuals and totalities produced by individuals.[71]

Catalano's methodological description of Sartre's dialectic resonates with many aspects of Lévi-Strauss's approach. For, Lévi-Strauss has also been accused of imposing an "abstract schema" on the facts. Lévi-Strauss's schemas, like Sartre's, are constructed from the empirical data and thus have no a priori or transcendental basis. Hénaff observes that "as Lévi-Strauss demonstrates in all his work, a structure is precisely a constant relation between contents (a relation that can thus be formalized). There is therefore no question of *its being applied* to them."[72] And Lévi-Strauss's approach can also be described as nominalist, as when he asserts that "'social structure' has nothing to do with empirical reality but with models which are built up after it."[73]

70. Sartre, *Critique,* 69.
71. Catalano, *A Commentary,* 65.
72. Hénaff, *Claude Lévi-Strauss,* 108 (original emphasis).
73. Lévi-Strauss, *Structural Anthropology,* 279.

Clearly, some of the intellectual methods and positions of Sartre and Lévi-Strauss, particularly with regard to the question of history, have more in common than either would care to admit and than the gulf that is typically assumed between existentialism and structuralism would lead us to believe. Though on some questions, namely the question of freedom, Sartre and Lévi-Strauss are certainly irreconcilable, Sartre's careful attention to *The Elementary Structures* in his *Critique* and the fact that Lévi-Strauss allowed himself "to borrow a certain amount of Sartre's vocabulary"[74] in *The Savage Mind* reveal a good faith effort to find common ground.

74. Lévi-Strauss, *The Savage Mind*, 245.

MARCEL HÉNAFF

Living with Others: Reciprocity and Alterity in Lévi-Strauss*

The question of reciprocity is a central theme of Lévi-Strauss's oeuvre. It is at the heart of his first major work, *Elementary Structures of Kinship*, which devotes a substantial chapter to it; it persistently reappears in *Mythologies* as a kind of counterpoint; and it often returns in the last books on Native American myths. It is never separated—and is probably not separable—from another important question, that of alterity. Thus the relation of reciprocity is for Lévi-Strauss inconceivable outside a clear distinction between self and nonself, a difference that is at once ontological, logical, and ethical, as well as perfectly embodied in systems of kinship, social classification, and in the complex narrative forms we call myths.

However, at a certain point in his career—roughly the decade of the 1950s—Lévi-Strauss appears to retreat from the arguments advanced in *The Elementary Structures of Kinship* (1949). The concepts of reciprocity and otherness seem to be absorbed into the idea of "communication." Some have attributed this apparent shift to the influence of game theory, information theory, and cybernetics, areas of research that developed in the United States during that period. But Lévi-Strauss never explicitly theorizes a shift and appears not even to have noticed it. It is clear, however, that he did not continue in this direction and that, with the publication in 1962 of *Totemism* and *The Savage Mind*, the early insights were, at least implicitly, restored. This trajectory is primarily what I propose to investigate and above all reassess in this essay, by calling on thinkers such as Charles Sanders

*This article first appeared in French as "Vivre avec les autres. Réciprocité et altérité chez Lévi-Strauss," in *Claude Lévi-Strauss et ses contemporains*, ed. Pierre Guenancia and Jean-Pierre Sylvestre (Paris: PUF, 2012), 157–80.

YFS 123, *Rethinking Claude Lévi-Strauss (1908–2009)*, ed. Doran, © 2013 by Yale University.

Peirce and Ludwig Wittgenstein as well as Vincent Descombes to assist me in this endeavor. However, what is at stake here is not merely an erudite question concerning one of Lévi-Strauss's positions but rather a certain way of defining social relations and a certain ethics of alterity.

RECIPROCITY AND THE INCEST TABOO: THE SEMANTIC FIELD OF ALTERITY

Let us enter the heart of the matter by examining the last lines of *The Elementary Structures of Kinship*, which appear to exemplify the question I want to treat. They are also well known:

> To this very day, mankind has always dreamed of seizing and fixing that fleeting moment when it was permissible to believe that the law of exchange could be evaded, that one could gain without losing, enjoy without sharing. At either end of the earth and at both extremes of time, the Sumerian myth of the golden age and the Andaman myth of the future life correspond, the former placing the end of primitive happiness at a time when the confusion of languages made words into common property, the latter describing the bliss of the hereafter as a heaven where women will no longer be exchanged, i.e., removing to an equally unattainable past or future the joys, eternally denied to social man, of a world in which one might *keep to oneself* [*vivre entre soi*].[1]

These words conclude a book whose principal aim was to demonstrate this essential point: that all human groups have felt the urge to resist the temptation of living in isolation and have accepted, according to various modalities, the necessity of living with others. Let us note that this does not amount to a refusal of living in a specific locality, with one's original language, beliefs, rituals, stories, and particular customs. Essentially, what Lévi-Strauss is concerned with here are the social forms of reproduction, i.e., sexual relations between men and women, which are not containable within the group and thus involve external relations; in short, life must come from elsewhere. The establishment of such relations is the specific role of systems of kinship.

As is well known, Lévi-Strauss reduces this necessity of going beyond the consanguineous group to a single formula: the incest prohi-

---

1. Claude Lévi-Strauss, *The Elementary Structures of Kinship*, trans. James Harle Bell, John Richard von Sturmer, and Rodney Needham (Boston: Beacon Press, 1969), 496–97.

bition. I am not going to dwell here on well-known arguments concerning this prohibition, namely, how it is presented as the transition from nature and culture, as the emergence of the rule as rule, in short, as the genesis of institutions.[2] What is important, from the perspective of the question I seek to address, is to understand this prohibition as a fundamental expression of the demand for reciprocity between human groups:

> Like exogamy, which is its widened social application, the prohibition of incest is a rule of reciprocity. The woman whom one does not take, and whom one may not take, is, for that very reason, offered up. To whom is she offered? Sometimes to a group defined by institutions, and sometimes to an indeterminate and ever-open collectivity limited only by the exclusion of near relatives, such as in our own society.[3]

The first aim of this prohibition is to make the consanguineous group exogamic, i.e., to force this group to seek another group to achieve what is absolutely fundamental for it: to reproduce as a group. Hence the denial of access to women of one's own group on the condition and with the immediate certainty that the other group will do likewise. But according to what logic? The answer is that a human group only exists as such by defining itself by the *marriage alliance*. Filiation is in some sense inscribed in the process of life; but if mate selection were based on this logic, the group would remain closed to the outside world. The prohibition is equivalent to the birth of society as such, as an entity larger than the consanguineous group: society begins with the marriage alliance, an agreement between Us and Them. The marriage alliance is a putting together of what is other; *sym-ballein*, symbol, means literally "putting together," the agreement between the one and the other. We can thus perhaps better understand Lévi-Strauss's aphorism: we must not seek to discover the social origin of symbolism, but rather to understand the symbolic origin of society.[4]

The marriage alliance occurs in the mutual exchange of wives, an exchange that exemplifies and consecrates the relations of the ceremonial gift, such as Marcel Mauss describes them in his seminal *The*

2. See Marcel Hénaff, *Lévi-Strauss and the Making of Structural Anthropology*, trans. Mary Baker (Minneapolis: University of Minnesota Press, 1998), Chs. 2 and 3.
3. Lévi-Strauss, *The Elementary Structures*, 51.
4. "Mauss still thinks it possible to develop a sociological theory of symbolism, whereas it is obvious that what is needed is a symbolic origin of society" (Lévi-Strauss, *Introduction to the Work of Marcel Mauss*, trans. Felicity Baker [New York: Routledge & Kegan Paul, 1987], 21).

Gift: The Form and Reason for Exchange in Archaic Societies (Essai sur le don, 1924). Lévi-Strauss acknowledges Mauss's essay as the main inspiration for his work on kinship. But to perceive this relation we must understand that the gift that is ritual, reciprocal, and public is profoundly different from two other types of gift: the generous unilateral gift (which is therefore not reciprocal and may or may not be public); and the gift of solidarity (which involves useful goods rather than precious ones). The ceremonial gift is primarily a prestation that ensures the reciprocal recognition of two groups; the relation is agonistic and involves the prestige and honor of the parties. Of all its forms explored by Mauss, the matrimonial alliance—about which he has little to say—is actually the most decisive, since it involves the life of the group and its generational survival. From this perspective, as Lévi-Strauss remarks, "it would be false to say that one exchanges or gives gifts at the same time that one exchanges or gives women. For the woman herself is nothing other than one of these gifts, the supreme gift among those that can only be obtained in the form of reciprocal gifts."[5] In the final pages of the book, he adds that the incest prohibition is ultimately "the supreme rule of the gift."[6]

But first we must address one aspect of the argument that I see as crucial: for this exchange to take place, there must be an element of alterity. This is manifested in the sexual instinct, which, as Lévi-Strauss says, is "man's only instinct requiring the stimulation of another person."[7] But this is only an initial condition, which allows one to situate the relation on the level of sexuality. Only the marriage alliance transforms this biological necessity into social reality. If the woman plays the central role, it is because of her ability to create life and thus simultaneously represent the group's possibility of self-transcendence. This is effectively illustrated in P. Elkin's study of marriage relations in Australian tribes, which emphasizes the paradoxical status of women in the group. Lévi-Strauss comments:

> The sole reason is that she is *same* whereas she must (and therefore can) become *other*. Once she becomes *other* (by her allocation to men

5. Ibid., 65.
6. Ibid., 481.
7. Ibid., 12. It is a question of "overcoming the contradiction by which the same woman was seen under two incompatible aspects: on the one hand, as the object of personal desire, thus exciting sexual and proprietorial instincts; and on the other, as the subject of the desire of others, and seen as such, i.e., as the means of binding others through alliance with them" (ibid., 496).

of the opposite moiety), she therefore becomes liable to play the same role, *vis-à-vis* the men of her own moiety, as she originally played to the men of the opposite moiety. In feasts, the same presents can be exchanged; in the custom of *kopara*, the same women that were originally offered can be exchanged in return. All that is necessary on either side is the *sign of otherness*, which is the outcome of a certain position in a structure and not of any innate characteristic.[8]

Now this essential alterity, understood as a requirement of the incest prohibition, becomes a kind of value that propagates in all kinds of behaviors, situations, and relationships; in short, it forms an extensive network of connotations in a wide variety of contexts. Lévi-Strauss vividly demonstrates this fact in his study of several forest tribes in Malaysia. For these tribes, certain serious transgressions will provoke a raging storm; the list of transgressions appears to be completely heterogeneous: marriage between close relatives; a father sleeping too close to his daughter or a mother sleeping too near her son; making insulting speeches; speaking disrespectful words; playing too loudly (in the case of children); imitating the cry of certain animals; laughing at one's own face in a mirror; dressing a monkey as a man and mocking him. What relationship exists between all these behaviors included under the same type of misconduct? Before responding, we should note some of the explanations given by the natives: one should not laugh at one's own reflection because the reflected image cannot defend itself; however, we can laugh at another human being because he is capable of self-defense; the same logic holds with the monkey costume: the monkey is treated as if it were a human who lacked the means of self-defense; and, similarly, imitating the cry of insects and birds usurps their language and position; speaking loudly or shouting is tantamount to an offensive use of the exchange of words. In short, in all these cases one either ignores the other's alterity by denying him the ability to respond, or one abuses the means of exchange and communication. For words are not merely a neutral medium of communication; they are bearers of *value*; they are offered to others as something that comes from us. Hence Lévi-Strauss's conclusion:

> These prohibitions are all thus reduced to a single common denominator: they all constitute a *misuse of language*, and on this ground they are grouped together with the incest prohibition, or with acts evocative of incest. What does this mean, except that women them-

8. Ibid., 114.

selves are treated as signs, which are *misused* when not put to the use
reserved to signs, which is to be communicated?[9]

Women are thus signs of alterity and pledges of the matrimonial alliance. In short, speaking, marrying, relating to other human beings
or animals, always highlights the fact that a relationship is only just
and worthy—i.e., it avoids abuse and contempt—if it is reciprocal and
recognizes the alterity of all—human or nonhuman—others.

Lévi-Strauss offers other examples of this logic: for example, he
writes that "during Polynesian ceremonial exchanges it is required
that goods be exchanged within the group of near paternal relatives,
but must as far as possible go to other groups and into other vil-
lages. To fail in this duty is called *sori tana*, 'eating from one's own
basket.'"[10] Here we have what Lévi-Strauss called "a sort of social
incest."[11] Hence the formula: "Incest in the broadest sense of the
word consists in obtaining by oneself, and for oneself, instead of by
another, and for another."[12] Yet it is interesting to note here that the
prohibition, as in the case of exogamy, is not only primarily a positive rule of reciprocity, but mostly focuses on specific goods such as
rich food—for these, marked by signs of alterity, are recognized as
privileged symbols of the demand for exchange; and this is true of
the other precious goods; they are immediately perceived as social
goods, which means, according to Lévi-Strauss's analysis, that they
are perceived as goods that must be shared, that is, as given to or
received from others. These are precious rather than useful goods in
that they are symbols of mutual recognition. Like women, they are
signs of alterity in the consanguineous group; they are part of the
logic of reciprocity; they are designated as belonging to the order of
the marriage alliance, which is identical to society as such, as that
which transcends the mere reproduction of life; it is this new order
that defines the marriage alliance as an institution.

Has this logic disappeared from our practices? Have we lost this
strong sense of reciprocity? It does not appear so, according to Lévi-
Strauss, who, in explaining this logic (which accounts for the incest
prohibition), does not hesitate to cite a seemingly trivial contemporary example, a practice he has observed in some small restaurants

9. Ibid., 495–496.
10. Ibid., 57–58 (translation corrected).
11. Ibid., 58.
12. Ibid., 489.

in southern France: customers sitting down to lunch find a small bottle of wine next to their plate (the wine is included as part of the meal); each customer then serves the person sitting opposite, who does likewise, and the conversation begins—a seemingly bizarre type of exchange since nothing is gained or lost. Nevertheless something important has happened: through this gesture, each customer has acknowledged the other, has expressed a desire to interact. Why has wine made this exchange possible? Because unlike food that concerns only subsistence, wine falls under the category of precious goods, and is thus better able to signal a consideration for others; it is a festive sign, a desire to manifest the social relationship itself, as these strangers are led to do; for without this local ritual that allows them to overcome the discomfort of the face-to-face encounter and engage with their counterpart, they might otherwise choose to ignore one another:

> This is the fleeting but difficult situation resolved by the exchanging of wine. It is an assertion of good grace which does away with mutual uncertainty. It substitutes a social relationship for spatial juxtaposition. But it is also more than that. The partner who was entitled to maintain his reserve is persuaded to give it up. Wine offered calls for wine returned, cordiality requires cordiality . . . and receiving makes one obligated, and always beyond what has been given or accepted.[13]

COMMUNICATION THEORY AND THE COMMERCIAL MODEL: LEVI-STRAUSS IN THE 1950S

This strong conception of reciprocity, which includes an equally strong condition of alterity (and which consecrates the marriage alliance as a relation of ritual gifts), appears, surprisingly, to be completely abandoned in a group of texts published in various journals during the 1950s and collected in *Structural Anthropology* (1958). The texts that interest us here concern the relationship between anthropology and linguistics. Along with his "Introduction to the Work of Marcel Mauss" (1950), these texts largely defined the theoretical position of Lévi-Strauss's structuralism. We cannot dwell here on the details of this debate around structuralism, except to examine the concept that manifestly dominates Lévi-Strauss's new formulations: that of *communication*—i.e., any system of relations that, as a bearer of information, conveys a message. To speak about communication

13. Ibid., 59.

in this case means first of all to define information as a reversible relationship between a sender and a receiver. The reference to a general theory of communication appears for the first time in 1950, in his programmatic "Introduction to the Work of Marcel Mauss":

> by associating more and more closely with linguistics, eventually to make a vast science of communications, social anthropology can hope to benefit from the immense prospects opened up to linguistics itself, through the application of mathematical reasoning to the study of phenomena of communication.[14]

References to communication are even more numerous in *Structural Anthropology*, in two texts in particular: one from 1952 entitled "Social Statics or Structures of Communication," which forms part of Chapter XV; the other, from 1956, which is included as a postscript to Chapters III and IV, both of which are devoted to the relationship between language and kinship. Lévi-Strauss sees the concept of communication as a "unifying concept"[15] for the project of renewing the human sciences.

In what sense is this concept unifying? In that, we are told, it allows us to treat, in a similar fashion, three major but seemingly very different areas, which fall under the principal systems of collective organization and relationships between individuals: kinship, economic exchange, and language. These correspond exactly to the three social science disciplines that have managed to approximate the kind of rigor achieved by the exact sciences: the anthropology of kinship, economics, and linguistics. Lévi-Strauss does not hesitate to generalize this similarity of approach as follows: "in any society, communication operates on three different levels: communication of women, communication of goods and services, communication of messages."[16] The same idea is stated in 1956, in a more precise form:

> [it is a matter of] treating marriage regulations and kinship systems as a kind of language, a set of processes permitting the establishment, between individuals and groups, of a certain kind of communication. That the mediating factor, in this case, should be the *women of the group*, who are *circulated* between clans, lineages, or families, in place of the *words of the group*, which are *circulated* between indi-

---

14. Lévi-Strauss, *Introduction to the Work of Marcel Mauss*, 43–44.
15. Claude Lévi-Strauss, *Structural Anthropology*, 300.
16. Ibid., 296.

viduals, does not at all change the fact that the essential aspect of the phenomenon is identical in both cases.[17]

Lévi-Strauss does not put forward such a model without reservations: each type, he notes, operates at a different strategic level and according to its own rhythm; thus relations of kinship can be very slow compared with the more rapid exchange of messages. On the other hand, in systems of kinship women are both signs and values, and above all they are persons. However, the dominant concept in this model is still that of "circulation"; no one would deny that this is a suitable term for goods and messages in general, but to speak about the "circulation of women" is in some sense to forget that the partners in the marriage alliance are the two exogamous groups. This amounts to erasing their role as agents in a reciprocal relationship that determines them as givers and receivers in every instance. In the assignment of a wife, the group's self is at stake, just as the speaker's self is at stake in the exchange of words; whereas in economic exchange—which aims, on the contrary, to preserve the neutrality of things in circulation as well as the neutrality of the partners in the transaction—this commitment of self has no place. Ignoring this fundamental difference leads to a conflation of the marriage alliance with the commercial contract.

One can certainly wonder how three major books—*Game Theory* (1944), by John Von Neumann and Oskar Morgenstern, *Cybernetics* (1948), by Norbert Wiener, and *The Mathematical Theory of Communication* (1949), by Claude Shannon and Warren Weaver—published in the United States between the writing of *The Elementary Structures of Kinship* and the appearance of *Structural Anthropology*, could have had a decisive influence on the views of Lévi-Strauss. We now know that the formulation of his regulation hypotheses about kinship systems owes nothing to Wiener (Lévi-Strauss's book was completed before *Cybernetics* appeared).[18] We also know that in the immediate postwar period, the famous Macy Conferences were instrumental in the development of concepts and theories that were then emerging from cognitive science.[19] But Lévi-Strauss did not participate in these gatherings. At most, we can assume that he heard echoes of

17. Ibid., 61 (original emphasis).
18. See Ronan Le Roux, "Lévi-Strauss, une réception paradoxale de la cybernétique," *L'homme* 169 (2009): 165–90.
19. Jean-Pierre Dupuy, *The Mechanization of the Mind: On the Origins of Cognitive Science*, trans. M.B. DeBevoise (Princeton, NJ: Princeton University Press, 2000);

the Macy Conferences from Gregory Bateson, Margaret Mead, and Roman Jakobson, all of whom did attend. We should also note that in the scholarly circles of New York of the period there was an atmosphere of conceptual innovation from which Lévi-Strauss benefited a great deal more than he ever acknowledged.[20] But this is not our concern here. We are interested in how the recourse to the concept of communication alters the approach to reciprocity developed in *The Elementary Structures*.[21]

The 1952 essay "Social Statics or Structures of Communication" is explicit in this regard and reveals the extent of the shift. Believing it is time to reconcile economic theory with anthropology, Lévi-Strauss writes: "since Mauss's pioneer papers and Malinowski's book on the *kula*—by far his masterpiece—every attempt in this direction has shown that the economic system provides sociological formulations with some of their more fundamental invariants."[22] The works in question are *The Gift* and *Argonauts of the Western Pacific* (1922),[23] two classic texts that describe and theorize the ritual exchange of gifts precisely as not being economic in nature. Moreover, it was by drawing on these works that Lévi-Strauss was able to describe the relation of reciprocity that governs marriage alliances, and thus to account for the incest prohibition; in short, these texts allowed him to make the theoretical breakthrough for which he is rightly recognized

---

reissued in 2009 on MIT Press (Cambridge, MA) as *On the Origins of Cognitive Science: The Mechanization of the Mind*.

20. In an interview that appeared in *Esprit* 301 (2004), I had the opportunity to pose these questions directly to Lévi-Strauss (see esp. 93–96). Here is the essence of his response: "In going from the point of view of exchange to that of communication, one achieves a higher level of abstraction where the incompatibilities that seemed to be irreducible at the previous level are removed. And likewise with respect to the exchange of gifts and of commercial exchange, which you so strongly emphasize in your recent book [*The Price of Truth: Gift, Money, and Philosophy*]. This is true in terms of exchange and in placing it under the rubric of what one could call, in the language of Auguste Comte, the 'subjective synthesis,' but it ceases to be so under the rubric of communication, of which commercial exchange, like gift exchange, represents only the modalities that are expressible in a common language" (96).

21. One could mention the objections of Daniel Sperber in his *Le structuralisme en anthropologie* (Paris: Seuil, 1973). He proposes a necessary distinction between structures of *code* and structures of *network*. Sperber observes that although language rules are able to create sentences and govern the linguistic code, the rules of kinship do not create the women who circulate in marriage networks.

22. Lévi-Strauss, *Structural Anthropology*, 297.

23. Bronisław Malinowski, *Argonauts of the Western Pacific* (New York: Dutton, 1922; reprint, 1961).

in the field of kinship studies. All this would be nullified if we now accepted that these two books primarily described the circulation of useful goods according to a new model of generalized communication, that is to say, as commodities for consumption, as all economic goods are.

Such a reversal or even inconsistency may seem somewhat surprising. However, it should be said that this equivocation is not new. It was already present in one of Lévi-Strauss's earliest articles, entitled "War and Trade in the Native Populations of South America" (1943),[24] where gifts and commercial goods are thrown together with surprising indifference. Though Lévi-Strauss never included this text in his collections of essays *Structural Anthropology* or *The View from Afar*, this is most probably due to the fact that the text had already been incorporated twice before: at the end of Chapter V of *The Elementary Structures* and in Chapter XXVIII of *Tristes tropiques*, but with interpretative differences that are particularly significant.

These texts treat a tense encounter between two rival groups in Nambikwara, an Amazonian tribe: after some verbal quarrels and aggressive gestures, the participants begin shouting at one another; after this preamble they show each other their earrings and various other ornaments, first to solicit and obtain them, then to offer them more freely. At this point a whole range of exchanges of goods develops peacefully, which Lévi-Strauss describes as a huge barter. In the article of 1943, he encapsulated his analysis in this often-quoted formula: "Commercial exchanges are peacefully resolved wars, and wars are the result of unsuccessful transactions." Yet it is interesting to note that in 1949, in the last two pages of Chapter V (on reciprocity) of *The Elementary Structures*, Lévi-Strauss, while returning to the analysis of 1943, dropped the word "commercial" in favor of the more inclusive notion of "transaction." Better still, he adds this crucial remark: "Thus it is a question of reciprocal gifts, and not of commercial operations."[25] But with *Tristes Tropiques* in 1955 (thus in the middle of a decade when his work was dominated by the theory of communication), he returns to a large extent to the commercial hypothesis. Certainly, he is not wrong to point out that an exchange of gifts can

24. "Guerre et commerce chez les Indiens d'Amérique du Sud," *Renaissance* 1/ 1–2 (1943): 122–39.
25. Lévi-Strauss, *The Elementary Structures*, 67.

be the prelude to successful commercial exchange; but to make the second the purpose of the first is quite questionable. As Mauss had already made clear, it is the exchange of gifts that ensures peace, for it expresses what is meaningful: it confers respect, confirms prestige, and maintains honor. It is a matter of mutual recognition between groups as opposed to mere business.

Other texts from the 1950s corroborate this interpretative equivocation. We cannot therefore deny the impression that Lévi-Strauss, who so ably identified the logic of the gift (which, in the case of exogamous marriage, is public, reciprocal, and ritualistic), no longer perceives—or at least does not perceive clearly—this logic as soon as it is a matter of goods rather than of persons (the spouses in matrimonial alliances). The great intuition of *The Elementary Structures* appears to have evaporated, it would seem; the great lesson of reciprocity and mutual recognition of the restaurant patrons whose indifference is transformed into conviviality appears to have been forgotten. We thus need to take a different approach to the problem.

GIFT, ALTERITY, AND RECIPROCITY: THE LESSONS OF PEIRCE AND WITTGENSTEIN

What seems to have disappeared (at least temporarily) is the *condition of alterity*, a necessary condition for the relation of reciprocity— that is, a relation between two parties that is neither accidental nor merely external. To better theorize this requirement and to define such a relation, we shall consider Charles Sanders Peirce's concept of the triad, which he distinguishes from the monad and the dyad.

According to Peirce, there are three types of propositions. The first type, the *monad* (for example: "the wall is white"), is a statement that assigns a quality or defines a status; there is a single logical subject (or propositional actant). The second type, the *dyad*, involves two logical subjects (as in "Cain killed Abel"); it implies the use of transitive verbs and thus accepts the transformation of the active into the passive; it indicates an action as at least potentially intentional (since one can kill another by accident). With the third type of relationship, which Peirce calls the *triad*, we are dealing with a different level, even a *different order*; here intentionality is explicit; the relationship between the terms is a mental, as opposed to a purely physical relation; the intention concerns an *action*, and the proposition contains three logical subjects ("Peter brings the hammer to Paul"). The best examples are provided by double-complement verbs: direct and indirect verbs that grammarians call "trivalents": *verbs of saying* (like asserting, announcing, learning) or *verbs of giving* (such as bringing, granting, providing, conferring, assigning, giving up, offering, granting, allocating; these verbs are associated with the gift in the most general sense, since the list also contains verbs such as lending, selling, and paying).

If, with the triad type of proposition there is a change in *order* (in the Pascalian sense), it is because the triad can absolutely not be formed by simply adding a term to the dyad. The triad opens up another space, that of plural relationships: it is in fact the beginning of a polyad. Dyads are still mere factual observations. But the triad immediately indicates an *intentional relation* between the terms; monads and dyads cannot be isolated within it. As Vincent Descombes observes: "no description of raw dyadic facts can account for any intentional triadic facts."[26] Descombes makes an eloquent parallel between Bertrand Russell's positions and those of Peirce. In *Meaning and Truth* (1940), Russell proposes to reduce complex propositions (such as those used to formulate trivalent verbs) to atomic propositions. Thus the statement "A gives book B to C" can be divided into two units: "A gives B"; "C receives B." Russell admits that his formulation is "phenomenalist," in the sense that it amounts to presenting the action as the addition of two physical events bereft of intentionality. In short, this amounts to "determining the relations between persons and objects while ignoring the relations between persons. One thus treats the giver-receiver relation as a simple logical consequence of the succession of two relations to the object."[27] Russell's position is diametrically opposed to that of Peirce. For the latter, no physical description, no addition of raw facts, can account for the *intentionality* embodied in the expression: "A gives book B to C," as he explains in a letter to Lady Welby (a pioneer in the field of semiotics):

> If you take any ordinary triadic relation, you will always find a *mental* element in it. Brute action is secondness, any mentality involves thirdness. Analyze for instance the relation involved in "A gives B to C." Now what is giving? It does not consist in A's putting B away from him and C's subsequently taking B up. It is not necessary that any material transfer should take place. It consists in A's making C the

26. Vincent Descombes, *Les institutions du sens* (Paris: Minuit, 1996), 236.
27. Ibid., 239.

possessor according to *Law*. There must be some kind of law before there can be any kind of giving—be it but the law of the strongest.[28]

This text is remarkable not only because it states a fundamental requirement of any gift relation, but because it reveals a logic inherent in any human relationship understood as a social relation. What remains to be correctly understood is what Peirce is saying when he speaks of *Law*. From the outset we realize that for him the concept of law is inseparable from the dimensions that have already been laid out: namely, that the gift relation is a *mental thing*, that is, *intentional* and therefore not reducible to raw facts, and that there is an encompassing element that is the purposive relation between the terms of the triad. *Law* means here that there is a necessary connection between the three terms of the triad. That is, one cannot isolate this relationship in pairs: each term (whether subject or actant) is the mediator of the other two according to its position; interrelations between persons are inseparable from their relations to things.

But this involves another dimension, which is also a necessary condition: that of *alterity*. In this context one can appeal to Ludwig Wittgenstein. Descombes reminds us again of a passage from the *Philosophical Investigations* that is useful for this debate: "Why can't my right hand give my left hand money? — My right hand can put it into my left hand. My right hand can write a deed of gift and my left hand a receipt. — But the further practical consequences would not be those of a gift."[29] Indeed, Wittgenstein adds the question: "And now what follows?" The answer can only be: nothing. The gift relation can only occur between *persons who are autonomous and real*. Such is the specifically social relation. The gift relation does not occur with the representation of the other (as can still happen in an intersubjective relationship), but with the other *in person*. It is in this sense that Wittgenstein's remarks on the relation between the two hands (my right hand giving to my left hand) becomes significant. Giving, in Peirce's sense, is only possible if one assumes that giver and receiver are not the same person. I cannot be the beneficiary of a gift (or more generally of a prestation) that I give to myself.

---

28. Charles Sanders Peirce, *Collected Papers*, Vol. 8 (Cambridge: Harvard University Press, 1958), 225–26 (§ 331).

29. Ludwig Wittgenstein, *Philosophical Investigations*, trans. G.F.M. Anscombe (New York: Prentice Hall, 1973), § 268. Quoted in Descombes, *Les institutions du sens*, 241–42.

EXCHANGE AS THE LAW OF RECIPROCITY

At this point we have two types of fruitful arguments with which to reconsider the relation of reciprocity and the condition of alterity in Lévi-Strauss.

Let us take the first question. It can be said that the model of relationality used by Lévi-Strauss corresponds exactly to Peirce's triad.[30] We find such a formulation in the "Introduction to the Work of Marcel Mauss," which echoes the one outlined in *The Elementary Structures*. Let us start with the formulation found in the former, which is the most explicit. In it, Lévi-Strauss takes up the central problem of Mauss's *The Gift*, which is that of the obligation to return (illustrated by the famous theory of the *hau*, the spirit of the thing given, which, in native Maori thought, seems to be the source of the imperative to return the gift). Lévi-Strauss first credits Mauss for having understood that

> *exchange* is the common denominator of a large number of apparently heterogeneous social activities. But exchange is not something he can perceive on the level of the facts. Empirical observation finds not exchange, but only, as Mauss himself says, "three obligations: giving, receiving, returning." So the whole theory calls for the existence of a structure, only fragments of which are delivered by experience—just its scattered members, or rather its elements.[31]

In a certain sense, Mauss indicates the locus for the missing explanation. The answer, for Lévi-Strauss, is that "the primary, fundamental phenomenon is *exchange* itself, which gets split up into discrete operations in social life."[32] This formulation corresponds exactly to the difference between the dyadic and the triadic in Peirce's theory. What Lévi-Strauss calls *exchange* is the totality of a relation that must immediately be understood as integrating the moments and elements of which it is composed; it is this structure of which experience offers only fragments. Hence the avuncular relation: "We do not need to explain how the maternal uncle emerged in the kinship structure: He does not emerge—he is present initially [*il en est la condition*]."[33] In

30. It is curious that Descombes does not notice this, though he devotes most of his eighteenth chapter, entitled "Essays on the Gift," to the discussion and refutation of Lévi-Strauss's objections to Mauss.

31. Lévi-Strauss, "Introduction," 45–46 (original emphasis).

32. Ibid., 47 (my emphasis).

33. Lévi-Strauss, *Structural Anthropology*, 46.

an exchange—such as the matrimonial alliance—it is indeed a matter of a *structure* linking immediately and necessarily all the terms or, in Peirce's words, a relation according to a law: a triad. Such is the fundamental meaning of the concept of exchange in Lévi-Strauss; this concept defines primarily a relation of *reciprocity* (a fact that has rarely been understood). But with this concept of exchange, Lévi-Strauss goes beyond Peirce. It is not a matter of merely understanding the intentional, triadic link between giver/receiver/thing given. It is a matter, at this second level, of understanding another type of intentionality, that which consists in *accepting* what is offered, and above all, in *giving in return* (not the same thing and not right away). Just as the triad is indivisible, so too, and at a more complex level, *exchange understood as reciprocal movement* is as well. It consists of its three moments: giving, receiving, returning, and in this respect it has a structure analogous to that of a two-person game.

This question is crucial because it helps us to understand *obligation*: one receives a ball and one must return it, not because it would be moral to do so, or illegal not to do so, but simply to stay in the game. In this sense, reciprocity is primarily a matter of the internal logic of the acceptance of a rule or system of rules (without doubt this is the logic of the *hau* and of all ritual procedures of sumptuary prestations). Seeing things from this point of view (made possible by the detour via Peirce and Wittgenstein) allows us to reread this well-known paragraph from *The Elementary Structures*, in which the universal nature of "mental structures" is asserted:

> It seems there are three: the exigency of the rule as rule; the notion of reciprocity regarded as the most immediate form of integrating the opposition between self and others; and finally, the synthetic nature of the gift, i.e., that the agreed transfer of a valuable from one individual to another makes these individuals into partners, and adds a new quality to the value transferred.[34]

With the "rule as rule," we enter into the order of the convention, the implicit pact; with the "notion of reciprocity," we are in a triadic structure from the outset; with the "synthetic character of the gift," we are in the domain of recognition guaranteed by goods transformed into symbols.

<hr />

34. Lévi-Strauss, *The Elementary Structures*, 84.

Let us now take up with greater specificity the requirement of alterity. The impossibility that Wittgenstein describes—of making a gift to oneself—means that giving necessarily presupposes a real addressee, that is, *another person;* yet this requirement is, on the institutional level, perfectly homologous with the obligation of a group to transcend itself and link up with another that is sufficiently different (such as the cross-cousins whose blood-line, unlike that of parallel cousins, is always different than that of the Ego). As we have seen, it is by means of this going outside/beyond itself that society is established as transcending consanguineous groups. Thus the *marriage alliance* sets this process in motion, the process of going outside of oneself posited as an obligation in the incest prohibition. We have now returned to the domain of semantics explored in an earlier section, where we spoke about the extension of an incest connotation to all sorts of activities and practices, all sorts of attitudes connoting the doubling of the same,[35] the withdrawal into the self, the lack of attention to others, the private consumption of public goods. The alterity condition is all the stronger due to its being a condition of a reciprocal relation and thus of the possibility of a structure of exchange in the strong sense (i.e., that which involves a movement of return).

Yet it is this constitutive reciprocity and alterity that appear to have been eliminated from the model of communication. The agonistic relation of the partners is missing, neutralized in the technical figures of the two poles of transmitter and receiver. Such was the (too) seductive generalization of the theory. Fortunately, it was soon implicitly challenged by the empirical diversity of the ethnographic materials that Lévi-Strauss began to study. Starting with *Totemism* and *The Savage Mind,* the systems of classification of persons and things (i.e., the social functioning of highly differentiated groups) required a reassessment of the forms of reciprocity. But it is especially in *Mythologies*—with its multitude of narratives dealing with the modalities of social life, such as the rule of the proper distance, the obligation of civility toward others, the necessity to give in return, and the taking of responsibility for the division of labor—that this reassessment will take place. It is these texts that dominate *The Origin*

---

35. See the insightful analyses of Françoise Héritier on this subject: "Symbolique de l'inceste et sa prohibition," in *La fonction symbolique,* ed. Michel Izard and Pierre Smith (Paris: Gallimard, 1979): 209–244.

of Table Manners and *From Honey to Ashes*, which relate at once to cosmology, the social order, the affirmation of sexual difference, and morality.

It is in this vein that Lévi-Strauss will treat a series of myths on honey and tobacco. Two metaphorical modes of cooking are compared and opposed: on one side, there is honey, that is to say, a precooked food—one that is "cooked" by nature and therefore consumable without the mediation of a ritual or of any specifically human activity. In this sense, honey is dangerous and seductive: it is part of the undeveloped ("nature"), while giving the illusion of belonging to the developed (the "culture"). Hence the figure of the Girl-Crazy-for-Honey, who, fascinated by this spontaneous, uncooked food, consumes it eagerly and by herself; she thus forgets social mediation and finds that, without the necessary intercessions, she is herself consumed. Tobacco occupies a position opposite to that of honey: it is consumable only if it is "overcooked," that is to say, first dried (exposed to sunlight), and, finally, reduced to ashes; however, this overcooking does not provide food, but smoke. Here we have a sort of cultural excess: this is why tobacco is related to the spirit-world, to the invisible. In short, honey occupies an infra-culinary position and tobacco a super-culinary one. Between these two extremes, myths invent all sorts of mediating figures, intermediate series that form various narrative variations. This is why honey and tobacco, as ways of connoting *excess*, can "code" behaviors and articulate a sociology with a moral. Thus honey, as a natural precooked product, is associated with the figure of the seductive woman, the Girl-Crazy-for-Honey, who offers union outside the marriage alliance, or a diversion toward a private usage of what must remain an institutional behavior. It is then up to the group to restore the equilibrium by pulling in the opposite direction: toward the overcooked, the consumption of tobacco. But if it is a female figure who is here designated as suspicious, it is because the woman must be this "sign of alterity" (and maintain herself as such) that designates her as the mediator and gage of the marriage alliance. Her role is thus that of the mistress of the hearth; she ensures the mediation between the extremes and incorporates within herself all the modalities of this role—from the grill pan to the pot—all the states, all the combinations of the cooked and the raw, the smoked and boiled, that allow human beings to measure their relations with the surrounding world, which is the source of their food, and with the other human beings with whom life is organized, reproduced, and sometimes celebrated.

Thus Lévi-Strauss finds in the narrative material of numerous indigenous myths of the Americas the conditions of reciprocity that are at the heart of kinship systems and to which the incest prohibition testifies above all. The reductive tendencies in Lévi-Strauss's texts of the 1950s-1960s transformed the relations of the marriage alliance into a circulation of spouses analogous to that of goods and messages and thus reducible to a structure of communication on the model of information theory; the agonistic exchange of gifts was thus confused with profitable exchange. We have demonstrated in our analyses that this tendency appears to have been definitively rejected, even if Lévi-Strauss never explicitly admitted to this reversal of position.[36]

CONCLUSION: LIVING WITH OTHERS OR THE LESSON OF THE SAVAGES

Looking back over the last few lines of *The Elementary Structures*, where Lévi-Strauss points out that it is impossible to pretend that "the law of exchange could be evaded, that one could gain without losing, enjoy without sharing,"[37] we clearly understand that this law is not that of the mere circulation of goods or commerce: it is that of the risk of generosity—specific to the gift/counter-gift structure—and of agonistic reciprocity—knowing how and when to give in return. The social relation is neither an assemblage of isolated individuals nor a movement of members of a group regulated only by institutional logics; it is essentially a relationship between agents who meet and confront one another as different and autonomous, who must negotiate their constitutive alterity, and who know how to oblige one another to do so through reciprocal constraints.

The risk is thus not only "living on one's own"; it is not only being enclosed within the circle of the Same; it is also about not knowing the right distance to maintain with others—not too close—or making the distance excessive, thereby becoming a stranger in one's own home—not too far. From this standpoint, the last part of the *The Origin of Table Manners*, entitled "The Rules of Good Breeding," shows us many examples of the necessity of reciprocal civility

36. One must admit that Lévi-Strauss's own absence of clarification of his positions in this area is very regrettable and has led to numerous misunderstandings; the texts from the 1950s have been projected onto the periods immediately preceding and following these years, giving rise to constant misinterpretations, particularly with respect to the notion of exchange.

37. Lévi-Strauss, *The Elementary Structures*, 497.

as well as of the balanced management of worldly relations that play such an important role in the Native American myths. The book concludes with a reflection that appears to respond to the last lines of *The Elementary Structures*, which were quoted at the beginning; these pages, which are highly critical of our civilization, represent a kind of urgent plea to finally learn how *to live with others*:

> The inherent ethic of the myths runs counter to the ethic we profess today. It teaches us, at any rate that the formula "hell is other people," which has achieved such fame, is not so much a philosophical proposition as an ethnographic statement about civilization. [. . .] When they assert, on the contrary, that "hell is ourselves," savage peoples give us a lesson in humility which, it is to be hoped, we may still be capable of understanding. In the present century, when man is actively destroying countless living forms, after wiping out so many societies whose wealth and diversity had, from time immemorial, constituted the better part of his inheritance, it has probably never been more necessary to proclaim, as do the myths, that sound humanism does not begin with oneself, but puts the world before life, life before man, and respect for others before self-interest.[38]

When Lévi-Strauss warns against the temptation "to outwit the law of exchange, win without losing, enjoy without sharing," we now better understand what the term *exchange* means in his thought: returning when one has received, and deferring to the—human or non-human—other in the regulated and improbable game of relations that make all communal existence possible.

—Translated by Robert Doran

---

38. Lévi-Strauss, *The Origin of Table Manners*, trans. John and Doreen Weightman (London: Cape, 1978), 507–508.

ELEANOR KAUFMAN

Do Dual Structures Exist?
Deleuze and Lacan in the
Wake of Lévi-Strauss

There is a quite radical strain of mid-twentieth-century French thought, one culminating in Gilles Deleuze's 1967 essays "How Do We Recognize Structuralism?" and "Michel Tournier and the World without Others," that in essence attempts to envision a world not mediated by the gaze of the other.[1] Insofar as the question of alterity—of interpolation by the other (Hegel, Sartre, Althusser), of mimetic rivalry with the other (Girard), or even of non-reciprocal exchange with the other (Bataille, Levinas, Baudrillard)—is a mainstay in twentieth-century French philosophy, and expressed in a variety of guises and valences,[2] it is hard to envision a realm in any clear sense apart from such relations. This is even more the case in the French anthropological tradition, with its rich development of the idea of gift economy, in which there is an absolute dependence on models of exchange, if not reciprocity. And this would certainly seem to be the framework not only of Claude Lévi-Strauss's important "Introduction" to Marcel Mauss's *The Gift* but also the stakes of his magisterial *The Elementary Structures of Kinship*, which are predicated on the endogamous and exogamous exchanges of women, above all in the marriage relation.[3] Yet, just as Jacques Derrida will pose the

1. Gilles Deleuze, "How Do We Recognize Structuralism?," in *Desert Islands and Other Texts, 1953–1974*, trans. Michael Taormina, ed. David Lapoujade (New York: Semiotext(e), 2004); and "Michel Tournier and the World without Others," appendix to *The Logic of Sense*, trans. Mark Lester with Charles Stivale (New York: Columbia University Press, 1990).

2. These would all be, after a fashion, "valences of the dialectic." See Fredric Jameson, *Valences of the Dialectic* (London: Verso, 2009).

3. See Claude Lévi-Strauss, "Introduction," in *Works of Marcel Mauss*, trans. Felicity Baker (London: Routledge and Kegan Paul, 1987); and *The Elementary Structures of Kinship*, trans. James Harle Bell, John Richard von Sturmer, and Rodney Needham

YFS 123, *Rethinking Claude Lévi-Strauss (1908–2009)*, ed. Doran, © 2013 by Yale University.

question of whether anything such as "gift" actually remains when exchange is considered through the full lens of reciprocity, thereby introducing a void or inexistent entity at the heart of the exchange economy, so, too, I would like to suggest that in *Structural Anthropology* Lévi-Strauss, perhaps inadvertently, provides the model if not the development of a thought of structure bound neither by an other-oriented nor by a reciprocity-driven economy.[4] Indeed at stake is not so much an *elementary structure*, but a structure so reduced to its elementary state that it is unary, *aneconomic*, and removed from the human dimension of the other.

This is effectively the model that Deleuze puts forward in his analysis of Tournier's first rewriting of the Robinson Crusoe story, *Vendredi ou les limbes du Pacifique*, in which he examines the transition that the protagonist Robinson undergoes on the desert island: from being caught up in the world of what Deleuze calls the "structure-Other," essentially the concern for the regard of other humans, to transcending the other-oriented realm entirely so as to become one with the material elements of the island itself. As Deleuze writes,

> In the Other's absence, consciousness and its object are one. . . . Consciousness ceases to be a light cast upon objects in order to become a pure phosphorescence of things in themselves. Robinson is but the consciousness of the island, but the consciousness of the island is the consciousness the island has of itself—it is the island in itself. We understand the paradox of the desert isle: the one who is shipwrecked, if he is alone, if he has lost the structure-Other, disturbs nothing of the desert isle; rather he consecrates it.[5]

I have outlined elsewhere[6] the remarkable convergence of a series of seemingly un-Deleuzian preoccupations from this pivotal moment in the late 1960s—the world without others over the structure-Other, the Freudian death instinct over life, sadism over masochism, and

---

(Boston: Beacon Press, 1969); and Marcel Mauss, *The Gift: The Form and Reason of Exchange in Archaic Societies*, trans. W. D. Halls (New York: W.W. Horton, 1990).

4. See Jacques Derrida, "The Time of the King," in *Given Time I: Counterfeit Money*, trans. Peggy Kamuf (Chicago: University of Chicago Press, 1992); and Lévi-Strauss, *Structural Anthropology*, trans. Claire Jacobson and Brooke Grundfest Schoepf (New York: Basic Books, 1963).

5. Deleuze, "Michel Tournier and the World without Others," 311.

6. See Eleanor Kaufman, "Extreme Formality and the World without Others," in Kaufman, *Deleuze, the Dark Precursor: Dialectic, Structure, Being* (Baltimore: The Johns Hopkins University Press, 2012).

static empty time over a world of becoming—and I would simply note here the additional convergence of these preoccupations with Deleuze's essay on structuralism, published several years later in 1972, but written (according to the first paragraph) in 1967.[7]

In "How Do We Recognize Structuralism?," Deleuze uses Lévi-Strauss to distinguish two structural components of structure itself, the differential aspect and the singular one. He links the differential aspect to Lévi-Strauss's mode of operation in *The Elementary Structures of Kinship* and the singular to his four-part mapping of the Oedipus myth in *Structural Anthropology*. I quote at length:

> When Lévi-Strauss undertakes the study of elementary kinship structures, he not only considers the real fathers in a society, nor only the father-images that run through the myths of that society. He claims to discover real kinship phonemes, that is, *kin-emes* [*parentèmes*], positional units which do not exist independently of the differential relations in to which they enter and that determine each other reciprocally. It is in this way that the four relations—brother/sister, husband/wife, father/son, maternal uncle/sister's son—form the simplest structure. And to this combinatory system of "kinship names" correspond in a complex way, but without resembling them, the "kinship attitudes" that realize the singularities determined in the system. One could just as well proceed in the opposite manner: start from singularities in order to determine the differential relations between ultimate symbolic elements. Thus, taking the example of the Oedipus myth, Lévi-Strauss starts from the singularities of the story (Oedipus marries his mother, kills his father, immolates the Sphinx, is named club-foot, etc.) in order to infer from them the differential relations between "mythemes" which are determined reciprocally (overestimation of kinship relations, underestimation of kinship relations, negation of aboriginality, persistence of aboriginality).[8]

I will return in more detail to the model of the Oedipus myth, but here I would note two associations that Deleuze proceeds to make with respect to this dual aspect of structure. The first is to Lévi-Strauss's distinction between "names" and "attitudes": "Another side of the question lies in the important attempt to correlate static positions in the kinship structure (as defined by terminology) with dynamic attitudes expressed, on the one hand, in rights, duties, ob-

7. Deleuze, "How Do We Recognize Structuralism?," 170.
8. Ibid., 177.

ligations and, on the other, in privileges, avoidance, etc."[9] This corresponds in effect to the distinction Lévi-Strauss makes earlier in the same essay between social structures "outside the time dimension" and social organization as such, "where time re-enters" (this also corresponds to the "'mechanical' time, reversible and non-cumulative" of anthropology itself, as opposed to the methodology of the discipline of history, which is grounded in "empirical observation").[10] The first and seemingly favored dimension seems to find a parallel in the first of three different notions of time in the Hopi kinship system, which Lévi-Strauss evokes briefly at a later point in the same essay. This is what he refers to as "an 'empty' time, stable and reversible, illustrated by the father's mother's and mother's father's lineages, where the same terms are consistently applied throughout the generations."[11] Deleuze does not elaborate here on this pattern of preferential opposition in Lévi-Strauss between two models of time: on the one hand, anthropological, static, mechanical, and empty; and, on the other, historical, empirical, dynamic, and irreversible.

However, Deleuze goes on in the next section to translate this dual model of structure into what will become the fundamental framework of his 1968 opus *Difference and Repetition*. He links the favored *differential relations* to 1) the total structure; 2) the virtual; 3) differentiation (t); and "distinct species," whereas *singularities* are linked to 1) the partial structure or singular points; 2) actualization; 3) differenciation (c); and 4) "the parts and extended figures which characterize each species."[12] In other words, the higher order, if this expression be permitted, in Deleuze's great work of so-called post-structuralism—namely, the celebrated notion of the virtual—aligns precisely with Lévi-Strauss's static, ahistorical model of structure. But beyond this, both works simultaneously gesture to the way in which the favored term of the two categories (the mechanical/ the differential) is itself comparable to a "total structure"[13] that in some sense goes beyond the dualism of the two categories, just as

9. Lévi-Strauss, "Social Structure," in *Structural Anthropology*, vol. 1, 310.

10. Ibid., 286.

11. Ibid., 301.

12. Deleuze, "How Do We Recognize Structuralism?," 178–79. A few pages earlier, Deleuze also puts his argument in the framework of what will become the dominant one of his other major synthetic work from this period, *The Logic of Sense* (1969), namely, the generation of sense from nonsense, as exemplified by the work of Lewis Carroll (175).

13. Ibid., 179.

the "world without others" goes beyond all duality implied by the "structure-Other." As Deleuze glosses it, and this not insignificantly in his brief discussion of Althusser and structuralist Marxism insofar as they privilege an analysis of the structural place holders of the capitalist system over and above the human subjects who fill those places: "The true subject is the structure itself: the differential and the singular, the differential relations and the singular points, the reciprocal determination and the complete determination."[14] If poststructuralist thought purportedly goes beyond dualism, we might say that Deleuze, like Lévi-Strauss, seeks more nearly to go to the heart of dualism. And this is a crucial distinction, for as Jacques Lacan allows us to see, it is only from the conscious interiority of dualism that its unconscious vanishing point becomes palpable.

There are at least two ways by which structural dualism becomes other to itself. On the one hand, as we have seen, one of the terms (such as the world without others) is elevated to the level of the totality. On the other hand, there is an empty term that serves as motor force for the whole. Deleuze explains the latter as follows:

> The whole structure is driven by this originary Third, but that also fails to coincide with its own origin. Distributing the differences through the entire structure, making the differential relations vary with its displacements, the object=x constitutes the differenciating element of difference itself. . . . Games need the empty square, without which nothing would move forward or function. The object=x is not distinguishable from its place, but it is characteristic of this place that it constantly displaces itself, just as it is characteristic of the empty square to jump ceaselessly. Lacan invokes the *dummy-hand* in bridge, and in the admirable opening pages of *The Order of Things*, where he describes a painting by Velasquez, Foucault invokes the place of the king, in relation to which everything is displaced and slides, God, then man, without ever filling it. No structuralism is possible without this degree zero. . . . And even Lévi-Strauss, who in certain respects is the most positive among the structuralists, the least romantic, the least inclined to welcome an elusive element, recognized in the "mana" or its equivalents the existence of a "floating signifier," with a symbolic zero value circulating in the structure.[15]

14. Ibid., 178.
15. Ibid., 186. Deleuze goes on to posit that it is the phallus that serves the function of "object=x" in Lacan's system: "But the phallus appears not as a sexual given or as the empirical determination of one of the sexes. It appears rather as the symbolic organ that founds sexuality *in its entirety* as system or structure. . . . the symbolic phal-

Rather than the "mana" in Lévi-Strauss's discussion of Mauss to which Deleuze refers, we might turn to another essay in *Structural Anthropology* that poses even more emphatically the problem of the empty or zero value: the 1956 essay "Do Dual Organizations Exist?," which will be discussed in more detail in what follows and in which the north-south axis of the Bororo village, which allows for a dualist reading of that space, is precisely the axis that has a *"zero value"* in that it appears to have no purpose other than to allow the social structure of Bororo life as such to exist:

> These institutions [here, the north-south axis] have no intrinsic property other than that of establishing the necessary preconditions for the existence of the social system to which they belong; their presence—in itself devoid of significance—enables the social system to exist as a whole. Anthropology here encounters an essential problem, one which it shares with linguistics, but with which it does not seem to have come to grips in its own field. This is the problem posed by the existence of institutions having no function other than that of giving meaning to the society in which they are found.[16]

In this way, there are three logics at play, or perhaps two logics with the second having two aspects. The first is the dual model of terms with the favored ones aligning on one side. Such a dualism would seem to correlate with the notion of the binary so squarely associated with structuralism. Yet the second logic entirely reorients the first in that it simultaneously elevates one side of the duality to a more absolute whole and in this manner shows the very idea of duality to be a fundamentally limited and limiting concept. And the third logic, which like the second undermines duality as such, nevertheless posits an empty structure that is not unlike the favored term of the duality (mechanical, empty time, the north-south axis, etc.), but which serves as the enabling motor force of the whole system and also remains in some sense apart from it. In the manner of the gift economy described above, structure cancels itself out from within and leaves as its indigestible remainder (perhaps what is central and raw and celibate in the fashion of the inner circle analyzed in "Do

---

lus is precisely that which does not coincide with its own identity, always found there where it is not since it is not where one looks for it, always displaced in relation to itself, *from the side of the mother*" (187, original emphasis). The question of the mother in Lacan's reading of *Hamlet* will be taken up in what follows.

16. Lévi-Strauss, "Do Dual Organizations Exist?," in *Structural Anthropology*, 159.

Dual Organizations Exist?") nothing short of the "structure itself."
At issue, then, is a thought of structure that uses its relentless logical
formalism to dismantle the very form of structure (in *Difference and
Repetition*, Deleuze evokes "the formless as the product of the most
extreme formality").[17] Yet, rather than being dismantled in the manner of what comes to be known as poststructuralism, here structure
is catapulted into a fully ontological domain, which is not the same
as the postmodern or poststructuralist rejection of all structure. This
process is ontological in that both the first term of the dualism (the
favored static, empty, and virtual aspect) as well as the interplay of the
second and the third anti-dualist positions, gesture to the "thing in
itself" of the entity rather than simply claiming that it cannot be arrived at and thus can only be approximated in epistemological terms.
At issue, then, is a rigorous undoing or weakening rather than something that simply falls apart (the subject, arguably, of all of Samuel
Beckett's fiction). Indeed, it is the affirmation of the otherworldly and
upending terrain that resides at the heart of a structure whose "center
does not hold" that, I will claim, marks the firmest embrace of a positive ontology of something like pure being that we are likely to find in
the entirety of the twentieth-century French philosophical tradition.

*   *   *

What I hope to isolate in its barest outline in the remainder of this
essay is what I will call the neo-Scholastic structural-ontological
synthesis, something that is cryptically advanced in a succession of
mid-twentieth-century works by Lévi-Strauss, Lacan, and Deleuze,
but never acknowledged as such by these thinkers. This is a synthesis that almost entirely vanished after the late 1960s, not only from
French thought in general but from the work of these specific thinkers, and my ambition is to suggest the outline of a counter-history of
twentieth-century French thought: what it might have looked like
post-1968 if its high-structural moment had not been so thoroughly
stamped out and disavowed, beginning in 1966 with its sudden and
transformative American appropriation.[18]

17. Deleuze, *Difference and Repetition*, trans. Paul Patton (New York: Columbia
University Press, 1994), 115.
18. This came in the form not only of the transatlantic enthusiasm for Foucault's
1966 book *Les mots et les choses* (*The Order of Things*, not published in English until

In appealing to Scholasticism, I am referring not so much to the extraordinary synthesis of Greek thought with Judaism, Christianity, or Islam as much as the *methodology* of Scholastic inquiry, which is a methodology that explores with extraordinary rigor, among other things, those categories that were considered as transcendental—above all being, truth, goodness, and unity. In short, any transcendental category worth its characterization as such is shown to contain both the thing and the form of the thing in a relation that is not simply inclusive but at times exclusive, in the fashion outlined above with respect to Lévi-Strauss and Deleuze. To take one of the principle examples from Scholastic thought, "being" signals the interplay of *esse* and *ens*, the general category of being (*esse*, to be) as distinguished from a particular being (*ens*), where the general category is thought at a level of abstraction such that it does not necessarily include the common sense notion of the particular entity.[19] That is, being as such in its absolute sense is only to be found in the realm of God, which is unchanging, perfect, eternal, and simple; this clearly does not much resemble a living being, so that what is ultimately at issue is whether God and creatures can even be measured in the same terms. The tradition of "divine names" takes up this question of whether God is entirely distinct from creatures (equivocity), is related by analogy to creatures (Aquinas), or is fundamentally coterminous with nature and creatures (Scotus and the lineage that followed him via Spinoza to Deleuze).

This emphasis on the structural bifurcation inherent in transcendental categories follows Eugene Thacker's argument in *After Life* that "life" has become a contemporary transcendental category insofar as there exists a bifurcation between "Life" and "the living" that can be traced back to Ancient and Scholastic thought.[20] In this way,

---

1970), but above all the famous conference at Johns Hopkins on the "The Languages of Criticism and the Sciences of Man" which brought together the likes of Lacan, Derrida, Roland Barthes, Paul de Man, and Jean Hyppolite. See *The Structuralist Controversy: The Languages of Criticism and the Sciences of Man*, ed. Richard Macksey and Eugenio Donato (Baltimore: The Johns Hopkins University Press, 2007); and François Cusset, *French Theory: How Foucault, Derrida, Deleuze & Co. Transformed the Intellectual Life of the United States*, trans. Jeff Fort (Minneapolis: University of Minnesota Press, 2008).

19. See Thomas Aquinas, *On Being and Essence*, trans. Armand Mauer (Toronto: The Pontifical Institute of Mediaeval Studies, 1968).

20. Eugene Thacker, *After Life* (Chicago: University of Chicago Press, 2010).

Thacker distinguishes between Life as a structural-ontological category that is not itself alive (essentially the *form* of *psuchē* as outlined in Aristotle's *De Anima*), and living beings (the actual beings that fall into Aristotle's three levels of *psuchē* or "soul," which are nutritive, sensitive, and intellective). In parallel fashion, though if anything at odds with the category of "life," I would propose that for a strain of French thought that runs from Lévi-Strauss to Lacan to Deleuze, the category of structure is in some sense catapulted to a transcendental, ontological category, and the question thus becomes how the fundamental bifurcation at the heart of this entity of "structure," as arrived at by a method of quasi-Scholastic transcendental inquiry, is itself to be thought within the framework of the totality of the structure that it simultaneously undoes.

The workings of this operation can be further specified by examining the way in which the Oedipus myth functions for each of the thinkers in question. If for Deleuze *The Elementary Structures of Kinship* is the mark of the differential operation of kinship relations, and the Oedipus myth the mapping of four singular transhistorical variants (grouped as positive or negative relations of filiation, marrying the mother/killing the father; and positive or negative relations to the earth, the club foot as positive valuation of chthonic birth/the killing of monsters, who spring from the earth, the negation of the chthonic), there seems nonetheless to be a differential operation at work in Lévi-Strauss's schematization of the Oedipus myth. Alongside the singularities of the narrative, there is a difference operator that sifts the human, the inhuman, and the elemental (here, the earth), so that these terms gain their significance also in relation to the potential for an inner bifurcation. The human is split between the familial and the chthonic, the inhuman between the murder of family and the killing of monsters, and the elemental between affirmation and negation. In Lévi-Strauss's hands, in short, this imminently human and familial tragedy becomes a dialectic of elements which, above and beyond the split between Life and the living, embodies the bifurcation between the Inhuman as Structure and the concrete singularities of human or inhuman action and anthropomorphic or non-anthropomorphic elements. There is the same problem of the "zero value" of the Inhuman Structure as formally distinct from the inhuman being or element, which at once encompasses those elements and dissolves them, just as in Scholastic discussions of truth the larger category of truth might encompass both truth and falsity as logical operators that both support an inquiry into truth and challenge its very foundations.[21]

Lévi-Strauss indeed poses Deleuze's problem of the differential and the singular, at least after a fashion, in the aforementioned "Do Dual Organizations Exist?" from *Structural Anthropology*. Here he analyzes the conflicting reports from informants in various Amerindian, Indonesian, and South American societies that explain how their clans are organized. One reported model is of a settlement divided by a straight line through the center into dual parts (the north-south axis discussed above); yet another model explains the arrangement as one of concentric circles in which the inner circle is the more elevated sphere (celibate, masculine, raw) and the other one the realm of women, the family, and cooked food. How can these different spatial models be reconciled? In an elaborate reading, Lévi-Strauss goes on to delineate how, depending on who is narrating, these models are not necessarily mutually exclusive but in fact can co-exist, especially if one regards the concentric circle model as an intermediary of sorts between the straight line division and a ternary model that is not described in detail. Thus may be posed the titular question of whether or not the well-established anthropological model of dual organization really exists. Whereas in his "Introduction" to the Work of Marcel Mauss, Lévi-Strauss critiques Mauss's tripartite model of gift exchange divided into giving, receiving, and returning and suggests that what is really at issue is the totality of exchange itself, in "Do Dual Organizations Exist?" he leaves this tension open, succumbing to the same "shortcoming" that he roundly criticizes in Mauss.[22] It is not so much the dual, concentric, and ternary organizational structures as it is the opening of the structural model itself to encompass all three in a non-contradictory manner that is indeed an approach that goes beyond dualism. For it is the latter that brings Lévi-Strauss in close proximity to the Deleuze who celebrates the loss of the

---

21. See John Buridan, *Sophisms on Meaning and Truth*, trans. T.K. Scott (New York: Appleton-Century-Crofts, 1966).

22. See Lévi-Strauss, "Introduction," 45. For more on the formidable lineage of responses to Lévi-Strauss's critique of Mauss with respect to questions of exchange and reciprocity, see: *The Logic of the Gift: Toward an Ethic of Generosity*, ed. Alan D. Schrift (New York: Routledge, 1997), which includes important selections by Derrida and Pierre Bourdieu among others; and Marcel Hénaff, *The Price of Truth: Gift, Money, and Philosophy*, trans. Jean-Louis Morhange and Anne-Marie Feenberg-Dibon (Stanford, CA: Stanford University Press, 2010); and Hénaff's most recent book *Le don des philosophes: repenser la réciprocité* (Paris: Seuil, 2012).

"structure-Other," in favor of a pure blending into a "phosphores-cence of things."

Thus "Do Dual Organizations Exist?" provides a framework not only for an ontological inquiry into the logic of "structure," but also for a phenomenology of reading that is not so much a "surface read-ing" in current parlance, but an alternate reading from the depths of structure, which are none other than the adjacent spaces of the vil-lages in question. This essay, along with Lévi-Strauss's other work from this period, explores the possibility of perceiving otherwise a seemingly mutually exclusive situation (such as the example of truth and falsity for the Scholastics). Yet this mode of perception is itself indissociable from a bumping up against the "navel" of the structure, which is also the space of the structure's vanishing. And it is this methodological opening to inexistence that is central to what I am calling the ontological enterprise that links Lévi-Strauss, Lacan, and Deleuze.[23]

*   *   *

This structural vanishing is, paradoxically, the point at which the structure nearly succeeds in creating a map—to use Borges's famous expression—that is coterminous with the territory. And it is in fact Lacan, above and beyond Lévi-Strauss and Deleuze, who recognizes

23. I draw the term "inexistence" from Alain Badiou's *Logics of Worlds*, trans. Alberto Toscano (London: Continuum, 2009) and other more recent writings. Whereas Badiou emphasizes the directionality of an inexistent factor that must become rec-ognized in order for the situation to be transformed into a properly evental one, I am gesturing to a structure that is already recognized as such (e.g., the north-south axis), but when it is considered more carefully appears to vanish or unravel. Marcos Zafi-ropoulous makes a direct influence argument with respect to Lévi-Strauss and Lacan, noting at one point the centrality of Lévi-Strauss's discovery of the zero value to Lacan: "The Bororo society is located at the heart of Lévi-Strauss's work and we have seen that the division between north and south had been a kind of enigma for him since the 1940s; he suddenly exhumed this enigma in 1956 and resolved it decisively by mak-ing it an archetype of the *zero-value institution*. In my opinion, the latter had inspired Lacan's own reflection from the time that he had first read Lévi-Strauss's preface to the work of Marcel Mauss," *Lacan and Lévi-Strauss or the Return to Freud (1951–1957)*, trans. John Holland (London: Karnac Books, 2010), 171. While this argument certainly underscores my claims here, I am not working as overtly with a notion of conscious influence between these thinkers. Other studies that pursue the line of direct influence include Alain Delrieu, *Lévi-Strauss lecteur de Freud: Le droit, l'inceste, le père et l'échange des femmes* (Paris: Anthropos, 1999) and *L'anthropologie de Lévi-Strauss et la psychanalyse: D'une structure l'autre*, ed. Marcel Drach and Bernard Toboul (Paris: La Découverte, 2008).

the vanishing or weakening point of the structure as something distinct from the motor force of the zero value "object=x" described above. This question of vanishing or *aphanisis*—which is technically the loss of sexual desire, but Lacan develops this in a more general sense—is the enigmatic kernel of Lacan's most structural-ontological seminar, "Desire and its Interpretations" (Seminar Six from 1958–59), which is also an extended reading of *Hamlet*. Whereas Lévi-Strauss demarcates the Oedipus myth under the rubric of four chiasmic parts, Lacan contrasts Oedipus and Hamlet as exemplifying two entirely different psychic dimensions. If Oedipus's actions reveal the imprimatur of the unconscious (Oedipus is unaware that he is marrying his mother and killing his father until after the fact), Hamlet by contrast is fully conscious of the vortex surrounding the father's murder into which he is catapulted, not insignificantly, by the murdered father himself, or, more precisely, by the dead father's specter. Lacan in fact repeatedly references the analysis of a dream Freud recounts in *The Interpretation of Dreams* of a man who has just lost his father, and dreams very poignantly of his father not knowing he is dead. Rather than focusing on the subject's almost certain wish for his father's death (for it seems the father suffered from a protracted illness in relation to which the son's wish for his death would be fairly unremarkable), Lacan contrasts the state of the father not knowing he is dead in the dream with Hamlet's all too death-conscious father.[24]

In the dream example from Freud, which parallels the case of Oedipus, there is a fundamental ignorance of the familial structure as it pertains to life and death. By contrast, Hamlet and his father the ghost are excellent readers of structures, for the father *knows* he is dead and is subsisting in purgatory (or worse); and the son is able not only to hear the voice of the father when others such as his mother cannot, but he is also able to devise a literary-structural replica of what the father knows (the play within the play).[25] Whereas Oedipus does not know (and his story is thus amenable to mapping schemas such as

24. See Lacan, "Desire and its Interpretation," Seminar Six, unpublished manuscript, readily accessible in the unofficial English translation by Cormac Gallagher, online or through Karnac Books, London, especially session 16, from April 8, 1959. See Sigmund Freud, *The Interpretation of Dreams*, trans. James Strachey (New York: Harper Collins, 1965), 466.

25. Lacan remarks that "[I]t is this community of knowing, of the fact that the father and the son both know, which is here the mainspring which creates the whole difficulty of the problem of the assumption of this act by Hamlet" ("Desire and its Interpretation," session 13, March 4, 1959).

Lévi-Strauss's and Deleuze's), Hamlet replicates what he knows to the point that it dissolves his cause. On the one hand, he is unable to kill his uncle at the moment the uncle, seemingly repentant after the play within the play, is praying (for the father has given his soul to these damning structural pursuits, whereas the uncle's soul would be freed if murdered while at prayer); on the other hand, as Lacan points out, Hamlet's desire is no longer with the structure that the father's ghost makes visible (if it ever was), but with the far less discernible desire of his mother Gertrude. As Lacan cites from *Hamlet* Act IV, "The body is with the king, but the king is not with the body."[26] Lacan will go on to relate this to the workings of the phallus, but we might say instead: the structure is with the father, but the father is not with the structure.

If Oedipus reflects the desire to kill the father and marry the mother, Hamlet for Lacan (in contrast to Ernest Jones's celebrated Oedipal reading of *Hamlet*)[27] stages the desire *of* the mother.[28] In other words, it is not that Hamlet desires his mother, as much as he embodies her desire—and this, then, is the part that is arguably not fully conscious for Hamlet. If he were not caught, like his mother, in the fundamental and immobilizing bifurcation of loyalty to the father and to the uncle, then certainly he would be able to act more efficiently. Whereas Oedipus pays for his sins, Hamlet does not.[29] According to Lacan, after the encounter with the ghost, Hamlet rids himself of the other-oriented Oedipal model (Deleuze's singular structure-Other), one preoccupied with rivalry with the father, the imaginary or aggressive relation to the mother, and a demand-oriented relation to the love object Ophelia (*objet petit a*).[30] Indeed this encounter with the otherless world of the specter not only brings out Hamlet's rejection of and cruelty toward Ophelia,[31] but it deflates Hamlet's reprimands to his mother in Act III (when he goes to her bedroom after the play

26. Ibid., session 14, March 11, 1959.

27. Ernest Jones, *Hamlet and Oedipus* (New York: Norton, 1976).

28. Lacan, "Desire and its Interpretation," session 15, March 18, 1959. Lacan explains that "what Hamlet has to deal with, all the time, what Hamlet is grappling with, is a desire which should be regarded, considered where it is in the play, namely very different, very far from his own, that it is not the desire for his mother, but the desire of his mother."

29. Ibid., session 13, March 4, 1969.

30. See ibid, session 15, March 18, 1959, for a discussion of the way in which Hamlet goes "beyond the other."

31. Lacan notes in session 17, April 15, 1959, that "Ophelia as I told you, is the trap . . . into which Hamlet does not fall."

within the play, in which the doomed Polonius is hiding, to admonish his mother for her sin of wedding his uncle without the appropriate delay: "the funeral baked meats/Did coldly furnish forth the marriage tables"),[32] throwing him into the space of weakness which is for Lacan the beyond of the other.[33] In thus rejecting the Oedipal dualism, Hamlet opens himself to a far more enigmatic space of desire, which is not so much the totality of the zero value, as developed above, but rather a faltering of the subject, an extraordinary weakness which is coincident with the recognition of this "hopeless," "truthless truth" of the situation.[34]

* * *

How does this relate back to Lévi-Strauss? It is through Deleuze, who develops these structural-ontological inquiries that are only gestured to in Lacan (though he leaves them aside once he embarks on his collaborations with Guattari), that we can perceive belatedly the way in which this idea of the structure "vanished" by its totalizing aspirations (or the structure for which its strength is also its weakness) is in fact anticipated in the form if not in the explicit methodology of Lévi-Strauss's analyses in *Structural Anthropology*. And these analyses provide the template, only recognizable in obscure and belated fashion, for the operation by which the structure that is the support and guiding framework of the entire system is shown to be, not a nothing, but precisely inexistent at the point of interpellation in language or naming. This is what accounts for Hamlet's waning enthusiasm for the revenge plan of his ghostly father, and for the loss of the structure-Other on the desert island in Deleuze's reading of Tournier. What I am calling the structural-ontological synthesis is difficult to extract from the thinkers in question, because, if anything, they make an ef-

---

32. Shakespeare, *Hamlet*, Act I, Scene 2.

33. Lacan notes that in *Hamlet* Act III, iv, 112, when the father's ghost in reference to the faltering Gertrude implores Hamlet to "[s]tep between her and her fighting soul," Hamlet himself falters in his reprimand to his mother: "we see here the oscillation between this which, at the moment of the collapse of Hamlet's discourse is something which is in the words themselves, namely the disappearance, the dying away of his appeal into something which is a consenting to the desire of his mother, laying down his arms before something which seems ineluctable to him; namely that the mother's desire here takes on again for him the value of something which in no case, and by no method can be raised up," session 15, March 18, 1959.

34. Ibid., session 16, April 8, 1959.

fort to disavow it: Lévi-Strauss at points renounces abstraction, such as when he critiques formalism for not returning to the concrete;[35] Lacan will repeatedly insist that he is training analysts and is thus not doing philosophy or ontology or structuralist analysis as such; Deleuze (not unlike Foucault) will look askance on his structuralist enthusiasm from the late 1960s, which is probably why he is so adamant to postdate his belatedly-published structuralism essay with the italicized enunciation "[t]his is 1967."[36] To revise Hamlet's wordplay cited above, we might say that the structure is with the textual/material support, but the textual/material support is not with the structure.

Lévi-Strauss is the only one of these thinkers who affirms his position as a structuralist, something that Lacan and Deleuze were reticent to do, and thereby provides the opening and impetus for situating the lineage of the thinkers in question under the rubric of the structural transcendental. We might say that it is Lévi-Strauss's avowal of the structuralist project, combined with Lacan's avowal of the tendency of the structure toward its own vanishing or weakness, that, alongside Deleuze's avowal of the positivity of the empty form and of the world without others (the undoing of dualism in the dual aspect of totality and collapse), allows the formulation of a structural-ontological synthesis derived from these three thinkers insofar as it is rendered visible at the point at which their respective works abandoned this line of inquiry. After *Structural Anthropology*, we see less of a penchant in Lévi-Strauss for the numerical distillation of structure in terms of two-, three-, or four-part mappings. After Seminar Six on "Desire and its Interpretations," Lacan is less focused on the *aphanisis* or the vanishing of desire but rather on its positive articulation in the figure of Antigone in Seminar Seven, in which he asserts that ethics is a matter of "act[ing] in conformity with the desire that is in you."[37] After this "dark" phase in the late 1960s, Deleuze embarks

35. See my extended discussion of this question in "Lévi-Strauss and the Joy of Abstraction" in Kaufman, *Deleuze, the Dark Precursor*.

36. Deleuze, "How Do We Recognize Structuralism?," 170.

37. Lacan, *The Ethics of Psychoanalysis*, trans. Dennis Porter (New York: W. W. Norton, 1992), 314. Notably in this seminar, Lacan also cites Lévi-Strauss in order to hold up Antigone as emblematic of precisely the intemporal ontology at issue in this essay: "This relationship to being suspends everything that has to do with transformation, with the cycle of generation and decay or with history itself, and it places us on a level that is more extreme than any other as it is directly attached to language as such . . . To put it in the terms of Lévi-Strauss—and I am certain that I am not mistaken

on his collaboration with Guattari and the terrain shifts entirely. After May '68, there is an interest in libidinal economy which in fact continues some of these structural-ontological pursuits in the form of a synthesis of Marx and Freud, but this line of inquiry itself entirely disappears by the mid-1970s and is replaced by a turn to the political over and above the structural-economic, and to political theology over and above the logical considerations of Scholastic theology.[38]

Even to think the structural-ontological synthesis that was so forcefully stopped in its tracks (why this stoppage took place will be reserved for a subsequent investigation) entails a necessarily speculative, if not a counter-factual approach. And of course, it might be asked, why would anyone wish to bother with a resuscitation of this type of high-structural, arguably ontotheological (but more nearly onto-logical), and quasi-nihilistic mode of abstraction? My answer is that such a form of thought represents an enhanced form of perception, one in fact gestured to in the farthest reaches of phenomenology—the late Merleau-Ponty of "The Intertwining—The Chiasm"[39]—that is no longer dominated by the reference point of the human perceiver but takes its dissipating motor force from a purely positive island-consciousness or structure-consciousness itself, which is perhaps more in line with both Lacan's and Deleuze's readings of Freud, in which they underscore that there is no negation, or "no," in the space of the unconscious.[40]

This is admittedly not a space of engagement (Sartre), event (in Badiou's sense), equality (Rancière), the common or the multitude (Hardt and Negri), or utopian dialectic (Jameson). Rather it is the domain of the "larval subject" that in its weakness has the capacity

---

in invoking him here, since I was instrumental in having had him reread *Antigone* and he expressed himself to me in such terms—Antigone with relation to Creon finds herself in the place of synchrony in opposition to diachrony" (285).

38. I have discussed the libidinal economy moment of French thought as it is crystallized in the work of Lyotard, Deleuze and Guattari, Baudrillard, and Klossowski in "The Desire Called Mao: Badiou and the Legacy of Libidinal Economy," *Postmodern Culture* 18/1 (September 2007). It might be argued that Derrida's reading of *Hamlet* and the "out of jointness" of messianic time in *Specters of Marx* (trans. Peggy Kamuf [New York: Routledge, 1994]), inaugurates the contemporary critical turn, or return, to political theology.

39. See Maurice Merleau-Ponty, "The Intertwining—The Chiasm" in *The Visible and the Invisible*, trans. Alphonso Lingis (Evanston, IL: Northwestern University Press, 1968).

40. See especially Deleuze's comments on *Beyond the Pleasure Principle* in "Coldness and Cruelty," in Deleuze, *Masochism* (New York: Zone Books, 1989), 30.

to withstand the most extraordinary onslaughts. As Deleuze writes, "thought is, rather, one of those terrible movements which can be sustained only under the conditions of the larval subject . . . Even the philosopher is a larval subject of his own system."[41] This system is an apparatus for using form and even formal logic to entirely alter common perception and notions of relationality. Like the larval subject that can tolerate rigorous upheaval because it is not yet mature, this thought was perhaps too disquieting for these thinkers to have sustained past the mid-point of their respective careers. Had these speculations been pursued, "French theory" would presumably have been less palatable to an Anglo-American audience. But then again, such speculations might be more perceivable and enticing precisely from the vantage point of the American dark continent.

41. Deleuze, *Difference and Repetition*, 118–19.

FRANÇOISE LIONNET

Consciousness and Relationality: Sartre, Lévi-Strauss, Beauvoir, and Glissant*

Claude Lévi-Strauss was personally acquainted with Simone de Beauvoir; yet he gives no impression of having intellectually engaged with her. Beauvoir's favorable 1949 review of *The Elementary Structures of Kinship* in *Les temps modernes*, for example, went unreciprocated. In fact, Lévi-Strauss never mentions Beauvoir in his written work, although they had become colleagues and friends in 1929 at the Lycée Janson-de-Sailly while doing their practice teaching on a team that included Maurice Merleau-Ponty. All three were preparing for the competitive *agrégation* exam; Beauvoir became an *agrégée* in 1929, Lévi-Strauss in 1931.

It is thus highly unlikely that Lévi-Strauss could have failed to notice the philosophical talent of the woman who, at the time of her *agrégation*, was regarded, in the words of Maurice de Gandillac, as *LA philosophe*.[1] One can, however, imagine several other reasons for the neglect, of which I will consider three. First, there is the all-too-usual, and all-too-unfortunate view of Beauvoir as a mere intellectual appendage, however talented, to Jean-Paul Sartre. If that were all she was, she would hardly have been deserving of the high esteem of her peers. Worthier of consideration is the view that Beauvoir's intellectual project was too remote from the concerns of Lévi-Strauss, or that he at least thought that this was the case, despite the fact that in *The Second Sex* (1949) she drew on *The Elementary Structures of Kinship*, specifically on its author's views about women as instruments

*My thanks to John McCumber and Robert Doran for their comments on earlier versions of this paper. Translations are mine unless otherwise specified.

1. Éliane Lecarme-Tubone, "Le couple Beauvoir-Sartre face à la critique féministe," *Les temps modernes* 619 (June-July 2002): 19–42 (esp. 21); Vincent Debaene and Frédéric Keck, *Claude Lévi-Strauss: L'homme au regard éloigné* (Paris: Gallimard, 2009), 25, 57.

YFS 123, *Rethinking Claude Lévi-Strauss (1908–2009)*, ed. Doran, © 2013 by Yale University.

of exchange among men. A third possibility, not entirely inconsistent with the previous one, is that Beauvoir's thought not only had a bearing on that of Lévi-Strauss, but that its critical impetus was so central and devastating to his own way of thinking that he was both unable and unwilling to see it as "thought" at all—in which case he suffered from the all-too-common blind spot stemming from the gender politics and economies of prestige of French intellectual life.[2]

In this essay, I want to reflect briefly on the notion of consciousness in Sartre, with a view toward discussing both Lévi-Strauss's critique of it and Beauvoir's correctives. I will suggest that it is possible to relate Lévi-Strauss's and Beauvoir's thought to that of Édouard Glissant, whose *Philosophie de la relation: Poésie en étendue* (2009, *Philosophy of Relation: Poetry at Large*)[3] addresses, in a postcolonial global context, issues that emerge directly (if implicitly) out of the same intellectual trajectory that links Lévi-Strauss and Beauvoir. Their respective theories of social cooperation or collaborative coalition represent similar efforts aimed at rejecting the transcendental orientation of Sartrean phenomenology. The fact that Lévi-Strauss never mentions Beauvoir or that Glissant acknowledges neither of his predecessors does not invalidate or impede my argument; rather it reveals the atomization of intellectual life that is but one of the seemingly inevitable consequences of the tradition of apodictic certainty that fuels Sartre's solipsism and against which the anthropologist and the feminist both push back.

Beauvoir strives, philosophically, to overcome this tradition of disembodied thought, to illuminate both the philosophical and social consequences of gender coding. For Lévi-Strauss, philosophy, narrowly construed according to the phenomenological model championed by Sartre, is a flawed discipline, which he ultimately rejects in favor of anthropology and a broader, more inclusive understanding of social and cultural histories.[4] Glissant, by contrast, develops an aesthetics grounded in a philosophical approach, which seems to me as indebted to Beauvoir's and Lévi-Strauss's logic of cooperative networks as it is

2. As Toril Moi has argued in *Simone de Beauvoir, the Making of an Intellectual Woman* (Oxford: Blackwell, 1994).

3. Édouard Glissant, *Philosophie de la relation: Poésie en étendue* (Paris: Gallimard, 2009).

4. Claude Lévi-Strauss, *The Savage Mind* (Chicago: University of Chicago Press, 1966), 245ff.

to the Deleuzian notions of the nomad and the rhizome.[5] Glissant would presumably never have agreed to such an assertion: he was known for his indifference to gender issues and to what he perceived as the "moral prescriptiveness"[6] of "political" approaches, and thus of feminist philosophy, in which he had no interest since he did not understand its premises.

While we do not have direct textual evidence of Lévi-Strauss's view of Beauvoir, we have solid knowledge of his opinions about Sartre (mostly of the later Sartre), whom he subjects to a withering critique in the final chapter of *The Savage Mind* (1962), which dissects Sartre's *The Critique of Dialectical Reason* (1960). If his critique of Sartre implicates Beauvoir as well, due to their similar philosophical commitments, there would be grounds, though not decisive ones, to relegate her work to that of a mere disciple, unworthy of Lévi-Strauss's attention. But as several philosophers have amply demonstrated, Beauvoir was an original thinker in her own right, whose 1947 *Pour une morale de l'ambiguïté* (*The Ethics of Ambiguity*) remains a powerful statement about human freedom.[7] It transcends the Sartrean under-

5. Glissant has been called "the most thoroughly Deleuzian writer in the francophone world" by Peter Hallward. See "Édouard Glissant between the Singular and the Specific," *Yale Journal of Criticism* 11/2 (1998): 441–64 (esp. 441–42).

6. The phrase is J. Michael Dash's. See *Édouard Glissant* (Cambridge: Cambridge University Press, 1995), 52.

7. See Nancy Bauer, *Simone de Beauvoir: Philosophy and Feminism* (New York: Columbia University Press, 2001); Eva Lundgren-Gothlin, *Sex and Existence: Simone de Beauvoir's "The Second Sex"* (London: Athlone, 1996), 67–82; John McCumber, *Time and Philosophy* (London: Acumen, 2011), 287–312; and *The Philosophy of Simone de Beauvoir*, ed. Margaret Simons (Bloomington: Indiana University Press, 2003), especially the essay by Stacy Keltner, "Beauvoir's Idea of Ambiguity," 201–213. According to the entry on Beauvoir in the on-line *Stanford Encyclopedia of Philosophy*: "There are some thinkers who are, from the very beginning, unambiguously identified as philosophers (e.g., Plato). There are others whose philosophical place is forever contested (e.g., Nietzsche); and there are those who have gradually won the right to be admitted into the philosophical fold. Simone de Beauvoir is one of these belatedly acknowledged philosophers. . . . Her enduring contributions to the fields of ethics, politics, existentialism, phenomenology and feminist theory and her significance as an activist and public intellectual is now a matter of record. English readers of *The Second Sex* have never had trouble understanding the feminist significance of its analysis of patriarchy. They might be forgiven, however, for missing its philosophical importance. So long as they had to rely on an arbitrarily abridged version of *The Second Sex* that was questionably translated by a zoologist who was deaf to the philosophical meanings and nuances of Beauvoir's French terms, it was difficult for them to see the ways that Beauvoir's critique of women's oppression is grounded in phenomenological-existential categories" (Debra Bergoffen, "Simone de Beauvoir," *The Stanford Encyclopedia of Philosophy* ed. Edward N. Zalta [Fall 2010 Edition] <http://plato.stanford.edu/

standing of human consciousness, entering into a territory that, I suggest, overlaps with Lévi-Strauss's concerns and announces Glissant's *Tout-monde* (a new concept of universalism).[8]

I have argued elsewhere that Beauvoir's definition of an "ethics of ambiguity"—as "one that will refuse to deny *a priori* that separate beings (*existants*) can, at the same time, be bound to each other, that their individual freedoms can forge laws valid for all"—announces Edward Said's "contrapuntal" reading of "discrepant" spheres of experience and that both thinkers search for non-coercive forms of universalism.[9] "Separation does not exclude relation," Beauvoir asserts, "it is part of [the mind's] function to make a multiplicity of coherent ensembles stand out against the single background of the world and, inversely, to comprehend these ensembles in the perspective of the ideal unity of the world."[10] In that short essay—which ought to be more widely studied—she begins to elaborate an original "non-Sartrean account of social existence" that allows her to overcome the "atomistic notion implicit in *Being and Nothingness*."[11] However, she does not fully explore the philosophical implications of this insight.

Glissant's project, on the other hand, his poetics and philosophy of *relation*, developed over roughly four decades (1969–2011) in numerous publications and interviews, dwells on the complexities of difference in a world that is One but also multiple and diverse, hy-

---

archives/fall2010/entries/beauvoir/>, accessed January 22, 2012). Unfortunately, even the new 2010 translation, although much more attuned to some of the nuances of the original, makes several philosophical mistakes. See Toril Moi, "The Adulteress Wife," review of Constance Borde and Sheila Malovany-Chevallier (translators), *The Second Sex* by Simone de Beauvoir, *London Review of Books* 32/3 (February 11, 2010), 3, 5–6. The 1952 translation is adequate for my purposes here.

8. In his *Traité du Tout-Monde* (Paris: Gallimard, 1997), published five years after the "novel" *Tout-Monde* (Paris: Gallimard, 1993), Glissant explains that he wants to discover the hidden commonalities behind the diversity of identities that make up our world and its plural archipelagoes. His project is to suggest the contours of a new and different universalism.

9. Simone de Beauvoir, *Pour une morale de l'ambiguité* (Paris: Gallimard, 1947), 26. *The Ethics of Ambiguity*, trans. Bernard Fretchman (New York: Citadel, 1948), 18. Edward Said, *Culture and Imperialism* (New York: Knopf, 1993), 43, 32. Françoise Lionnet, "Cultivating Mere Gardens? Comparative Francophonies, Postcolonial Studies, and Transnational Feminisms," in *Comparative Literature in an Age of Globalization*, ed. Haun Saussy (Baltimore: Johns Hopkins University Press, 2006), 100–13.

10. Beauvoir, *The Ethics of Ambiguity*, 122.

11. Sonia Kruks, "Beauvoir: The Weight of Situation," in *Simone de Beauvoir: A Critical Reader*, ed. Elizabeth Fallaize (New York: Routledge, 1998), 43–71 (esp. 54, 55).

brid and creolized, unpredictable and dynamic. In an interview on "Europe and the Antilles" given in Berlin in 1998, Glissant explains that "what is good now is that Europe is turning into an archipelago. That is to say that beyond national barriers, we see many islands taking shape in relation to one another."[12] This statement echoes the preoccupations of Lévi-Strauss, who points out, in *Race and History* (1952), that the "diversity of human cultures cannot be static . . . [it] depends less on the isolation of the various groups than on the relations between them."[13]

It is this concept of relationality, found in different forms in Beauvoir, Lévi-Strauss, and Glissant, that I want to consider here: its inter-individual dimensions in Beauvoir, and its intercultural and post-national ones in Glissant. But in order to have a better appreciation of Beauvoir's unique contribution to the *relational* development of human consciousness, we must first examine Lévi-Strauss's account of Sartre's shortcomings, as seen by the cultural anthropologist.

LÉVI-STRAUSS CONTRA SARTRE

Lévi-Strauss's critique begins from the claim that, in the wake of Husserl, Sartre treats consciousness as a self-enclosed realm, i.e., one that is unaffected by anything outside and that can therefore be explained only in terms of itself. For Husserl, to say that consciousness is entirely self-explanatory means that everything about it must be articulated in terms that are founded exclusively on consciousness as we experience it: on its presence-to-self. Sartre evinces a similar view in this statement on the "self-enclosure" thesis, from his early text *The Transcendence of the Ego* (1934):

> And this is just how the ego gives itself to reflection: as an interiority closed upon itself. It is inward *for itself, not for consciousness*. Naturally, we are dealing with a contradictory composite: for an absolute interiority never has an outside. It can be conceived only by itself, and that is why we cannot apprehend the consciousness of others (for that reason only, and not because bodies separate us).[14]

12. Andrea Schwieger Hiepko, "Europe and the Antilles: An Interview with Édouard Glissant," trans. Julin Everett, in *The Creolization of Theory*, ed. Lionnet and Shu-mei Shih (Durham, NC: Duke University Press, 2011), 255–61 (esp. 256).

13. Lévi-Strauss, *Race and History*, no translator (Paris: UNESCO, 1952), 8–10.

14. Jean-Paul Sartre, *The Transcendence of the Ego*, trans. Forrest Williams and Robert Kirkpatrick (New York: Noonday Press, 1957), 84; *La transcendance de l'Ego et autres textes phénoménologiques* (Paris: Jean Vrin 2003), 120.

To be sure, this self-enclosed ego is also, for Sartre, part of the world, which is why it is a "contradictory composite." But its involvement with the world, which phenomenology can grasp only formally, does not affect its basic structures. This self-enclosure makes Sartre, in Lévi-Strauss's words, the "prisoner of his Cogito." Referring to the *Critique of Dialectical Reason*, which is Sartre's philosophy of history and thus of groups, Lévi-Strauss adds, in the same book (*The Savage Mind*), that "by socializing the Cogito, Sartre merely exchanges one prison for another."[15] Nevertheless, Lévi-Strauss is appreciative of Sartre's achievement in the *Critique*. Sartre had moved from the formal account of the Ego (or consciousness), elaborated years earlier in *Being and Nothingness*, to a concrete, and therefore engaged, philosophy, from the empyrean of pure theory to social praxis:

> Sartre then does what every anthropologist tries to do in the case of different cultures: to put himself in the place of the men living there, to understand the principle and pattern of their intentions, and to perceive a period or a culture as a significant set. In this respect, we can often learn from him, but these are lessons of a practical, not a theoretical, nature.[16]

The move itself is problematic for Lévi-Strauss, because it began from a formal account of the ego that is impossible from the outset. For one thing, such a purely formal or transcendental approach, viewing the ego as unconditioned by anything outside itself, means looking at it as distinct from its opposite and thus as able to disengage itself from (or "nihilate") both the natural and the social world, from the "facticity"[17] of the body as much as from the world of the social that conditions its development; here, then, there is no "bridge" between man and nature. (Merleau-Ponty develops Sartre's ideas about embodied consciousness in his *Phenomenology of Perception*; and we should recall that Lévi-Strauss dedicated *The Savage Mind* to Merleau-Ponty.) To the extent that "primitive" societies and cultures do not appeal to or presuppose such a self-contained ego, they must be categorized as biologically conditioned to a greater extent than "advanced" societies, thus as closer to nature than such societies and as

15. Lévi-Strauss, *The Savage Mind*, 229.
16. Ibid., 250.
17. Sartre, *Being and Nothingness*, trans. Hazel E. Barnes (New York: Citadel, 1964), 282.

examples of deficient humanity.[18] Echoing Johann-Georg Hamann's 1784 critique of Kant's similarly "transcendental" account of the mind,[19] Lévi-Strauss also points out that such an approach cannot account for language, which is physiologically and psychologically conditioned.[20]

According to Lévi-Strauss, the failure or shortcomings of the self-enclosure thesis mean that any attempt at a purely formal or "transcendental" account of the ego is impossible; the ego must be explained in terms of "being-in-the-world." When, as Jean Pouillon points out, Lévi-Strauss continually views phenomenology as a form of empirical description, completely ignoring Husserl's (and Sartre's) transcendental orientation,[21] he is not merely engaging in an "astonishing" misreading; he is, by his own lights, being charitable. For Lévi-Strauss, the empirical side of phenomenology, developed by Sartre after his Marxist turn away from his focus on the economy of the individual consciousness—including its material (bodily) aspects and interpersonal relations—to history and collectivities, is what is valuable in Sartre's approach.

The crucial stepping-stone in Sartre's move from transcendental to empirical phenomenology is his concept of dialectical reason, a second target of Lévi-Strauss's critique. Dialectical reason and its counterpart, analytical reason, are in Sartre's hands complex and elusive concepts—as befits their nature, Lévi-Strauss might say, as *ad hoc* solutions to insoluble problems. Dialectical reason, a concept Sartre develops via a treatment of Hegel and Marx that is itself dialectical, amounts for Sartre to the "living logic of action."[22] As such, it constitutes the intelligibility of praxis itself, which Sartre (again following Marx) basically conceives as class struggle, and as a series of confrontations than can only be grasped via contradiction. The possibility of contradiction, and so of action, is grounded for Sartre in "the certainty of always being able to transcend," which "replaces the empty detachment of formal reason."[23]

18. Ibid., 248.

19. Johann-Georg Hamann, *Sämtliche Werke*, ed. Josef Nadler (Wien: Herder Verlag, 1949–1953), vol. 4 (1951), 283–89.

20. Lévi-Strauss, *The Savage Mind*, 252.

21. Jean Pouillon, "L'œuvre de Claude Lévi-Strauss," in Lévi-Strauss, *Race et histoire* (Paris: Gonthier -UNESCO 1961), 87–127 (esp. 109, n. 27).

22. Sartre, *Critique of Dialectical Reason*, 38.

23. Ibid., 21.

The certainty of always being able to transcend is the beginning of Sartre's move to the concrete, for it is given in the basic character of Sartrean consciousness: to become aware of something is to see that thing as not-identical with oneself, which, as early as *Being and Nothingness* (1943), means taking up a distance from it:

> The being of consciousness qua consciousness is to exist *at a distance from itself* as a presence to itself, and this empty distance which being carries in its being is Nothingness. Thus in order for a *self* to exist, it is necessary that the unity of this being include its own nothingness as the nihilation of identity.[24]

Nihilation (*néantisation*) is, then, the way consciousness comes about, and, true to the self-enclosure thesis, it is an "absolute event,"[25] i.e., one that can be explained only by itself. This understanding of the Cogito, according to Sartre, moves us beyond Husserlian apodicticity, for, since nihilation has no nature of its own, it is defined entirely by what it nihilates. The objects of which I, as the "for-itself," am aware—the "in-itself" in general—are, though distinct from my consciousness, also essential to it, though in a negative manner:

> The for-itself is perpetually determining itself not to be the in-itself. This means that it can establish itself only in terms of the in-itself and against the in-itself. . . . The concrete, real in-itself is wholly present at the heart of consciousness *as that which consciousness determines itself not to be.*[26]

Returning now to the *Critique of Dialectical Reason*, the logic of praxis requires that we be able to transcend the given, that we be able to change our world, an enterprise that begins with a refusal of that world. Such refusal is the basic structure of Sartrean consciousness, and the grasping of it as such is dialectical reason. Analytical reason, by contrast, is founded not on refusal but upon acceptance: it is thus a matter of abiding by fixed distinctions; in Lévi-Strauss's words, analytical reason "defines, distinguishes, classifies and opposes."[27]

The negation of the given, the "perpetual self-determination" of the for-itself not to be the in-itself, is thus for Sartre universally human; but that he should call its philosophical form "dialectical rea-

---

24. Sartre, *Being and Nothingness*, 54.
25. Ibid., 55.
26. Ibid., 61, my emphasis.
27. Lévi-Strauss, *The Savage Mind*, 245.

son" betrays that, in his view, the most complete negation of the given is to be found in what Marx would call "revolutionary praxis": only in revolution can we negate the entirety of what is around us in capitalism. Revolutionary Man, i.e., Modern European Man, thus becomes the privileged paradigm of humanity itself.

In Lévi-Strauss's view, Sartre has misconstrued the relation of these two forms of reason, and in two different ways: he either views them as entirely separate, or he confounds them altogether.[28] The former strategy maintains the strict independence of dialectical reason from the analytical variety, but fails because Sartre is unable to give an account of dialectical reason without appealing to analytical procedures: to maintain the mutual independence of the two types of reason, one must define, distinguish, classify, and oppose them.[29] Identifying the two forms, however, comes at the price of identifying their goals: there is a single truth aimed at by both. In which case, why think that dialectical reason can do any job that analytical reason cannot?[30]

The true solution for Lévi-Strauss is that dialectical reason should be understood as analytical reason *"en marche"* (in action).[31] Once this "primacy of the analytical" is established, however, the claim of dialectical reason to comprehend a distinct domain of being—human history—falls away; and with it goes Sartre's attempt (in Lévi-Strauss's eyes, anyway) to identify humanity itself with dialectical praxis, and so with modern conceptualities. Whereas for Marx and Sartre, modern Western humanity is the exemplar of historical praxis and thus the paradigmatic realization of humanity itself, for Lévi-Strauss such privileging is unacceptable: history can only be partial or incomplete. History is a "chronological coding" that "conceals a very much more complex nature,"[32] parts of which are thus bound to remain unknown or *opaque*.

A somewhat similar idea of opacity becomes a central concept in Glissant's poetics and philosophy. Although a leitmotif in much of his writings, the idea of the opacity of history receives its most concise elucidation in a six-page chapter of Glissant's *Poetics of Rela-*

28. Ibid., 245–46.
29. Ibid., 245.
30. Ibid., 246.
31. Ibid., 251.
32. Ibid., 258.

tion.[33] But it was up to the critic Michael Dash, in his monograph on the Caribbean thinker, to make clear, though only in passing, the link (unstated by Glissant) with Lévi-Strauss, which I too will address at the end of this essay, albeit all-too succinctly.[34]

LÉVI-STRAUSS'S ALTERNATIVE TO SARTRE

Lévi-Strauss's critique of the formal character of Sartre's account of the ego is not unique to him; it connects him to a strand of thought that began, as noted above, with Hamann's critique of Kant and is continued, for example, in Merleau-Ponty's critique of Husserl in the "Preface" to *The Phenomenology of Perception*.[35] This history places Lévi-Strauss under a burden: if Sartre's theory of the empirical ego as self-enclosed—that is, as bracketing the world though it is necessarily *in* the world—runs into such devastating problems, what sort of account is he to give?

For Lévi-Strauss, in contrast to Sartre, "human societies are never alone; when they appear to be most divided, the division is always between groups or clusters of societies" (sous forme de groupes ou de paquets).[36] The basic problem with Sartre is not that he seeks underlying invariances within the changing multiplicity of human societies, but that he locates such invariances within modern Western society conceived as an isolated system. Thus, whereas for Descartes and Husserl transcendental truth was accessible to the isolated individual ego, for Sartre it is accessible to the isolated society: "Descartes, who wanted to found a physics, separated Man from Society. Sartre, who claims to found an anthropology, separates his own society from others."[37]

Sartre has merely "exchanged prisons": instead of seeing individual egos as isolated totalities, he sees societies in that way. The conceptual vehicle of such isolation is dialectical reason itself. If the basic nature of the ego is nihilation, the rejection of the conscious object, then revolutionary praxis is its ultimate realization. Since only

33. Glissant, *Poetics of Relation*, 189–194.

34. Dash, *Édouard Glissant*, 152.

35. Maurice Merleau-Ponty, *Phenomenology of Perception*, trans. Colin Smith (London: Routledge & Kegan Paul, 1962), vii-xix.

36. Lévi-Strauss, *Race et histoire*, 16; *Race and History*, 10. Note that these groups or "paquets" suggest the formation, in Glissantian terms, of *archipelagoes*.

37. Lévi-Strauss, *The Savage Mind*, 250.

modern Western societies contain an overtly revolutionary praxis, only such societies are allowed to be truly human. Dialectical reason is thus wedded to the isolation of modern society as something that can be explained only in terms of itself. The task of conceiving of society otherwise—of understanding a given society not as isolated, but as interrelated with others—must thus fall to analytical reason.

For Lévi-Strauss, a society, like a morpheme for Saussure, is defined by its difference from other societies:

> Moreover, side by side with the differences due to isolation, there are others equally important which are due to proximity, bred of the desire to assert independence and individuality. . . . We should not, therefore, be tempted to a piecemeal study of the diversity of human cultures, for that diversity depends less on the isolation of the various groups *than on the relations between them.*[38]

Opposing the Sartrean treatment of societies as isolated units, we have in Lévi-Strauss the concept of societies as cooperating in "coalitions."[39] Lévi-Strauss illustrates the way such a coalition functions with an example from roulette. Suppose a sequence 21–22 has come up. The chances of getting 23 are greater the more tables are in the game.[40] Thus, if history has readied humanity to produce things like chassis, wheels, gears, and engines, putting those things together into a car has a greater chance of happening the more people, and diverse people, are aware of those different components and are looking for a more efficient means of transport. That it happened first in Stuttgart is not unimportant, but it is not crucial either: somebody would have done it eventually.

The cooperative coalition thus begins from diverse individuals, or societies, confronting a common situation and reacting to it in different ways to produce what eventually becomes a common response. The initial diversity is thus, inevitably, reduced by the cooperation: "for the inevitable consequence of the practice of playing as a syndicate [*jeu en commun*], which is the source of all progress, is, sooner or later, to make the character of each player's resources uniform [*homogénéisation*]."[41] The resulting homogeneity or uniformity, would, on the theoretical level, be an agreed upon repertoire of

38. Lévi-Strauss, *Race and History*, 10, my emphasis.
39. Ibid., 46.
40. Ibid., 41.
41. Ibid., 46.

concepts, classifications, and distinctions: the "theory," for example, of the motorcar. Thus, we can say that analytical reason itself not only permits us to understand cooperative activity; it comes about itself through the cooperative activity of a coalition, whether of societies or of individuals. It is this coming about of analytical reason that is, for Lévi-Strauss, dialectical reason. He writes:

> In my view dialectical reason is always constitutive: it is the bridge, forever extended and improved, which analytical reason throws out over an abyss; it is unable to see the further shore but it knows that it is there, even should it be constantly receding.[42]

Dialectical reason is thus the cooperative transition from one phase of analytical reason to another. But this process, according to Lévi-Strauss, is contradictory:

> If men [les hommes] are to progress, they must collaborate; and in the course of their collaboration, the differences in their contributions will gradually be evened out, although collaboration was originally necessary and advantageous simply because of those differences.[43]

Note also that for the structuralist anthropologist, only men are agents of collaboration; women are mere objects of exchange that facilitate the exogamous cooperation and associations necessary to a fruitful—and increasingly interconnected—set of social practices that culminate in various forms of identification. Hence the use of "les hommes" here: it does not refer to universal humanity, but specifically to males.

Enter Simone de Beauvoir, whose thinking about gender dynamics in The Second Sex[44] obliges us to rethink such social relations— although Lévi-Strauss (like most of her peers) never explicitly acknowledges her contributions.

LÉVI-STRAUSS, BEAUVOIR, AND GLISSANT

We now have two questions with which to approach Beauvoir. Can Lévi-Strauss's critique of Sartre also be applied to her, or does her more ambiguous or singular position (i.e., as a feminist) elude it? If it is the latter, is she outside philosophy altogether, so that her reflec-

42. Lévi-Strauss, The Savage Mind, 246.
43. Lévi-Strauss, Race and History, 48.
44. Beauvoir, The Second Sex, trans. and ed. H. M. Parshley (New York: Knopf, 1952).

tions would not be relevant to Lévi-Strauss's own project? Or does she present an account of the ego that deserves to be called philosophical, but that nevertheless differs in a fundamental way from both Lévi-Strauss and Sartre, thereby rendering an engagement with her work more difficult, if not impossible?

We can begin by noting that for Beauvoir, men and women must also cooperate. But such cooperation, obviously, cannot produce identification: the difference between the sexes is for her, at least on the biological level, inexpungible. It is not surprising, then, that Beauvoir orients her account of male/female relations with respect to Hegel's dialectic of "lordship and bondage" in the *Phenomenology of Spirit* (often called the "battle for prestige" or the "Master-Slave Dialectic").[45] Hegel's battling consciousness has the general character of a Sartrean ego in that it is an entirely empty self-enclosed realm that consists, *à la* Sartrean nihilation, in the immediate distancing of itself from all its contents: "as self-consciousness it is movement; but since what it distinguishes from itself is only itself as itself, the difference, as an otherness, is immediately superseded for it."[46] Defined as it is by distanciation—i.e., by the supersession of all difference or, as one could say, the rejection of all content as it arises—such a consciousness must reject other human beings in particular: as Beauvoir writes, it is characterized by "a fundamental hostility to every other consciousness."[47] Only in such terms, she points out, can we make sense of Lévi-Strauss.

Collaboration, for Hegel as for Lévi-Strauss, is necessary: not only for Hegel's battlers, but for man and woman, and for society in general. Indeed, as Aristotle wrote, the cooperation of man and woman is the most basic form of all, because without it the species cannot continue.[48] But for Hegel, as for Beauvoir, the collaboration that comes out of the original hostility is impoverished: the master and the bondsman cannot communicate because, as John McCumber has shown, they share only a rudimentary language, which allows each to define himself only as *not* the other.[49] Beauvoir suggests that this sort

45. G. W. F. Hegel, *Phenomenology of Spirit*, trans. A. V. Miller (Oxford: Oxford University Press, 1979).

46. Ibid., 105 (§167).

47. Beauvoir, *The Second Sex*, xli.

48. Aristotle, *Politics* in *The Basic Works of Aristotle*, ed. Richard McKeon (New York: Random House, 1941), 1113–1316.

49. John McCumber, *Poetic Interaction* (Chicago: University of Chicago Press 1989), 40–45.

of uncollaborative collaboration or minimal cooperation applies better to the relation of man to woman than to that of master to slave.[50] We thus have, at the center of *The Second Sex*, a form of cooperation that does not culminate in identification and so remains unthought by Lévi-Strauss.

In *The Ethics of Ambiguity*, such "cooperation" is framed less antagonistically: in terms of childhood. For the child, adults—parents and teachers—are, like the "master" for the "slave": divinities.[51] The world they inhabit is the real world, which has being in a "definite and substantial way"[52] and so has the characteristics of the Sartrean in-itself. The child is excluded from this world, which she "is allowed only to respect and obey."[53] But again, like the Hegelian slave, for whom "thinghood is the essential characteristic,"[54] she takes herself to have the kind of definite and substantial being she sees in adults.[55] Childhood, in Sartrean terms, is thus the domain of the in-itself.

The child and her caregivers hardly constitute a Lévi-Straussian "coalition": they are not a culturally "diverse" group of similarly situated individuals and so cannot be equal.[56] Rather, the child imbibes what Lévi-Strauss calls, in *Race and History*, "a complex system of criteria, consisting in value judgments, motivations and centers of interest."[57] As with Beauvoir, the child does not distance herself from these structures, that is, she does not have to nihilate them; rather, she identifies with them.[58]

The crucial difference between Beauvoir and Lévi-Strauss is that for Lévi-Strauss, the assimilated structures of one's society are not what is most basic. His account of them is given in the context of an

50. Beauvoir, *The Second Sex*, 68.

51. Beauvoir, *The Ethics of Ambiguity*, trans. Bernard Frechtman (New York: Citadel, 1968), 35 ff.

52. Ibid., 36.

53. Ibid., 35.

54. Hegel, *Phenomenology of Spirit*, 115 (§ 190).

55. See Beauvoir, *The Ethics of Ambiguity*, 36.

56. Childcare arrangements in a globalized world have never been limited to monocultural arrangements, from slave societies to contemporary urbanized families with nannies who hail from the global south. This vital sociological question has no place in Lévi-Strauss's ethnographic scenario of traditional kinship arrangements.

57. Lévi-Strauss, *Race and History*, 25.

58. This identification across racial and cultural lines in the case of children raised and nurtured by racial others is another salient question examined, for example, by Ann L. Stoler in *Race and the Education of Desire: Foucault's History of Sexuality and the Colonial Order of Things* (Durham, NC: Duke University Press, 1995).

appropriation of Einstein's theory of relativity; the individual child is like an Einsteinian observer, and the norms children imbibe are analogous to Einsteinian coordinate systems. Over and above the plurality of cultures and coordinate systems, however, are the structures of observation itself: the speed of light, for Einstein, and the quantity of information, for Lévi-Strauss. It is the capacity to observe coupled with the conceptual procedures of analytical reason that, for Lévi-Strauss, permits the ethnographer to free himself from his own culture by disengaging the basic structures of the human—not the culturally relative—world.[59] And it is the capacity to observe that accounts for the willed diversity of different cultures: because the "desire to assert independence, to distinguish and to *be oneself*" (le désir de s'opposer, de se distinguer, *d'être soi*)[60] can only follow from the observation of other cultures.

For Beauvoir, by contrast, even basic structures of consciousness —such as the fact that, as we saw above, consciousness, as Sartre puts it, "can establish itself only in terms of the in-itself and against the in-itself"—originate in the experience of childhood: "The misfortune which comes to man as a result of the fact that he was a child is that his freedom was first concealed from him and that all his life he will be nostalgic for the time when he did not know its exigencies."[61] Childhood, as noted above, is for Beauvoir the domain of the in-itself. But it is not just a domain where those structures predominate: it is *because* we were once children that we must define ourselves, later on, as opposed to, and hence as nostalgic for, the in-itself. Indeed, the consciousness of freedom—and so, as Sartre recognizes, our freedom itself[62]—comes about for Beauvoir when the child discovers the imperfections of adults.[63]

In her account, then, consciousness begins by transferring to itself the categories of the in-itself it *finds* in the quasi-divine adults who care for it. Further experience teaches it that those adults are eminently fallible, as a result of the questions that have already plagued it—"Why must I act this way? What good is it? And what will happen

59. Cf. Lévi-Strauss, *Race et histoire*, 22; *Race and History*, 12.

60. Ibid., 17/10, my emphasis.

61. Beauvoir, *The Ethics of Ambiguity*, 40.

62. "My possibility can exist as *my* possibility only if it is my consciousness which escapes itself toward my possibility" (Sartre, *Being and Nothingness*, 61).

63. Beauvoir, *The Ethics of Ambiguity*, 38–39.

if I act in another way"[64]—and that have become definitive for it. At that point, consciousness becomes aware of its own freedom, and it constitutes its freedom in that awareness. This process is perhaps, in a broadly Hegelian sense, dialectical. However, it is hardly a case of Marxian revolutionary praxis. The child's original relation to the adult world is not that of a neutral observation of it but of an imbibing of it; it is not an activity of analytical reason, but its primary acquisition. And it does not culminate in an agreed homogeneity of concepts and values but in the questioning of these and therefore in the assumption of one's own individual subjectivity.[65] Beauvoir thus provides a *genetic* account of consciousness that is foreign to both Sartre and Lévi-Strauss.

Indeed, we can say that Lévi-Strauss's approach to family structure obscures such a genetic understanding. His emphasis on exogamy tends to reduce family to kinship structures. But kinship structures do not nurture; indeed, the nurturing is not, as Beauvoir recognizes, performed entirely by relatives, but by other caring adults as well, such as teachers. Lévi-Strauss's (limited) approach to family structure in fact begins not with the nurturing of the child, but with the question of the lonely adolescent as he ventures out on his own to become a man: with whom can I couple?

But the logic of nurture is not analytical, for it does not repose on the homogenization of diversity. Nor, therefore, is it dialectical, either in Sartre's post-Marxian sense of the comprehending of action (the child or adolescent does not truly "act") or in Lévi-Strauss's sense of the transition from one phase of analytical reason to another. From the respective points of view of these thinkers, then, Beauvoir's approach has no logic at all: it is not what they can call "philosophical." Though her attention to the logic of nurture places her in a philosophical tradition that runs from Aristotle through Hegel and beyond to Deleuze and others, it subtracts that portion of her thought from the apodictic project that Lévi-Strauss identifies with philosophy itself. From that perspective, it is perhaps understandable why Beauvoir's undertaking would be passed over in silence.

But once it has been admitted that nurturing is not only philosophical but philosophically primary, a number of consequences fol-

64. Ibid., 39.
65. Ibid.

low. Interpellation, the unwilled positing of an individual by an external force, is not always exercised by the state, as for Louis Althusser, nor is it always ideological. Nurturing is the action of a human individual (or at most a few of them). Instead of reducing an individual to her place in a system, as in classical concepts of interpellation, and thereby foreclosing her future, nurturing aims to facilitate the arrival of a future that the nurturer(s) will not see and which, being unknown, cannot be foreclosed. As Glissant puts it in *Philosophie de la relation*, "the fertile play of change and transformation belongs to us and is in us . . . and human solitude is no longer a walled-in self-enclosure."[66]

Nurturing is thus a *relation* that seeks, not to abolish difference or make all relation into self-relation, but to establish the difference of another, the nurtured one. As such it approaches what Glissant calls "relationality": "the concrete sum of all differences in the world" (la quantité réalisée de toutes les différences du monde).[67] The primary binary of Sartre, that of consciousness and non-consciousness or of the for-itself and the in-itself, is replaced by a symphony of interrelated differences: "Being receptive to differences and to their points of encounter . . . means arriving at an understanding of plural diversities, which are the form and the substance . . . of the *Tout-monde*."[68] Relationality thus describes a dynamic similar to the one underscored by Beauvoir in her understanding of "nurture," since it enables and sustains the other in his or her difference.

Beauvoir's legacy and her possible rapprochement with Glissant become even clearer when we detach nurturing from the adult/child context in which I have presented it and think of it as reciprocal— for people can, of course, nurture, enable, and support each other. To recognize this in a global context is to focus on a "new" imaginary: one that values flows of reciprocity and interrelatedness rather than static systems of ideology. We are then in a different domain of ontology and a more respectful regime of epistemology. For Glissant, the set of interrelated differences that are thus opened up by what he calls "la Relation" cannot function in a single panopsis or "system of the world,"[69] but rather as a gradual and wandering formation, a

66. Glissant, *Philosophie*, 30.
67. Ibid., 42
68. Ibid., 30.
69. Ibid., 52.

form of *errance* that is analogous to a process whereby a "continental" entity becomes an "archipelago."[70] This process is the antidote to the ruptures caused by, among other things, analytical reason (and its divisive, classificatory thrust) against which Beauvoir so quietly protests. For the nurturing reason uncovered by the critical eye of *LA philosophe* is neither a separate domain of historical praxis nor a mere moment of transition between two phases of analytical reason. It neither informs us nor liberates us; it brings us about *as human* and therefore as members of collectivities grounded in the diverse social and anthropological networks foregrounded by Lévi-Strauss and imagined by Glissant in terms of interconnected but distinct islands, those Creole archipelagoes that inspire Glissant's inclusive vision of a *Tout-monde* and echo Lévi-Strauss's notion of "a world-wide coalition of cultures, each of which would preserve its own originality."[71]

Glissant's philosophy takes to a global level the understanding of intersubjective networks that are for Beauvoir constitutive of individual consciousness. Whereas Sartre can argue that the empirical ego brackets and nihilates the "Other" to achieve transcendental subjectivity in a context where "Being" must posit the Other's "Nothingness" as constitutive of the self, both Beauvoir and Glissant see others (plural, small "o") as separate *existants* in a multiplicity of possible relations with the self, together forming the "ideal unity of the world" that they both posit as their horizon. Glissant's assertion, in the final elaboration of his *Philosophie de la relation* (published two years before his death) that "Being quivers, but it now includes all of us, and as being-as-becoming" (l'Être frémit, mais pour nous tous, et en être-comme-étant)[72] is, in the final analysis, the postcolonial iteration of an on-going philosophical reflection that underscores the diverse material (genetic, familial, and social) processes that can help build solidarities beyond the limits of Sartrean philosophy, as Lévi-Strauss and Beauvoir demonstrate each in his and her own distinct and complementary way.[73]

70. Ibid., 62.
71. Lévi-Strauss, *Race and History*, 45.
72. Glissant, *Philosophie*, 62.
73. For a more complete discussion of questions of race and identity, opacity and solidarity in France and in the Creole world, see Françoise Lionnet, "Continents and Archipelagoes: From *E Pluribus Unum* to Creolized Solidarities," *PMLA* 123/5 (Oct. 2008): 1503–1515.

THOMAS PAVEL

Reflections on the Oedipus Myth*

An early study of Claude Lévi-Strauss by Edmund Leach compares his work with the achievements of two influential social anthropologists in the English speaking world, Sir James Frazer and Bronisław Malinowski.[1] Frazer examined myths and rituals from every culture and historical period to learn how the human psyche works, while Malinowski concentrated on a single community in Melanesia, focusing on the way it functioned as a social system. Leach argues that Lévi-Strauss is closer to Frazer's tradition, if not to his style, insofar as the French anthropologist takes as his object the operation of the human mind rather than social organization. But whereas Frazer's analyses highlight rituals and mythical meanings that are accessible to collective consciousness, Lévi-Strauss is interested in the way abstract, impersonal semantic structures operate independently of their ostensible aspects.[2]

Thus, in his influential article "The Structural Study of Myth," published in 1955, Lévi-Strauss contends that the Oedipus myth—considered in all its versions, including the one sketched out much later by Sigmund Freud—always relies on two semantic oppositions: 1) *the overrating of blood relations* versus *the underrating of blood relations*; and 2) *the assertion of the autochthonous origin of mankind* versus *its denial*.[3] Oedipus's killing of his father exemplifies the underrating of blood relations, while his marriage to Jocasta illustrates the overrating of such relations. The killing of the Sphinx,

*I am particularly grateful to Robert Doran, the editor of this issue, for his generous guidance and advice.
  1. Edmund Leach, *Lévi-Strauss* (London: Fontana/Collins, 1970), 7.
  2. Ibid., 51.
  3. Claude Lévi-Strauss, *Structural Anthropology*, trans. Claire Jacobson and Brooke Grundfest Shoepf (New York: Basic Books, 1963), 215.

YFS 123, *Rethinking Claude Lévi-Strauss (1908–2009)*, ed. Doran, © 2013 by Yale University.
  118

a chtonian monster, denies that mankind is born from Earth, while Oedipus's name, which means "lame foot," signifies the difficulty of standing upright, therefore asserting that man is born from Earth. An even more abstract, quasi-algebraic formula is supposed to underlie the structure of all myths in all cultures.[4] The algebraic speculations notwithstanding, the four elements of the semantic oppositions found by Lévi-Strauss are grounded in human experience and human attempts to interpret it. Although Lévi-Strauss presents them as elements that *shape* human understanding, they are in fact, like any interpretive notion, the *result* of human understanding. Lévi-Strauss himself seems to be to some extent aware of this aspect. He never explains how the pair of oppositions translates into the actual myth of Oedipus, but neither does he claim that his reading of this myth is definitive. On the contrary, he is fully aware that his interpretation might not be "acceptable to the specialist."[5] He wants only to illustrate a specific technique of myth analysis that detects abstract, general semantic elements, even though the use of this technique "is probably not legitimate in this particular instance."[6] And he compares his demonstration with the actions of a "street peddler, whose aim is not to achieve a concrete result, but to explain, as succinctly as possible, the functioning of a mechanical toy which he is trying to sell to the onlookers."[7]

Lévi-Strauss's honesty is admirable. The two semantic oppositions that, in his view, form the core of the Oedipus story are to be understood as mere examples of a kind of myth-analysis that deliberately goes beyond easily reached comprehensibility, rather than as an accurate interpretation of this particular myth. The kind of analysis he wants to promote is based on tentative assumptions that fall within the province of early French structuralism, in particular on the convictions that "myth belongs to the same category as language, being, as a matter of fact, only part of it,"[8] and that natural languages

4. Lévi-Strauss was persuaded that the validity of this abstract structure would easily be proven if only French anthropologists had enough space for "vertical boards about six feet long and four and a half feet high, where cards can be pigeon-holed and moved at will. [. . .] Furthermore [he adds], as soon as the frame of reference becomes multidimensional [. . .] the board system has to be replaced by perforated cards, which in turn require IBM equipment" (ibid., 229).

5. Ibid., 213.

6. Ibid.

7. Ibid.

8. Ibid., 210.

can be exhaustively described as systems of oppositions. The present discussion will not focus on these assumptions, which I have examined elsewhere.[9] Instead, I will look at the Oedipus myth and its versions,[10] to show that the semantic oppositions mentioned above, while grasping something interesting and important about this myth, need to be supplemented, as Lévi-Strauss himself appears to intimate, with a richer, more diversified interpretation. Therefore, at every step in my analysis of Lévi-Strauss's structuralist interpretation, I will supplement Lévi-Strauss's abstract notions with readings that highlight intuitively accessible aspects of this myth. It will become clear that Lévi-Strauss's abstract approach, far from contradicting a more intuitive way of looking at this myth, is ultimately based on rather common insights about human experience.[11]

Among the two oppositions, the one that contrasts *the assertion of the autochthonous origin of mankind* with *its denial* is, when understood literally, less noticeable than the debate about blood relations; but, as we shall see, it nevertheless plays a role as a deeper, more general reflection on the mission human beings fulfill in the world. Lévi-Strauss argues that in myths about humans born from the Earth, they walk clumsily when they emerge from the depths, a clumsiness to which Oedipus's name is presumed to allude. Lévi-Strauss's Native American examples, drawn from Pueblo and Kwakiutl mythology, are convincing; it is nevertheless difficult to forget that the slow—very slow—learning of how to walk is a feature of *actual* human beings, the only mammals that require a year's growth before standing

9. See Thomas Pavel, *The Spell of Language: Post-Structuralism and Speculation* (Chicago: University of Chicago Press, 2003).

10. Timothy Gantz, *Early Greek Myth: A Guide to Literary and Artistic Sources*, vol. 2 (Baltimore: Johns Hopkins University Press, 1993), 488–502.

11. At about the same time, Noam Chomsky's *Syntactic Structures* (The Hague: Mouton, 1957) proposed a set of mathematical models that underlie linguistic performance: a finite-state, an immediate constituent, and a transformational model. These models are truly abstract in the sense that they are first constructed mathematically and only then checked against the actual sentences of natural languages. Chomsky's project is perhaps best understood with reference to the cybernetic dream of solving the mind-body problem. See Jean-Pierre Dupuy, *The Mechanization of the Mind: On the Origins of Cognitive Science* (Princeton, NJ: Princeton University Press, 2000; reissued in 2009 on MIT Press [Cambridge, MA] as *On the Origins of Cognitive Science: The Mechanization of the Mind*), which offers an incisive history and critique of this dream.

upright, in contrast to four-legged mammals, which can walk almost immediately after birth.

To be sure, stories about humans born directly from the Earth are present in Greek mythology, for instance in the tale of Deucalion and Pyrrha, the only survivors of the deluge unleashed by Zeus to punish Lycaon's sacrifice of his own son. Deucalion and his wife, who is now too old to have children, are instructed by an oracle to repopulate the earth by throwing the bones of their mother over their shoulders. Realizing that their mother is Gaïa, the Earth itself, they pick up and throw rocks which, when these touch the ground, become human beings. But in the myth of Deucalion and Pyrrha the issue is not that of *creating* mankind from the Earth, but rather of *restoring* it after the Father of the gods has virtually exterminated it as a punishment for an outrageous crime. Moreover, in this story the humans born from Earth's bones do not totter, stagger, or walk clumsily. Neither do the armed warriors who, in Cadmos's myth, menacingly rise from a dragon's tooth planted in the Earth by Oedipus's valiant ancestor. Thus, in the mythical imagination, being born from the Earth does not necessarily involve walking clumsily.

Oedipus's name alludes to a swollen foot because his parents, wanting to get rid of the infant to avoid the prophecy that warned them against having children, had instructed a shepherd to leave the child exposed in the Kithairon mountains with his ankles pierced by an iron pin. Later in the story, the Sphinx's riddle makes a clear reference to this possibility: a creature that in the morning goes on four legs (and later, at noon, on two and finally, in the evening, on three) can well use the four of them to crawl away. As for limping, Asklepiades's version of the riddle specifies that "when it [this creature] goes supported on three . . . feet, then the speed of his limbs is weakest."[12] Weak legs in this case are, quite plausibly, a sign of age, not of chtonian birth.

At this point I should specify an important difference between Lévi-Strauss's approach and the one proposed here. For the French anthropologist, the story told by a myth only *seems* to be a linear succession of actions and events linked to each other by intentions, causality, chance, or fate. Going beyond this temporal unfolding or succession,

---

12. Gantz, *Early Greek Myth*, 496.

the anthropologist establishes a bi-dimensional chart of events and actions, classified according to their semantic similarity, e.g.:

Column I	Column II	Column III	Column IV
		Cadmos kills the dragon	
	Oedipus kills his father		
		Oedipus kills the Sphinx	
			Oedipus = *swollen foot*
Oedipus mar- ries his mother			
	Eteocles kills his brother Polyneces		
Antigone buries her brother Polyneces			

The chart's columns illustrate the main oppositions: I—overrating of blood relations; II—underrating of the same; III—denial of Earth origin; IV—assertion of it. Although they have a definite semantic content, the above columns operate not unlike grammatical categories that designate the syntactic functions fulfilled by words in a sentence. Consider the two sentences "The cat jumps on the couch" and "John takes the cat on his lap." By analyzing them one can go beyond the concrete meaning of the words and find the following abstract sequences:

Column I	Column II	Column III	Column IV
Subject	Verb	Direct Object	Indirect Object/ Prepositional phrase
The cat	jumps		on the couch
John	takes	the cat	on his lap

But, obviously, the speakers who utter these sentences in conformity with the rules of English grammar do not mean to say: "Subject + Verb + Direct Object + Indirect Object." They *use* the grammar and the vocabulary *to speak about* the cat, about its jumping on the couch, about John, and about him taking the cat on his lap. Similarly, the story of Oedipus might well *involve* the semantic oppositions illustrated by the Lévi-Strauss's columns; but what the story *tells* us is that Oedipus did this and that, for this or that reason, in such and such a context, and that what he did and what happened to him give rise to a variety of possible meanings.

The same is true about the story of Deucalion and Pyrrha. Its resolution does involve the birth of a multitude of human beings from the Earth, but the entire story tells us much more. It affirms the divine origin of human beings and emphasizes the unity of humankind and its dependency on the rule of the gods. Zeus governs the world and requires worship and obedience. By punishing the whole human race for Lycaon's sacrifice of his son, Zeus makes it clear that the worship he requires from all humans should never infringe upon the natural duties of parents to their children. Human sacrifice, in particular the sacrifice of one's children, is prohibited. The biblical story of Abraham and Isaac has similar implications: Yahweh, who requires Abraham's absolute devotion, asks him to sacrifice his son Isaac. In the end, however, he prevents this cruel deed, and in the place of Isaac, Abraham sacrifices a ram. In the Bible, this moment is understood as a manifestation of divine generosity: Yahweh graciously renounces something he himself had earlier asked for. In the Greek myth, human sacrifice, seen from the beginning as a transgression, is punished very severely once it takes place, intimating that Lycaon should have known how scandalous it was to offer his son to Zeus, who had never asked for such a sacrifice. As for the deluge and quasi-extermination of the entire human race as punishment for its corruption, something similar occurs in the biblical narrative as well, where the flood is meant as a response, as in the Greek myth, to the moral decay of humans. In both cases, a single couple is saved, perhaps as a reminder that humans (and in the Bible, animals too) are born from the sexual union of their parents. Mother Earth's presence in the story of Deucalion and Pyrrha invites its audience to realize, in addition, that humans are not *simply and only* born of their parents, but are equally indebted to the gods and to nature. Humans should therefore be grateful—in a wise way—to all those who made their existence possible.

Taken as stories, myths do not merely convey abstract semantic oppositions, but narrate concrete actions and their consequences, imagine origins and describe ways of the world, often in order to shed light
on prevailing religious and moral obligations.

In the case of the Oedipus myth, one of the most stable elements
in its ancient versions is the child's being cast off by his royal parents
and adopted by another royal couple. The human ability to decipher
blood relations is indeed part of the topic here, for, in a species in
which infants are for a long time defenseless, being unable to walk,
talk, and remember what happens to them, it is as easy to get rid
of one's newborn children as it is difficult for them later to figure
out who their true parents are. Similar separations between infants
and their parents can be found in many traditions—in the biblical
story of Moses, for instance, whose mother sends him afloat on the
Nile in a tiny basket soon to be picked up by Pharaoh's daughter. In
one of the versions of the Oedipus story, Laius's son is also placed
in a chest that floats on a river until it is found by king Polybos of
Corinth. Later, in ancient Greek romances and their Renaissance and
early modern imitations, the main character often does not know his/
her true origin until late in the story: thus, Chariclea in Heliodorus's
Ethiopian Story believes that she is the daughter of the Greek mer-
chant Charicleus, while in reality her mother, the Queen of Ethiopia,
noticing that the newborn girl's skin was white (as a result of the
Queen's looking at a portrait of Andromeda at the very moment of
conception), has given her daughter up for adoption in order to avoid
the accusation of adultery. Such stories emphasize the difference between the biological parents and the adoptive ones, between birth
and education, or, in Lévi-Strauss's terms, between nature and culture. Humankind, they remind us, is the only species that weaves a
cultural curtain able to cover and hide natural blood links. All these
stories concern *ignorance* of blood relations. But while Moses and
Chariclea, once they discover their true origin—Hebrew for Moses,
royal Ethiopian for Chariclea—happily merge into their newfound
real family, in Oedipus's story ignorance is fatal. Rather than merely
opposing the overrating and the underrating of blood relations, the
Oedipus myth reflects on the difficulty of gauging them correctly and
on the high price one must pay for a mistaken assessment. The *epistemic* element is crucial, for in none of the myth's ancient versions
does Oedipus know who his real father is. Incidentally, when Freud
speculated that small boys feel close to their mothers and are jealous

of their fathers, his use of the Oedipus myth (recast as the Oedipus *complex*) is not entirely suitable. Supposing that such attachments and jealousies do occur in small children, they can be said to develop in situations in which the boy in question knows that this woman and this man are his parents. In Oedipus's case, however, the tragedy takes places precisely because its hero *is unaware of* the blood links binding him to Laius and Jocasta.

In Freud's use of the myth, the emphasis falls on the attraction the little boy is assumed to feel for his mother, presumably replicating Oedipus's marriage with Jocasta. But in the ancient versions of the myth, the marriage of the young hero to a woman who later turns out to be his own mother does not always take place. The murder of Laius, in contrast, is always present. Moreover, in at least one version, Oedipus, still without knowing what he is doing, kills both his father and his mother. Even when his father is the only victim, the murder is surrounded by a complex of circumstances that do not involve Oedipus's awareness and even less his guilt. Laius has long before been warned by oracles that he must refrain from having children if he wants to avoid either his own death or the destruction of his city, Thebes. The reason for this interdiction varies. Some versions refer to an earlier serious transgression that has upset Apollo. In other versions, Laius is portrayed as a lustful, bisexual man who in his youth abducted and raped Chrysippos, the son of Pelops, thus offending Hera, the goddess of marriage. In some cases, the oracle who informs Laius that his child will kill him specifies that this is Zeus's answer to the prayers of angry Pelops (but in other versions Pelops accepts the relationship between Laius and Chrysippos). Moreover, Laius is unable to respect the interdiction of having children. Never presented as a model of self-mastery, Laius, in at least one version of the myth, forgets the oracle in a fit of lust and drunkenness. Finally, he attempts to cheat fate and the gods by getting rid the infant. In Ancient Greece, infant exposure did not qualify as murder, since most often the abandoned child was left not far from the parents' house where he could be rescued by others. But by ordering the child to be exposed on the top of a mountain with his ankles pierced, Laius does not merely abandon an undesirable progeny; he wants to make sure that the infant, left in the wilderness and unable to crawl, will die.

The myth's various versions thus portray Laius as someone who deserves his fate. Seen in this light, Oedipus is the instrument used by fate and the gods against his father. By punishing Laius and his family in a horrible way, fate and the gods highlight rather than question the importance of blood links. These links get polluted and broken because the retribution for Laius's transgressions, in particular for his turning a deaf ear to the oracle's warning, is designed to target and destroy the most basic, vital ties between humans. Those who fail to respect the gods' rules (a situation that was, in fact, rather difficult to avoid in a world in which the gods' requirements so often contradict each other) pay a high price. And precisely because of the very tightness and significance of family relations, fate and the gods punish transgression by striking indiscriminately at the whole family rather than at one single individual.

Equally important is Oedipus's belonging to Thebes as a city—a law-governed union of related families. Just as Oedipus, an abandoned infant, cannot remember his genuine family, no reliable clue will later tell him in which country he was really born. Adopted and raised by the king of Corinth, he has no reason to believe that he is a Theban. When he leaves Corinth and arrives in Thebes—in some versions because he learns that he is destined to murder his father and, wanting to avoid this fate, runs away from the king of Corinth, in other versions because Thebes had offered a reward to the person who defeated the Sphinx—Oedipus and the Thebans are persuaded that he is a stranger. This stranger magnificently saves the city, is adopted by it, and is invited to marry the Theban queen. Considered a foreigner, Oedipus is revered as the savior of the city, the husband of its queen, and its wise king. Ignorance about one's actual place among one's fellow human beings is again a trap set by fate and the gods. For, when it turns out that this foreigner is, in fact, a native, his parricide and incest will weigh heavily on his and his city's conscience. If only he were truly a foreigner! If only he had known he was a Theban! The myth, particularly in the form Sophocles gave to it in his *Oedipus Rex*, intimates that the glory is that of the stranger and the shame that of the native. To run away from one's country is a blessing, as Oedipus, having left Corinth, learns after his victory over the Sphinx. To be rooted is a tragedy, as the revelation of his Theban origin teaches him. In conformity with this view, in Sophocles's tragedy Oedipus's remains are said to be buried in Colonus, far from the city of his birth (an episode not found in other versions of the myth). Human beings, Sophocles seems to say, cannot and should not always be bound to the place of their birth.

As much as these qualities raise Oedipus above mere mortals, the power of his mind—in Sophocles's version—and his personal strength and courage—in those versions of the myth in which, absent the riddle, Oedipus fights and kills the monster—do not suffice to keep him in this exalted position. His mind as well as his courage may well outshine everyone else's, but he is present in this world only because he was born into a family and in a city and, as such, he willy-nilly carries along the guilt, the debts, the mistakes, and the crimes of his kin. In Sophocles's version, in particular, Oedipus's intelligence and rectitude, so obvious when he acts without knowing his origin, are set in contrast to his being crushed by fate when he discovers it. The question "How to define an individual human being?" has two, tragically different answers: on the one hand, humans are what their gifts and actions make them; but, on the other, humans are a product of their origin. In most versions of the myth, but especially in Sophocles's version, the tension between these two answers is left unresolved. Among many other things, the Oedipus myth also speaks about the heartrending conflict between what it means to be a praiseworthy human being and what it means to be deeply-rooted in one's original family and city. In a vivid, non-abstract way, the issue of humankind's autochthonous origin is thus present in this myth. I wonder what Simone Weil, who has so aptly defended the need for roots, would have thought about this last point.[13]

This myth, finally, raises a fundamental question concerning human involvement in action. Is the person who performs a deed fully responsible for it? In all versions, Oedipus, fated to murder his father, performs this act in ignorance of the full reality of what he is doing. He is thus both the main agent, because Laius dies at his hands, and a mere instrument of fate, because he unwittingly fulfills the oracle's prediction. Human beings, the myth seems to say, are not fully in charge of their acts, not only because destiny governs their lives, but also because their grasp of the world in which they live is partial, inadequate, and deceptive. And yet their deeds are unmistakably *theirs*. To emphasize this point, Sophocles included in his tragedy two elements that were not always present in the other versions of the myth: Oedipus's marrying Jocasta and their having children together. The

13. See Simone Weil, *The Need for Roots*, trans. Arthur Wills (London: Routledge & Kegan Paul, 1952).

incestuous consequences of Oedipus's lack of knowledge are vividly presented on stage. The story of Oedipus asks whether human beings are the true source of their deeds or—to use a contemporary philosopher's terms—a mere *complement* that these deeds require in order to be achieved.[14]

These considerations have taken us far beyond Lévi-Strauss's simple and elegant view of the Oedipus myth. To defend his structural approach, one might argue that it deliberately bypasses details and nuances to seek what this myth means *in the last analysis.* I suspect, however, that here looms what could be called "the final analysis fallacy." In the final analysis, human beings are sets of atoms, but each field of, for instance, medical research operates at the more complex levels of molecular biology and organ physiology. In the last analysis, a novel is a set of sentences, but to confine literary study to this level is to miss the plot, the characters, the staging, the underlying ideals, the message, the period, the expectations of the readers, and the talent of the author. Far from being required to perform a *last* analysis, disciplines—be they exact sciences or cultural disciplines—are expected to find and target the *appropriate* level of analysis at which their work becomes relevant. I therefore doubt that in the study of myth and, more generally, of cultural phenomena there is such a thing as the "last analysis." Those who seek to achieve it by devising, as Lévi-Strauss intended to do, a general semantic framework, may end up discovering an illuminating set of notions. Since such notions are ultimately based on human experience, myth and literary analysis can considerably benefit from them. Lévi-Strauss's own study of the legend of Asdiwal is a splendid model of structural analysis precisely because the author sees and makes visible a content that is present in the story.[15] This kind of analysis, however, is not the last word on myth and literature: other insights capturing widely shared human interests remain possible, welcome, and even necessary.

14. Vincent Descombes's *Le complément de sujet* (Paris: Gallimard, 2004) analyzes the human agent as a complement of the verb designating the action. Other complements may indicate the target, the place, the time, and the cause of the action. While traditional analyses privilege the subject of the action, Descombes makes the interesting point that the subject, that is, the agent, is simply one among several complements that surround the verb.

15. Lévi-Strauss, *Le geste d'Asdiwal* (Paris: Imprimerie Nationale, 1958), translated as "The Story of Asdiwal," in Lévi-Strauss, *Structural Anthropology*, vol. 2. (Basic Books, New York, NY, 1976): 146–94.

JEAN-MICHEL RABATÉ

Lacan's Dora against Lévi-Strauss

"Is there cold on ye, doraphobian? Or do yu want yur primafairy schoolmam?" [1]

—James Joyce

ou toi apoblêt' esti theôn erikudea dôra
Never to be cast away are the gifts of the gods, magnificent,
hossa ken autoi dôsin, hekôn d' ouk an tis heloito
which they give of their own will, no man could have them for wanting them. [2]

—Homer

I am writing this in October 2011, just two years after the demise of Claude Lévi-Strauss. It is also the moment when a series of talks, books, and debates on French radio and television have paid homage to Jacques Lacan's work in Paris, thirty years after his death (in 1981). One can hardly avoid connecting the two names. Lacan and Lévi-Strauss often stand side by side in library or bookstore shelves, where they have been linked for posterity in what is presented as a French invention, structuralism—whereas "post-structuralism" seems to be of British, German, or American descent. Some excellent books (by Alain Delrieu, Markos Zafiropoulos, Marcel Drach, and Bernard Toboul) [3] have recently been devoted to new assessments of Lacan's debt to Lévi-Strauss. They all mention the confusions and obfuscations produced by the unifying label of structuralism.

Late in his career, when the discussion about structuralism had lost urgency and relevance, Lacan gave a talk at M.I.T. in which he surveyed the field. This was in December 1975. Lacan began his pre-

1. James Joyce, *Finnegans Wake* (London: Faber, 1939), 478.
2. Homer, *Iliad*, III, 65–66.
3. See Alain Delrieu, *Lévi-Strauss, lecteur de Freud* (Paris: Anthropos, 1999); Markos Zafiropoulos, *Lacan et Lévi-Strauss, ou le retour à Freud* (Paris: PUF, 2003); and *L'anthropologie de Lévi-Strauss et la psychanalyse*, ed. Marcel Drach and Bernard Toboul (Paris: La Découverte, 2008). The latter collection has a good bibliography on Lévi-Strauss and psychoanalysis.

YFS 123, *Rethinking Claude Lévi-Strauss (1908–2009)*, ed. Doran, © 2013 by Yale University.

sentation by repeating an answer he had just given to the American philosopher Willard Quine, who was also present at the talk. Yes, Lacan said, he owed a great deal to Lévi-Strauss, perhaps even everything. But he followed this remark with a qualification: "This does not prevent me from having a very different idea of the concept of structure."[4] In order to better understand how their notions of "structure" diverged, I will examine Lacan's reading of the Dora case, to show first how his interpretation was influenced early on by Lévi-Strauss's pronouncements on myth and symbolic structures, and then how he took off in his own direction.

The books by Delrieu and Zafiropoulos and the edited collection by Drach and Toboul explore the arc of Lacan's adoption of models found in Lévi-Strauss's works, from their first meeting in 1949 to their parting of ways in the mid-sixties. Lacan's seminars and essays from the 1950s are full of references to famous works by Lévi-Strauss: to *Structural Anthropology*, to "Introduction to the Work of Marcel Mauss," and to the *Elementary Structures of Kinship*. But some reservations start cropping up after 1965. This is most visible in "Science and Truth" from *Écrits*, an essay in which Lacan first enumerates what he borrowed from his friend's work: the combinatory analysis of social rituals and codes; the perception of the structures of kinship and myths displayed in a mathematical grid; the structural analysis of myth according to a linguistic model; the idea of a collective unconscious made up of social rules of exclusion and inclusion; the concept of a symbolic order that determines subjects' actions and even their volition, etc. But then Lacan expresses a reservation, which is not so much his own, but rather the one he anticipates from Lévi-Strauss:

> I believe, however, that Lévi-Strauss would have reservations about the introduction, during the collection of documents, of a psychoanalytically inspired approach, a sustained collection of dreams for example, with all that would entail by way of a transferential relationship. But why would he, when I maintain to him that our praxis, far from altering the subject of science—the only one about which he can or wants to know anything—is entitled to intervene only when it tends toward this subject's satisfactory realization in the very field that interests Lévi-Strauss?[5]

4. Jacques Lacan, "Conférences et entretiens dans des universités nord-américaines," *Scilicet* 6/7 (1976): 53.

5. Lacan, *Écrits*, trans. Bruce Fink (New York: Norton, 2006), 732.

Lacan's main argument is that when one attempts to draw a graph or a grid pointing to the structure's determining function one should take the subject into account, and the subject is present first in "transferential" relations to others. This restates the main idea that, for Lacan, there is no structure without a subject. A structure only functions for a subject, even if it may be shown that it is the structure that determines subjectivity, and not the reverse. This is what Lacan tried to explain earlier to a somewhat baffled American audience at Johns Hopkins University in 1966, with a rather impenetrable lecture entitled "Of Structure as an Inmixing of Otherness Prerequisite to Any Subject Whatever." In this text, Lacan refers to Frege's and Russell's logical theories and explains that the idea that the unconscious is "structured as a language"—whose formulation he may have owed to Lévi-Strauss's famous article on "Symbolic efficacy"[6]—is in fact a simple tautology, since the expressions "structured" and "as a language" are synonymous.[7] Hence, going back to the foundation of structural linguistics, he adds that all a signifier can do is represent a subject, not for another subject, as one would expect, but for another signifier.[8] Lacan's slogan, "A signifier represents a subject for another signifier," suggests that language mediates between non-transparent subjects. One should not bother looking for improbable correspondences of signifiers and referential objects in the world. The lessons that psychoanalysis has learned from the study of a poetic language governed by metonymy and metaphor apply to the Freudian unconscious. Whenever I dream, I become both a Surrealist poet and a Structuralist ethnographer. The felicitous parapraxes that proliferate in everyday life remind me that if my language circumscribes my world, this language is already inhabited by the discourse of the Other.

At the time of the 1966 conference, Lacan and the Lacanians (such as Guy Rosolato, another participant) had shifted significantly from the linguistic theories of Saussure to encompass those of Jakobson and Benveniste. Jakobson's "shifters" lead to the "subject of the enunciation" that never fully coheres with the "subject of the enounced." The task of linguistics, as it was perceived in 1966, was also to describe the formal apparatus of enunciation, that is, the set of coded

6. See Darian Leader, "Lacan's Myths," in *The Cambridge Companion to Lacan*, ed. Jean-Michel Rabaté (Cambridge: Cambridge University Press, 2003), 37.

7. Ibid., 188.

8. Ibid., 194.

devices allowing a person to say or write "I." These terms had been introduced by Lacan as early as in 1964, in his seminar entitled *Four Fundamental Concepts of Psycho-Analysis*. Thus subjectivity matters, even if it is determined by a formal apparatus enabling the utterance of the self reduced to the linguistic "I."

These terms should be kept in mind to understand how Lacan interpreted transference and how he slowly changed his position regarding it. I will examine a single case, that of Dora, Freud's famous hysterical woman, to show first what Lacan had learned from Lévi-Strauss and then how he ultimately diverged. Lacan had alluded repeatedly to Dora in his extended discussion of Freud's seminal text on "Psychogenesis of a Case of Feminine Homosexuality." But it was a few years earlier, in January 1957, in the context of his Seminar on Object Relations,[9] that Lacan returned to Freud's treatment of the Dora case armed with concepts borrowed from Lévi-Strauss, thereby modifying the reading of the Dora case that he had presented in a 1951 text entitled "Presentation on Transference." The differences between the 1951 text and his 1957 seminar testify to the depth of the impact made by Lévi-Strauss on his work, especially when it came to a systematic rereading of Freud.

The first talk, given in 1951 at the Conference of French-speaking Psychoanalysts, was published in the *Revue française de psychanalyse* in 1952.[10] Lacan's starting point in "Presentation on Transference" was Freud's remark to Dora that she had played the part of an accomplice in a sexual comedy of betrayals. In very strong terms, Freud stated that Dora had "made herself an accomplice in the affair, and had dismissed from her mind every sign which tended to show its true character."[11] Or again: "it was quite certain that the reproaches which (Dora) made against her father of having been deaf to the most imperative calls of duty and of having seen things in the light which was most convenient from the point of view of his own passions— these reproaches recoiled upon her head."[12] Freud proceeded to turn against Dora the charges she had leveled against her father—that is, exploiting his bad health to further an illicit amorous liaison. Freud

9. Lacan, *Le séminaire IV: La relation d'objet* (Paris: Seuil, 1994). I will also refer to Freud's case study as *Dora* for Sigmund Freud, *Dora: An Analysis of a Case of Hysteria*, ed. P. Rieff (New York: Touchstone Books, 1997).

10. In Lacan, *Écrits*, 176–85. For the discussion of the Dora case, see 178–84.

11. Freud, *Dora*, 29.

12. Ibid., 31.

wanted Dora to take a good look at herself, which she did—the only successful moment in the treatment. Dora immediately complained of gastric pains, which Freud quickly identified as imitative symptoms; Dora was reproducing the pains experienced by a close cousin, who was jealous of the fact that her younger sister had got engaged. Freud then asked: "Whom are you copying now?" He was able to show her that she was willing her disease, using it as a weapon. Alas, his triumph was to be short-lived: if Freud had "hit the mark,"[13] he had hit it only once.

In 1951, Lacan saw Freud's art as an art of dialectical reversal. He admired the masterful inversion of the line of questioning, with Freud effectively turning the tables on Dora. This led to a further series of dialectical reversals, of which Lacan distinguished three moments. The first, as we have observed, was when Freud sends Dora back to her unexamined function in the "quadrille," linking her to Mr. K, Frau K, and her father. This was an eye-opening disclosure that allowed her to become aware of her objective collusion in the little drama. The second moment occurred when Freud asked Dora to be aware that her jealousy concerning her father's love for Mrs. K. concealed something else. The third moment corresponded to a new attraction: her infatuation with her father's mistress, Mrs. K., disclosed what was really at stake, namely her fascination with the mystery of femininity.

It is clear that, in 1957, Lacan had not renounced his thesis on Dora, but felt the need to update the language used to discuss it. Lacan thus sought to revise his "dialectical" reading of transference, even if in 1957 he did not radically change his point of departure. Lacan began in a similar manner, by letting Freud ask Dora the same initial question: "Isn't what you attack as a disorderly state of affairs something in which you yourself have participated?"[14] Indeed, as Freud had noted, Dora agreed to be instrumental in making the tryst between her father and Mrs. K. possible, for instance by being a devoted baby-sitter, thus allowing Mrs. K. to go out with her father.

For Lacan, referring to Hegel's dialectics seemed entirely justified in 1951, and even functioned as a gateway to a deeper understanding of the case. Lacan had noted the troubling similarity between Dora's predicament and Hegel's canonical analysis of the "beautiful soul."

13. Ibid., 31.
14. Lacan, *La relation d'objet*, 137.

The whole Hegelian reading applied to Dora: she protested her purity, denounced the chaos and the confusion outside while being blissfully unaware of her own murky role and of her obvious contradictions.[15] Hegel was probably thinking of his own sister's pathology (she ended up institutionalized) when he described the "beautiful soul" in *The Phenomenology of Spirit*, even though he was ostensibly referring to Molière's *Misanthrope*, a play in which Alceste embodies the pattern of the *schöne Seele*. In Hegel's analysis, the only outcome for the "beautiful soul" is madness:

> The "beautiful soul," lacking an *actual* existence, entangled in the contradiction between its pure self and the necessity of that self to externalize itself and change itself into an actual existence, and dwelling in the *immediacy* of this firmly held antithesis [. . .] this "beautiful soul," then, being conscious of this contradiction in its unreconciled immediacy, is disordered to the point of madness, wastes itself in yearning and pines away in consumption.[16]

Thus for Hegel, the "beautiful soul" is someone who, for purely "sentimental" reasons, refuses to see what he or she gives and is given. The "beautiful soul" deliberately remains blind to the network of actual gives and takes that defines interactions in the symbolical realm. The "beautiful soul" wants to veil the cruel realities underpinned by an abstract Symbolic system and therefore denies or bypasses the foundation of all social relationships.

Lacan's seminar of January 23, 1957 takes up the examination of the Dora case with a more critical edge. Instead of praising Freud's genius or his clinical expertise in the handling of transference via dialectical reversal, Lacan begins by stating that Freud had blundered. This is what immediately strikes most readers: Freud's confusion or even blindness as to the real object of desire for Dora. Freud admitted that he had missed her homosexual attachment to Mrs. K. because of his unanalyzed assumption that Dora should "normally" have been attracted to her husband, Mr. K. Yet, even if his belated admission was necessary, one cannot completely discard Mr. K.'s role in the dialectic of Dora's desire. Lacan relates this ambiguity to a clinical observation that he sees as foundational for all structures of hysteria: hysterics love by proxy and therefore have a problem with being an

---

15. Lacan, *Écrits*, 179.
16. G.W. F. Hegel, *The Phenomenology of Spirit*, trans. A. V. Miller (Oxford: Oxford University Press, 1957), 407 (original emphasis).

object of heterosexual desire; moreover, the hysteric's object is fundamentally homosexual.[17]

Dora's ego contains a deep identification with Mr. K., and it is this identification that accounts for her transformation into a virile character: "In other words, it is through the intermediary of Mr. K., it is in so far as she is Mr. K. at the imaginary point constituted by the personality of Mr. K., that Dora is attached to the character of Mrs. K."[18] Mrs. K derives her importance from the fact that, beyond her election to the status of object of desire, she embodies Dora's most essential preoccupation.

Dora rehearses what hysterics have in common: they have been blocked on the way to an Oedipal resolution of their desires. They both can and cannot overcome the Oedipal crisis. For Dora, what is of prime importance is that her father, though rich (*vermögend*), is also impotent (*unvermögend*). What function does the father occupy in the Oedipal pattern in Lacan's grid? The father should normally be the agent who gives, symbolically, the missing object or the phallus. In this case, Dora's father cannot give it because he does not have it. The phallic lack of the father is crucial in that it yields a new twist in the dialectics of giving. This is how Lacan develops the idea:

> What is giving? Isn't there another dimension that is introduced in the object relation when it is brought to a symbolical level as an object that can be given or not? In other terms, is it ever the object that is given? Such is the question, and with Dora we see one of its outcomes, one which remains exemplary.[19]

Thus, Dora remains exclusively attached to a father whose virile gift she can never receive.

If Dora's problems appear at the time of her struggle facing her Oedipal entanglement, this will entail an increase in her love for her father: the more her father is wounded or seen as deficient, the more she loves him. Thus, her love for the maimed father is proportional to the diminution of the father's status. This assertion can be generalized: there is no greater gift, no truer sign of love, than the gift of what one does not have. In true structuralist fashion, Lacan stresses that the cultural meaning of the gift is determined by the framework of the symbolic law. As sociologists have shown since Marcel Mauss,

---

17. Lacan, *La relation d'objet*, 138.
18. Ibid.
19. Ibid., 139.

a gift is something that circulates; the gift you give is always something you have received. "But when it comes to a gift between two subjects, the cycle of the gifts comes from elsewhere, since what establishes the love relationship is that the gift is given, if one may say so, for nothing."[20] Thus "nothing for nothing" is the formula of this type of exchange. It might look like the expression of interest, but it is in fact the formula for pure gratuity. In the love gift, something is given for nothing, and this something is a nothing.

> What constitutes the gift is that a subject gives something in a gratuitous manner, for as much as behind what he gives there is something that is lacking, and thus the subject sacrifices beyond what he has. The same happens with the primitive mode of the gift that one can see as the effective root of all human exchanges under the shape of the *potlatch*.[21]

Lacan comments that if someone is extremely rich, a gift from him or her will lose proportionally in value. Thus, in the same way, if God is thought of as infinitely rich and endowed with attributes, there is no reason to love him for his gifts—except if we suspect that he is lacking in being. "There is no reason to love God, except that perhaps he does not exist."[22]

Thus, Dora loves her father for what he does not give her. But he then initiates another act, an act that is partly brought about by Dora. We can speak of a ternary relationship:

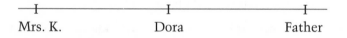

| Mrs. K. | Dora | Father |

It looks as if Dora had only to ask the question: "What does my father love in Mrs. K.?" Clearly, she does not know what it is. What she is looking for is the phallic object insofar as it can be given. As we have seen, for Lacan, a woman can only enter into the dialectic of the symbolic order through the gift of the phallus. Desire aims at the phallus when it can be received as a gift; when the phallus is raised to the dignity of the gift, the subject can be introduced into the dialectics of all subsequent exchanges.

20. Ibid., 140.
21. Ibid.
22. Ibid.

We can now understand why Dora's main issue is the reiteration of an old riddle: "What is a woman?" Thus Mrs. K. embodies the whole of the feminine function. As a myth, she allegorizes the riddle of femininity as such. As an object of the father's love, Mrs. K. is an object that he loves beyond Dora. This is why Dora is so fascinated by her. Dora remains positioned between her father and Mrs. K., and indeed, as long as her father loves Mrs. K., Dora is satisfied. The position of the impotent father in love is compensated by symbols of munificence, which are multiplied. These include material gifts that are showered equally on the mistress and on the daughter, who even share them. Dora participates in the symbolic function displayed here, but at a remove, as it were. Soon, alas, this will not suffice: Dora will try to reestablish a triangular situation that implies Mr. K.

Mr. K.

Mrs. K.   Dora   Father[23]

Because she is still haunted by her question, which is the riddle of femininity, Dora believes that Mr. K. has to bring into the bargain his own adoration of his wife, an adoration that is clearly expressed when she superimposes the Sistine Madonna on Mrs. K. When Freud notices that the reference to "two hours" in Dora's second dream corresponds to the two hours she once spent contemplating the Sistine Madonna in Dresden, he asks what attracted her. She answers in an enigmatic and tautological manner. "When I asked her what had pleased her so much about the picture she could find no clear answer to make. At last she said: 'The Madonna.'"[24] Mrs. K. has to be adored by all who are close to her, including, of course, Dora. If Mr. K. can provide an element of normality, it is because of his masculinity that he must take his own wife and not Dora as an object of desire.

This is why Dora slaps Mr. K., *not* when he courts her or when he declares his love to her, but only when he tells her that he is not in love with his own wife, and that she is nothing to him: "Ich habe nichts an meiner Frau." This ominous phrase is repeated in the case

---

23. Ibid., 142.
24. Freud, *Dora*, 88.

study as it migrates from Dora's father to Mr. K., referring to their respective wives. It serves to reintroduce the "nothing" as an empty space comparable to Mauss's *hau*, which is reinscribed by Lévi-Strauss into a circuit. This can be schematized in the following diagram:

Mrs. K.   Mr. K.
the question   with *whom Dora identifies*

Dora   Father
                       Remains the Other par excellence

For if Dora can admit that her father "loves" through her, "loves" what is beyond her, that is, Mrs. K., Mr. K. can only be tolerated if he remains in an inverse and stabilizing position. When Mr. K. blurts out that he is interested only in Dora and that his wife is "for nothing" (*pour rien*) in the circuit, this suggests conversely to Dora that her father might also be interested only in Mrs. K. and that henceforth she would be "for nothing" in the quadrille. This is what she cannot accept and what brings about the crisis with her complaints.

This reading of Dora is filtered by Lévi-Strauss's structuralist anthropology. Lacan quotes Lévi-Strauss's *Elementary Structures of Kinship* on several occasions. According to Lacan, Lévi-Strauss's basic rule of kinship and exogamic exchange can be summed up by the formula: "I have received a wife and I owe a daughter."[25] Lacan comments that such a principle of exchange governing a symbolic economy of culture will transform any woman into a simple object of barter. This is precisely what Dora refuses with her utmost energy. Dora cannot bear having been excluded as an active agent from the institutions of the gift and of the law. If she has not renounced the paternal phallus as the object of the gift, it is because there is nothing that she can accept from anyone else, at least not from any other man. This is why, as soon as she sees herself reduced to a pure object, Dora rebels and concludes that her father is merely selling her to someone else to further his extra-marital intrigue.

When Mr. K. confesses that he is not part of the circuit in which Dora can either identify with him or think that she is the object he is aiming at beyond the wife he is supposed to adore, all the fragile

25. Lacan, *La relation d'objet*, 143.

but dense links that had connected the four partners fall away. Dora herself "falls" from her own justifications and into a violently querulous attitude. All of a sudden she claims a need for what she might hitherto have thought had been given to her (although obliquely via the intermediary of another), namely her father's love. And since this love is absolutely refused to her, she must claim it all the more exclusively.[26]

However, Dora will then be caught in a metaphor that traps her and provides no exit. This metaphor of the *court* (*Hof*) finds an expression in the recurrent use of signifiers in her dreams: jewel box, *Bahnhof, Friedhof, Vorhof*. These signifiers keep repeating—*hof*, that multivalent "courtyard." They have to be multiplied because, fundamentally, they point to the fact that Dora cannot situate herself anywhere else. She does not know who she is anymore, what her place is, and, in her structural liminality, she cannot fathom love's use or meaning. Though she knows something about sex, it is love that remains a tantalizing riddle, and it hinges on the mystery of femininity. The only way to unknot all this would have been for her to remain on a purely symbolic level.

Such an insight allows Lacan to understand Freud's basic mistake: he blundered most when attempting to introduce something in the real, that is, when he tried to tell Dora something that touched upon her feelings. For instance, he tried to convince her that "in fact" she was "*really*" in love with Mr. K. Freud did not see that the introduction of Mr. K. as a normalizing object of heterosexual love should have remained metaphorical and that this was Dora's last attempt to comply with the law of symbolic exchanges.[27] Since Dora could only accept the idea of being an object of desire once the riddle of femininity had been solved for her, what she was looking for in Mrs. K. was less an object of same-sex desire than an insight into how a woman could become an object of desire. It is this insight that she failed to grasp.

What stands out in this survey of Lacan's second reading of Dora in 1957 is that it is highly structuralist. Structuralism entailed a break with Hegelian dialectics. Let us recall that in 1951, Lacan could present Hegel and Freud as having a comparable program: "The analytic neutrality derives its authentic meaning from the position of

26. Ibid., 144.
27. See ibid, 146.

the pure dialectician who, knowing that all that is real is rational (and vice-versa), knows that all that exists, including the evil against which he struggles, is and always shall be equivalent to the level of its particularity."[28] When he turned into a structuralist à la Lévi-Strauss, Lacan abandoned this hyper-rationalist discourse and paid more attention to the "manipulation" of the psychoanalyst. Following Lévi-Strauss's comparison of the agency of the shaman and the psychoanalyst in "The Effectiveness of Symbols,"[29] Lacan sought to explore universal patterns contained in the laws of exchange and of language.

This more distant point of view on culture also allowed Lacan to separate himself more clearly from Freud's embarrassing sexist prejudices. Whereas in 1951 Lacan still asserted that Dora would have benefited from a link with Mr. K. and that her infatuation with Mrs. K. was a "regression," in 1957 he had adopted a more systematic view of exchanges so as to take into account Marcel Mauss's theory of the gift and of *potlatch*.[30] In the earlier essay, he dismissed Dora's fascination with the Virgin Mary seen by Dora in Dresden—this Madonna that transformed her love for Mrs. K. into a mystical riddle—as equivalent to the traditional "solution which Christianity has given to this subjective impasse, by making woman the object of a divine desire, or else, a transcendent object of desire," which in effect, would imply telling Dora: "Get thee to a nunnery, go!" But by contrast, in 1957, Lacan analyzed the drama of a double impossibility: because she was structurally attached to her father and his economies, Dora could love neither a man nor a woman. Having meditated Lévi-Strauss's structural analysis, Lacan was moving away from the concept of transference as "positive non-action aiming at the ortho-dramatization of the patient's subjectivity."[31] The new systemic and structuralist approach of 1957 would allow for a more generous appre-

28. Lacan, *Écrits*, 184.

29. In Lévi-Strauss, *Structural Anthropology*, trans. C. Jacobson and B. G. Schoepf (New York, Basic Books,1963), 202.

30. See Marcel Mauss, *The Gift: The Form and Reason for Exchange in Archaic Societies*, trans. W. D. Halls (New York: Norton, 1990), and Bronisław Malinowski, *Argonauts of the Western Pacific* (New York, Dutton, 1961). Malinowski published his book in 1922 and Mauss in 1925. See also *The Logic of the Gift: Toward and Ethic of Generosity*, ed. Alan D. Schrift (New York, Routledge, 1997), for a good collection of texts on the gift. It includes Lévi-Strauss's "Introduction to the Work of Marcel Mauss."

31. Lacan, *Écrits*, 184.

ciation of Dora's gifts. Paradoxically, Lacan's "economic" analysis of the circuit of exchange underpinning Dora's personal drama would be more faithful to the letter of Freud's text. Whereas his first Hegelianized reading of transference as a series of dialectical reversals implied a new spin on Freud's elaboration, his "structuralist" interpretation made good sense of one of the last successful interpretations given by Freud to Dora. Freud, very close to the solution, finds the key but does not know it. He tells Dora:

> As you say, the mystery turns upon your mother. You ask how she comes into the dream? She is, as you know, your former rival in your father's affections. In the incident of the bracelet, you would have been glad to accept what your mother had rejected. Now let us put "give" instead of "accept" and "withhold" instead of "reject." Then it means that you were ready to give your father what your mother withheld from him.[32]

Freud simply makes the blunder of adding that Dora was ready to "give to Herr K. what his wife withholds from him." This is what she refuses, not the main implication that the only way for her to become conscious of her entanglement is to think like an anthropologist who considers society as a network of exchanges and gifts. Dora could not accept the erroneous conclusion drawn by Freud that she must have wanted to give herself to Mr. K. What he had discovered then, but saw fully only later, was that this particular structure made her stick to her father and imitate him in his "love" for Mrs. K. If, as Lacan repeats, to love is to "give what one does not have," Dora can truly be said to "love," if "love" is to remain a mystery.

Indeed, the choice of "Dora" as a fictional name for Ida Bauer may prove to have been Freud's most lasting stroke of genius.[33] By making her name the Greek word that means "gifts" in the plural, Freud was no doubt aware of the fact that the plural *dora* meant not only "presents" but also "retaining fees" or "bribes." The legal overtones of the Greek plural hint at accusations against those who take bribes. However, if a gift involves the obligation to return (i.e., the counter-

32. Freud, *Dora*, 62.
33. As to the curious anonymity to which Freud consigns the real Peppina Zellenka and her husband, his decision to use the simple initial K. (which happens to be the initial of the most neglected character in the whole story recounted by Freud: Dora's mother was named Katharina or Käthe Bauer) seems to announce Kafka's fictional alter-egos.

gift), what gift will not ipso facto turn into a bribe? This is what Malinowski and Mauss had to ponder in their remarkable anthropological studies of the gift. Following Lacan, it is clear that as long as she can be given the father's "nothing," a nothing that condenses the impossibility of a "pure" gift, Dora will maintain her role in a structure that allows her to participate in the love of her father (in the double sense of the genitive, both objective and subjective). When another type of "nothing" was presented to her and forced her to renounce the other phallic substitutes that came up along the symbolic chain, she suddenly realized she had merely occupied the position of an object. As an object barely represented by metaphors, she fell out of the structure, since she was reduced to the function of a bribe. Bribe or bride? That would have to be her question. In this poststructuralist dilemma, Dora still earns our admiration for having refused the most basically "given" form of social exchange. As for Lacan, he was on the path toward a meditation on the "naming" power of language: Freud's interpretation could be condensed by a perfectly adequate choice of a pseudonym for his rebellious patient. In this simple gesture, Freud showed that he had anticipated Lévi-Strauss's basic principle, the conflation of language, the cultural unconscious, and the socio-economic patterns of exchange. What is more, in his failed treatment of Dora, Freud had almost seen—but missed—a fundamental principle, well systematized by Lévi-Strauss: the unconscious is not "full," like a reservoir of universal images and symbols (this would be Jung's idea), but is "empty," and it is by understanding this void as a dynamic or active function that the psychoanalyst's work is made possible.

This is how Lévi-Strauss opposes the unconscious to the preconscious. The preconscious is a reservoir of personal images, whereas the unconscious can be compared with an organ such as the stomach.

> The unconscious, on the other hand, is always empty—or more accurately, it is as alien to mental images as is the stomach to the foods which pass through it. As the organ of a specific function, the unconscious merely imposes structural laws upon unarticulated elements which originate elsewhere—impulses, emotions, representations, and memories.[34]

No wonder Freud's first efficacious remark was about Dora's gastric pains! The serious contention made by Lévi-Strauss in 1949, and

34. Lévi-Strauss, *Structural Anthropology*, 203.

wholly absorbed and systematized by Lacan, was that the "food" brought along by the preconscious is simply a vocabulary, while the syntax is provided by the unconscious: "this vocabulary becomes significant [. . .] only to the extent that the unconscious structures it according to its laws and thus transforms it into language."[35]

* * *

This leads us to the reasons for the gradual but undeniable divergence between Lacan and Lévi-Strauss. Lévi-Strauss's view of structuralism remained consistent since the forties, whereas Lacan's changed massively.

Lacan would have agreed with some of Jacques Derrida's strictures against Lévi-Strauss's tendency to fall into positivism or scientism. What is wrong with this scientism is not its faith in science, but a positioning of structures outside the perceiving or acting agent. When it comes to subjectivity, structures cannot be treated as if they were found objects waiting for a meaning granted to them by a dispassionate scientific investigation. Like Derrida, Lacan wants to pose the question of the structurality of structure, and to go back to a long history, at least as ancient as Western metaphysics. Pure structuralist anthropology cannot choose a position between an empirical approach and a critique of empiricism. Famously, Lévi-Strauss described his own activity as a *bricolage*, which is an idiosyncratic way of mediating between empiricism and dogmatism. Derrida warns him sternly:

> What I want to emphasize is simply that the passage beyond philosophy does not consist in turning the page of philosophy (which usually amounts to philosophizing badly), but in continuing to read philosophers *in a certain way*. [. . .] I have said that empiricism is the matrix of all faults menacing a discourse which continues, as with Lévi-Strauss in particular, to consider itself scientific. If we wanted to pose the problem of empiricism and *bricolage* in depth, we would probably end up very quickly with a number of absolutely contradictory propositions concerning the status of discourse in structural anthropology.[36]

35. Ibid.
36. Jacques Derrida, "Structure, Sign and Play in the Discourse of the Human Sciences," in *Writing and Difference*, trans. Alan Bass (Chicago: The University of Chicago Press, 1978), 288.

Derrida adds that Lévi-Strauss's structural schemata of kinship re-lations or creation myths are adduced as mere hypotheses allowing anthropologists to introduce some order into the baffling diversity of human practices. Empirical diversity is soon subsumed under an epistemic totalization provided by structures that fall under the cat-egory of universals or foundational constituents of the human mind reaching even into unconscious thought, finally stabilizing them-selves precariously between nature and culture, in the name of the very divide between nature and culture.

CAMILLE ROBCIS

Lévi-Strauss's Structuralist Social Contract

> The incest-prohibition is no longer a scandal one meets with or comes up against in the domain of traditional concepts; it is something which escapes these concepts and certainly precedes them—probably as the condition of their possibility. It could perhaps be said that the whole of philosophical conceptualization, systematically relating itself to the nature/culture opposition, is designed to leave in the domain of the unthinkable the very thing that makes this conceptualization possible: the origin of the prohibition of incest.
>
> —Jacques Derrida, "Structure, Sign, and Play in the Discourses of the Human Sciences"

During the last years of his life, Claude Lévi-Strauss was often described as apolitical. After a brief period of socialist activism during his youth, the story went, he had relinquished politics altogether to focus on his scientific research. Lévi-Strauss himself was partly responsible for propagating this myth. In his 1988 dialogue with Didier Éribon, he claimed to have "totally abandoned all political activities" after World War II, when he returned to France from his years of exile in New York.[1] In a 1980 interview, he explained that he had chosen to stay away from politics because he "did not believe that they could be the object of a theoretical reflection."[2] Similarly, he wrote to Alexandre Pajon: "by 1950, I was already very remote from politics. In fact, my scientific and political interests have evolved in opposite directions. They diverged—even though, at the time, I was not fully conscious of this—when I chose to explore the world instead of continuing to take part in my country's affairs."[3] In recent years, several scholars, including Pajon, have challenged Lévi-Strauss's political self-presentation as well as the chronology of his supposed "departure

1. Didier Éribon and Claude Lévi-Strauss, *De près et de loin* (Paris: Odile Jacob, 1988), 80.
2. "Interview with André Burguière and Jean-Paul Enthoven," *Le nouvel observateur* (5 July 1980): 18.
3. Alexandre Pajon, *Claude Lévi-Strauss politique: de la SFIO à l'UNESCO* (Toulouse: Privat, 2011), 9.

YFS 123, *Rethinking Claude Lévi-Strauss (1908–2009)*, ed. Doran, © 2013 by Yale University.

from politics." They have unearthed documents suggesting that Lévi-Strauss was not only active in the interwar period, but that he continued to write on politics, particularly on foreign relations, through the framework of the UNESCO.[4]

The question of Lévi-Strauss's politics resurfaced in the late 1990s during the controversy surrounding the Civil Pact of Solidarity or PACS (Pacte Civil de Solidarité), a law designed to give non-married couples—including same-sex couples—a set of rights and benefits comparable to those of marriage. Various scholars opposed to the PACS cited Lévi-Strauss to argue that heterosexual marriage was the universal and transhistorical foundation of society and of culture. Consequently, they asserted, the PACS was unacceptable not because it was naturally objectionable (as religious zealots would maintain), but rather because it was *culturally* impossible. This argument was articulated particularly forcefully by Françoise Héritier, one of Lévi-Strauss's most prominent students.

Héritier had inherited his chair at the Collège de France and was, at the time, running the Laboratoire d'anthropologie sociale founded by Lévi-Strauss in 1960 at the École des Hautes Études en Sciences Sociales. She was also routinely called as an "expert" in governmental committees pertaining to gender and sexuality. In an editorial in the French news daily *Le monde* titled "Let Us Not Leave the Critique of the PACS to the Right!" Héritier contended that with the PACS, "what was at stake was the fundamental upheaval of the imaginary and the symbolic structures of an entire society."[5] She pursued her critique of the legal recognition of same-sex unions in an interview with the Catholic newspaper *La croix* titled "PACS: No Society Ad-

---

4. For recent works on Lévi-Strauss's politics, see Stéphane Clouet, *De la rénovation à l'utopie socialistes: révolution constructive, un groupe d'intellectuels socialistes des années 1930* (Nancy: Presses Universitaires de Nancy, 1991); Vincent Debaene, "A propos de 'La politique étrangère d'une société primitive,'" *Ethnies* 33–34 (2009): 132–38; Debaene, "'Like Alice through the Looking Glass': Claude Lévi-Strauss in New York," *French Politics, Culture and Society* 28/1 (2010): 46–57; Debaene and Frédéric Keck, *Claude Lévi-Strauss : l'homme au regard éloigné* (Paris: Gallimard, 2009); Laurent Jeanpierre, "La politique culturelle française aux États-Unis de 1940 à 1947," in *Entre rayonnement et réciprocité: Contributions à l'histoire de la diplomatie culturelle* (Paris: Publications de la Sorbonne, 2002), 85–116; Laurent Jeanpierre, "Les structures d'une pensée d'exilé: La formation du structuralisme de Claude Lévi-Strauss," *French Politics, Culture and Society* 28/1 (2010): 58–76; Emmanuelle Loyer, *Paris à New York: intellectuels et artistes français en exil (1940–1947)* (Paris: Grasset, 2005).

5. "Ne laissons pas la critique du PACS à la droite!" *Le monde* (27 January 1999): Horizons, 14.

mits Homosexual Parenting."[6] According to Héritier, sexual difference was one of society's "unsurpassable limits of thought [*butoirs indépassables de la pensée*]" and as such, homosexual adoption was simply unthinkable from an anthropological perspective.[7]

The "experts" were not the only ones to cite Lévi-Strauss during the PACS debates. Within the Assembly, the Senate, and the courts, Lévi-Strauss's name and concepts returned again and again. The elected representative Renaud Dutreil brought *The Elementary Structures of Kinship* to the Assembly, reading it aloud to justify his opposition to the bill: "all human societies have produced a certain number of norms: exogamy, the prohibition of incest, and heterosexuality . . . Society enriches itself in otherness. Today, the other is the other sex. Homosexuality is the fear of the other."[8] Jacques Myard, another deputy, argued that homosexuals could not possibly constitute a family because, according to Lévi-Strauss, the "anthropological foundations of our society were constituted by two pillars: sexual difference and generational difference. All anthropologists, all ethnologists, have brought to light this fundamental structure which establishes the family."[9] According to the logic of these PACS opponents, homosexuality ought to be tolerated, even protected by a special set of rights, but in no way should the law recognize homosexuals as a "family," in the legal sense, because, since their kinship was not premised on sexual difference, it lacked a symbolic foundation.

Finally, in a letter dated from July 1999, the sociologist Éric Fassin, who had been one of the most active supporters of the PACS, asked Lévi-Strauss to take a position. Fassin, who told Lévi-Strauss that this "partisan use" of anthropology appeared to distort the scientific nature of his work, specified that his intervention at this moment in the discussion would be particularly meaningful. Lévi-Strauss sent Fassin the following response:

> The scale of human cultures is so large, so varied (and so easily manipulated) that we find without much trouble arguments supporting whichever thesis. Among the conceivable solutions to the problems of life in society, the role of the ethnologist is to distinguish and de-

6. Françoise Héritier, "Pacte civil de solidarité: 'Aucune société n'admet de parenté homosexuelle.'" Interview with Marianne Gomez, *La croix* 9 (1998): Société.

7. Ibid., 16.

8. Clarisse Fabre, "Des députés proposent d'étendre le pacte civil de solidarité aux fratries," *Le monde* (2 October 1998).

9. Débats Parlementaires, 7 November 1998.

scribe those which, in determinate conditions, have proved themselves viable. This familiarity acquired with the most diverse uses
teaches him—at best—a certain wisdom which cannot be useless to
his contemporaries; without forgetting nevertheless that the choices
of society belong not to the scholar as such, but—and he himself is
one—to the citizen.[10]

Fassin, who had been extremely critical of the experts who invoked
"anthropological transcendentals" to challenge the PACS, read Lévi-
Strauss's letter as an implicit condemnation of Héritier, as evidence
to support his position that the debate around same-sex unions was
specifically *political* (one involving citizens) rather than anthropological. Others, such as the anthropologist Jeanne Favret-Saada, interpreted Lévi-Strauss's laconic and purposefully noncommittal reply
as an example of his "legendary aversion to political debate."[11] Yet,
Lévi-Strauss's letter and his various statements on politics do raise
the question of where—if anywhere—the political lies in his work.

In what follows, I would like to consider this question in the
context of *The Elementary Structures of Kinship*, the book that was
most often cited in the debates around the PACS. Did Lévi-Strauss
indeed seek to simply "distinguish and describe" viable solutions to
the problems of life in society, or did his text carry a prescriptive
message? Was the structuralist model of kinship described and/or
prescribed in *The Elementary Structures* political? My argument in
this essay is twofold. First, I want to suggest that Lévi-Strauss's scientific and political interests did indeed evolve in reverse direction.
Lévi-Strauss returned to Paris in 1948 and published *The Elementary
Structures of Kinship* in 1949. His embrace of structuralism in this
work was an explicit act of distancing himself from politics, an act
that was strategic on both institutional and intellectual grounds. Second, I want to show that even though politics is absent in *The Elementary Structures*, the problem of *the political* figures prominently.
By "the political" I am referring to the overall framework of society,
the "principle or set of principles generative of the relationships that
men hold amongst each other and with the world," in Claude Lefort's

10. Eric Fassin, "La voix de l'expertise et les silences de la science dans le débat
démocratique," in Daniel Borrillo and Eric Fassin, *Au-delà du PACS: l'expertise fami-
liale à l'épreuve de l'homosexualité* (Paris: PUF, 2001), 110.

11. Jeanne Favret-Saada, "On n'est jamais si bien trahi que pas les siens," *Prochoix*
16 (2000): 31.

words.[12] Thus understood, *The Elementary Structures* can be read as a social contract theory describing the transition from a state of nature of discrete individuals to a structured social order. It offers a theory of the social bond, of social integration, an account of what gives society its foundation, its unity, and its basic coherence. This political force, the "glue" holding the social together is, for Lévi-Strauss, sexual difference. Heterosexual exchange is the condition for kinship and sociality, for publicness. Yet, Lévi-Strauss does not present this exchange as a temporally and geographically specific event but as a logical necessity, as a universal and transhistorical normative structure that he defines as "symbolic." Structuralism allows Lévi-Strauss to evacuate history and politics from his master narrative so that kinship and his social contract end up looking strangely *apolitical*. French scholars and legislators opposed to the PACS found solace in *The Elementary Structures of Kinship* precisely because of this apolitical quality of the social/sexual contract, which allowed them to bypass the political discussion of same-sex unions by focusing on the abstract and normative role of kinship.

THE DISCIPLINARY CONTEXT

As its title indicates, *The Elementary Structures of Kinship* was, on the surface, a study of kinship. It sought to outline marriage rules, nomenclature, and the system of rights and prohibitions that derived from these structures. However, Lévi-Strauss's ambitions for this project far transcended this narrow focus. *The Elementary Structures* represented a fundamental disciplinary move and a crucial philosophical intervention. Indeed, in a time of intense institutional competition and reshuffling, Lévi-Strauss conceived of his book as a theoretical manifesto for the new discipline he was founding: social anthropology. His purpose was, first of all, to demarcate himself from the tradition of French anthropology that had until then focused on physical anthropology. Throughout the nineteenth century, French anthropology was vibrant: the Société d'Anthropologie and the École d'Anthropologie were founded in 1859 and 1875 respectively; the Musée d'Histoire de l'Homme and the Musée d'Ethnographie were completed in 1879 in the Palais du Trocadéro. The members of these as-

12. Claude Lefort, *Essais sur le politique: XIXe-XXe siècles* (Paris: Seuil, 1986), 8.

sociations were primarily physicians and natural scientists interested in archaeology and the study of human "races." Many of them were linked to colonial missions and administration. Although the École aspired to study the human "races" in all their forms, its investigations quickly became restricted to the study of physical type and to the demonstration of a supposed correlation between physical type and the degree of development of a specific "race."[13] By 1940, several anthropologists of the École d'Anthropologie found in the policies of the Vichy government the possibility of putting into practice some of their intellectual hypotheses. Many proclaimed their allegiance to the National Revolution and others, such as Georges Montandon, were given institutional positions in the Vichy regime.[14]

As anthropology in France became synonymous with physical anthropology and with right-wing politics, sociology emerged as the privileged discipline for social and cultural analysis. In particular, French sociology found a new impetus in the work of Émile Durkheim and his students. For Durkheim, the goal of sociology was to discern the specificity of "the social," its totalizing and autonomous nature, the whole that was irreducible to the sum of its parts. Marcel Mauss, Durkheim's nephew and disciple, encouraged sociologists to study "total social facts": facts involving the totality or near totality of society and institutions, facts that were "at the same time juridical, economic, religious, and even aesthetic and morphological . . . political and domestic."[15] Moreover, to demarcate himself from the École d'Anthropologie's increasingly conservative positions, Mauss, who was a member of the French Socialist Party, the SFIO, and who wrote for the Communist paper *L'humanité*, preferred to describe his work as "ethnology" rather than "anthropology." Strongly affiliated with the left, Mauss, along with Paul Rivet and Lucien Lévy-Bruhl, founded the Institut d'Ethnologie in 1925, under the patronage of the

13. Donald Bender, "The Development of French Anthropology," *Journal of the History of Behavioral Science* 1 (1965): 142. See also Elizabeth A. Williams, *The Science of Man: Anthropological Thought and Institutions in Nineteenth-Century France* (Bloomington: Indiana University, 1983).

14. For more on the conservative strand of French anthropology, see Jean Jamin, "L'anthropologie et ses acteurs," in *Les enjeux philosophiques des années 50* (Paris: Éditions du Centre Pompidou, 1989): 99–114; Herman Lebovics, "Le conservatisme en anthropologie et la fin de la Troisième République," *Gradhiva* 4 (1988): 3–17.

15. Marcel Mauss, *The Gift: the Form and Reason for Exchange in Archaic Societies* (New York: Norton, 1990), 79.

Cartel des gauches.[16] Similarly, in 1937, he participated in the renovation of the Musée d'Ethnographie du Trocadéro, which would become the Musée de l'Homme. Funded by the Popular Front government, the new museum was meant to play a role in the democratization of knowledge that Mauss and his colleagues advocated.[17]

From his student years, Lévi-Strauss was personally and intellectually close to many of the members of the Institut d'Ethnologie. Mauss's influence was particularly evident in *The Elementary Structures of Kinship*, in which Lévi-Strauss characterized the incest prohibition as the "supreme rule of the gift."[18] The prohibition was indeed not simply negative: it forced men to marry outside of their clan and thus to forge social relations with the outside. Similarly, Lévi-Strauss made clear in his *Introduction to the Work of Marcel Mauss* that the prohibition—and kinship—needed to be understood as total social facts. One of his main points of contention with previous historical explanations of the prohibition (i.e., that they were the product of particular contexts, times, and places) is that these theories remain anchored in the contingent. "History provides examples," Lévi-Strauss explains, but "the problem"—his problem—"is to discover what profound and omnipresent causes could account for the regulation of the relationships between the sexes in every society and age."[19] What, in other words, makes kinship universal, total, and regular?

While Lévi-Strauss admired the French sociological school for trying to discern the specificity of the social and while he affiliated himself with this tradition in many ways, he was also critical of the empirical research of these ethnologists, many of whom had barely ventured abroad. Given this state of affairs, Lévi-Strauss's encounter with American anthropology during his exile was crucial. Lévi-Strauss greatly benefited from the wide collection of English-language sources at the New York Public Library where he wrote most of the

16. See Bender, "The Development of French Anthropology," 145. On Mauss's politics, see Sylvain Dzimira, *Marcel Mauss, savant et politique* (Paris: Découverte, 2007); Marcel Fournier, *Marcel Mauss* (Paris: Fayard, 1994).

17. Régis Meyran, "Races et racismes: Les ambiguïtés de l'antiracisme chez les anthropologues de l'entre-deux-guerres," *Gradhiva* 27 (2000): 65. See also Alice L. Conklin, "L'ethnologie combattante de l'entre-deux-guerres," in *Le siècle de Germaine Tillion*, ed. Tzvetan Todorov (Paris: Seuil, 2007): 39–60.

18. Claude Lévi-Strauss, *The Elementary Structures of Kinship*, trans. James Harle Bell, John Richard von Sturmer and Rodney Needham (Boston: Beacon Press, 1969), 480.

19. Ibid., 22–23.

Elementary Structures. Moreover, he established close ties with the most prominent American anthropologists, in particular Franz Boas, affiliated at the time with Columbia University, and many of his students, including Ralph Linton, Ruth Benedict, Alfred Kroeber, and Robert Lowie. Lévi-Strauss dedicated *The Elementary Structures* to the memory of Lewis Henry Morgan—one of the pioneers of American ethnography and one of the first scholars to systematically study kinship systems—partly to acknowledge his debt toward this empirically-oriented "American school of anthropology" that had so deeply shaped his work. *The Elementary Structures* was thus the product of this double heritage. In the exhaustiveness of his research, the range of scholarship he engaged with, and the sheer quantity of ethnographic data he had assembled, Lévi-Strauss inscribed himself within this "Anglo-Saxon" tradition of social and cultural anthropology that he admired. However, by considering the social as a whole, as a universal and as a total social fact, he remained committed to the theoretical enterprise of the French school of sociology. Lévi-Strauss thus located *The Elementary Structures of Kinship* at the crossroad of these two genealogies, but he also envisioned it as a solution to the impasses facing each one. As such, *The Elementary Structures* would serve as the prototype for a new kind of anthropology, and one that would also overcome the tainted politics of French anthropology during the Vichy years.

THE THEORETICAL INTERVENTION

The Elementary Structures of Kinship, however, was not merely innovative in institutional terms; it was also extremely ambitious on the level of theory. As Lévi-Strauss stated in the first pages of his book, his goal was to propose a definitive theory of how the social related to the biological, to determine, once and for all, where exactly "nature ends and culture begins."[20] Is human identity (physical and behavioral) determined by biologically innate and instinctual attributes, or is it the product of a complex interaction of our social, educational, and familial contexts? This question, according to Lévi-Strauss, had puzzled sociologists, biologists, and anthropologists for years. Given the inherent difficulty in isolating humans from any social interaction

20. Ibid., 4.

(even in the case of a newborn or the so-called "wolf-children"), social scientists have opted for a functionalist model that simply juxtaposes culture and biology, or have abandoned the question altogether. Similarly, social scientists had attempted to discern traces of culture in animal life, particularly among great apes. Chimpanzees for instance, are able to "articulate several monosyllables and disyllables but they never attach any meaning to them."[21] Although monkeys can utter sounds, these are never *signs* in the sense that a particular signified is attached to a particular signifier. To use one of Lévi-Strauss's most important concepts, animals are incapable of "symbolic thought." Most significantly, Lévi-Strauss argues, "the social life of monkeys does not lend itself to the formulation of any norm . . . Not only is the behavior of the single subject inconsistent, but there is no regular pattern to be discerned in collective behavior."[22] This lack of norms and regularity is particularly striking in the chimps' sexual activity, where "monogamy and polygamy exist side by side."[23] Thus, Lévi-Strauss claims, it is "this absence of rules [that] seems to provide the surest criterion for distinguishing a natural from a cultural process."[24] "Let us suppose," Lévi-Strauss famously concludes, "that everything universal in man relates to the natural order, and is characterized by spontaneity, and that everything subject to a norm is cultural and is both relative and particular."[25]

Within the overall structure of Lévi-Strauss's carefully constructed argument, this passage is key. Indeed, it comes as the answer, the only answer, to the "insoluble question" of where nature stops and culture begins, a question that, as Lévi-Strauss tells us, has haunted both philosophy and the social sciences. Without a proper understanding of nature and culture, any "understanding of social phenomena" is precluded.[26] Yet, as Lévi-Strauss makes clear in his examples of the newborn and the wolf-children, a pure state of nature is a hypothetical construction; it is by definition, foreclosed. Though a non-domesticated animal might be able to return to a form of natural behavior, "such cannot be expected of man, since the species has no

21. Ibid., 6.
22. Ibid.
23. Ibid., 7.
24. Ibid., 8.
25. Ibid.
26. Ibid., 4.

natural behavior to which an isolated individual might retrogress."[27] While "wild children may be cultural monstrosities . . . under no circumstances can they provide reliable evidence of an earlier state."[28] From birth, because of their innate capacity to symbolize, men are always already "in society." In other words, the state of nature is not a real or historical phenomenon, but a heuristic *structure* necessary to Lévi-Strauss's argument. As Lévi-Strauss puts it in the beginning of his book, "this distinction between nature and society, while of no historical significance, does contain a logic, fully justifying its use by modern sociology as a methodological tool."[29] It is in this sense also that we should understand Lévi-Strauss's assertion that "no empirical analysis . . . can determine the point of transition between natural and cultural facts, nor how they are connected."[30] Thus, Lévi-Strauss refers to his definitions of nature and culture according to norm and universality as proceeding from an "ideal analysis," as opposed to what he calls a "real analysis."[31] By ideal, Lévi-Strauss appears to indicate that he is relying on a priori concepts that need to be posited abstractly, since they cannot be deduced from experience. It is this ideal analysis that guides the remainder of *The Elementary Structures.*

Lévi-Strauss links his discussion of the nature/culture dichotomy to that of kinship through the prohibition of incest. If we define nature by universality and culture by the existence of relative and particular norms, Lévi-Strauss writes,

> we are then confronted with a fact, or rather a group of facts, which in light of the previous definitions, are not far removed from a scandal: we refer to that complex group of beliefs, customs, conditions and institutions described succinctly as the prohibition of incest, which presents, without the slightest ambiguity, and inseparably combines, the two characteristics in which we recognize the conflicting features of two mutually exclusive orders. It constitutes a rule, but a rule which alone among all the social rules, possesses at the same time a universal character.[32]

The prohibition of incest, Lévi-Strauss argues, is the only phenomenon with "the distinctive characteristics both of nature and of its

27. Ibid., 5.
28. Ibid.
29. Ibid., 3.
30. Ibid., 8.
31. Ibid.
32. Ibid., 8–9.

theoretical contradiction, culture. [It] has the universality of bent and instinct, and the coercive character of law and institution . . . [and, as such] presents a formidable mystery to sociological thought."[33] Just as sociologists have failed to give a definitive explanation of the distinction between nature and culture, they have been unable to determine the precise origin of the incest prohibition and to account for its sacredness, in all times and all cultures. Specifically, Lévi-Strauss contends, sociologists who have tried to explain the incest taboo have fallen into one of three methodological "traps," all resulting from an inadequate conceptualization of nature and culture. A first camp (which includes Lewis Henry Morgan and Henry Maine) has argued that the prohibition was imposed by societies who had become aware of the hazardous biological (i.e., natural) effects of consanguinity. Genetic foreshadowing, however, cannot justify the existence of the incest taboo, since the medical ramifications of incest have been fully grasped only recently and since biology alone cannot account for the arbitrariness regarding which unions are considered incestuous and which are not. According to a second camp (exemplified by Edward Westermarck and Havelock Ellis), the prohibition is merely the formal expression of a universal, deep-rooted instinct of *natural* repugnance toward incest. Again, Lévi-Strauss dismisses this "universal disgust" theory by claiming that not only do incestuous relations exist but, as psychoanalysis has shown, the only universal feeling when it comes to incest is an unconscious desire for it, as in the example of the Oedipus complex. Moreover, this theory of the "natural horror" produced by incest can hardly account for the aura of sacredness that the prohibition bears in most societies: as Lévi-Strauss contends, one would not need to forbid something so explicitly if it did not correspond to some widespread wish or longing. Finally, others (including Herbert Spencer, James Frazer, and Durkheim) have treated the prohibition as a purely *social* phenomenon, imposed by particular cultures at particular times. Most of these explanations, however, not only appear historically improbable, but they also present a larger and more critical logical issue:

> They attempt to establish a universal phenomenon on an historical sequence, which is by no means inconceivable in some particular case but whose episodes are so contingent that the possibility of this sequence being repeated unchanged in every human society must be

33. Ibid., 10.

wholly excluded . . . It is possible to imagine that, in a given society, the origin of some particular institution is to be explained by some highly arbitrary transformations. History provides examples. But history also shows that, according to the society considered, such processes may result in widely differing institutions, and that where analogous institutions have found independent origins in various parts of the world, the historical sequences leading up to their appearances are themselves highly dissimilar. This is what is termed convergence.[34]

Thus, to sum up, we could say that for Lévi-Strauss, natural explanations of the incest taboo can account for universality but not for the rule, whereas historical/sociological explanations can account for the rule but not for its universality.

It is in opposition to these two options that Lévi-Strauss sets up his own model of interpretation of the incest prohibition, which, he suggests, moves beyond the purely biological/purely historical accounts, beyond the nature/culture paradigm. "The problem of the incest prohibition," Lévi-Strauss writes, "is not so much to seek the different historical configurations for each group as to explain the particular form of the institution in each particular society. The problem is to discover what profound and omnipresent causes could account for the *regulation* of the relationships between the sexes in every society and age."[35] To pinpoint this problem of regulation, Lévi-Strauss makes the now famous argument that we must understand the incest prohibition as situated at the *transition* from nature to culture and that, as such, it is, by definition, both nature *and* culture: "The prohibition of incest is in its origin neither purely cultural nor purely natural, nor is it a composite mixture of elements from both nature and culture. It is the fundamental step [*démarche*] because of which, by which, but above all in which, the transition from nature to culture is accomplished."[36]

The prohibition of incest, Lévi-Strauss concludes, is the link between man's biological existence and his social existence.[37] It is, we could say, the necessary condition for the social contract, the struc-

34. Ibid., 22.
35. Ibid., 23 (my emphasis).
36. Ibid., 24. The term *démarche* here is interesting since it refers not only to the physical action of "stepping" but also to the intellectual activity of "moving forward" as in *démarche intellectuelle* or *démarche de pensée*.
37. Ibid., 24–25.

ture that brings men from the scattered state of nature into an integrated social framework:

Nature	Incest Prohibition	Culture/Society
Universality		Norms, Regularity
Spontaneous	$\longrightarrow$	Relative, Particular

In the diagram above, the arrow—the incest prohibition—goes in one direction only, because the state of nature, as Lévi-Strauss makes clear, is always already foreclosed. Lévi-Strauss confirms this idea when, describing the prohibition of incest as the link between nature and culture, he writes:

> This union is neither static nor arbitrary, and as soon as it comes into being, the whole situation [*la situation totale*] is completely changed. Indeed, it is less a union than a transformation or transition. Before it, culture is still non-existent; with it, nature's sovereignty over man is ended. The prohibition of incest is where nature transcends itself. It sparks the formation of a new and more complex type of structure and is superimposed upon the simpler structures of physical life through integration, just as these themselves are superimposed upon the simpler structures of animal life. It brings about and is in itself the advent of a new order.[38]

As this passage suggests, the incest prohibition and culture become at some point rhetorically synonymous. This "new order" is premised on the existence of the incest prohibition, but also on the dichotomy between nature and culture, one in which nature exists as a purely hypothetical construct that is nonetheless necessary for the logic of the argument.

If Lévi-Strauss consecrates the prohibition of incest as the "rule of rules" of his "new order," it is because he is primarily interested in the positive effects of his prohibition. Indeed, if men cannot marry the women in their own family or clan, they must look for the women of another family, and thus establish a connection—a social bond—with another family. In this sense, Lévi-Strauss adopts Mauss's paradigm of the gift. For Mauss, the act of giving is never free, pure, or disinterested, since it incurs the obligation to reciprocate. This, according to Mauss, creates a moral system in which giving, owing, and

38. Ibid., 25.

reciprocating open individuals to one another. As he puts it, "If one gives things and returns them, it is because one is giving and returning 'respects' . . . Yet it is also because by giving one is giving *oneself,* and if one gives *oneself,* it is because one 'owes' *oneself*—one's person and one's goods—to others."[39] Therefore, the exchange can only have meaning—or *signify*—in relation to other signifiers in that same system. In *The Elementary Structures,* it is through the exchange of women that individuals are linked to the collectivity, to the social world. In Lévi-Strauss's words:

> Exchange—and consequently the rule of exogamy which expresses it—has in itself a social value. It provides the means of binding men together, and of superimposing upon the natural links of kinship the henceforth artificial links—artificial in the sense that they are removed from chance encounters or the promiscuity of family life—of alliance governed by rule.[40]

Within this framework, incest is not so much morally or biologically objectionable as it is fundamentally anti-social and selfish: "incest, in the broadest sense of the word, consists in obtaining by oneself, and for oneself, instead of by another, and for another."[41] It is in that sense also that we should understand Lévi-Strauss's assertion that "incest is socially absurd before it is morally culpable."[42] Incest means the refusal to participate in the social contract—a refusal, however, that is theoretically impossible because man, as we have seen, is always already social.

As an illustration of this non-socialized subject who remains outside the system of exchange, Lévi-Strauss gives the example of a bachelor he met in Brazil who "rarely went out, except to go hunting by himself, and when the family meals began around the fires, he would as often as not have gone without if a female relative had not occasionally set a little food at his side, which he ate in silence."[43] From Lévi-Strauss's portrayal of this bachelor, we can conclude that the exclusion from the social contract is not only social: it also psychological. Described as anxious, wretched, and ill-looking, the bachelor testifies to the fact that "marriage is of vital importance for every in-

39. Mauss, *The Gift,* 46.
40. Lévi-Strauss, *The Elementary Structures of Kinship,* 480.
41. Ibid., 489.
42. Ibid., 485.
43. Ibid., 39.

dividual, being, as he is, doubly concerned, not only to find a wife for himself but also to prevent those two calamities of primitive society from occurring in his group, namely, the bachelor and the orphan."[44] Marriage, in other words, has both a psychic and a social benefit.

Kinship is thus "symbolic," according to Lévi-Strauss, not because of its content but because of its structure. As Lévi-Strauss explains in his introduction to the collection of Mauss's essays *Sociologie et Anthropologie*:

> Any culture can be as a combination of symbolic systems headed by language, the matrimonial rules, the economic relations, art, science and religion. All the systems seek to express certain aspects of physical reality and social reality, and even more, to express *the links that those two types of reality have with each other* and those that occur among the symbolic systems themselves.[45]

What is symbolic here is not something intrinsic to particular things, people, or events; it is rather the articulation between the "physical reality," which we could call nature, and the "social reality," which we could call culture. In this context, although Lévi-Strauss praises Mauss for attempting to think the link between the individual and the social in innovative ways, he criticizes him for not pushing his interpretation far enough: "Mauss still believes it is possible to elaborate a sociological theory of symbolism, when we clearly should be looking for the symbolic origin of society."[46] Lévi-Strauss makes a similar objection to Durkheim: "We cannot explain the social phenomenon; the existence of the state of culture is in itself unintelligible if symbolism is not treated by sociological thought as an a priori condition . . . Sociology cannot explain the genesis of symbolic thought, *it must take it as a given.*"[47] *The Elementary Structures* can be read, I have suggested, as an answer to this methodological impasse facing the French sociological school. Indeed, since Lévi-Strauss posits nature and culture as a priori categories and since the incest prohibition is defined as the link between the two, the incest prohibition—and the heterosexual exchange that brings it about—also needs to be taken

44. Ibid.

45. Lévi-Strauss, *Introduction to the Work of Marcel Mauss*, trans. Felicity Baker (New York: Routledge and Kegan Paul, 1987), 16 (my emphasis).

46. Ibid., xxii.

47. Lévi-Strauss, "La sociologie française," in *La sociologie au XXe Siècle*, ed. Georges Gurvitch (Paris: PUF, 1947), 526–27, original emphasis.

as an a priori condition, to understand social relations, culture, or *la pensée symbolique*.

BEYOND HISTORY

The implications of Lévi-Strauss's concepts of nature, culture, and the incest prohibition become apparent in the last chapter of *The Elementary Structures*. Lévi-Strauss begins by clarifying his critique of history through an analysis of Freud's *Totem and Taboo*. The choice of *Totem and Taboo* is significant, since this work represents one of Freud's most elaborate attempts to link the social to the sexual. In Freud's narrative, the brothers' murder of the Father and the sacrificial meal that follows mark the institution of the superego. Out of the brothers' guilt emerges the rule of law, morality, religion, but also, exogamy, since the Father can no longer keep all of the women for himself. The prohibition of incest marks the birth of culture, of the symbolic as such, "the beginnings of religion, morals, society, and art converge in the Oedipus complex."[48] For Freud, the structural equivalence between culture, morality, society, and psychic adjustment has a series of consequences. In particular, Freud suggests that being "outside" this social contract has not only social but also psychic implications. As he explains:

> The asocial nature of neuroses has its genetic origin in their most fundamental purpose, which is to take flight from an unsatisfying reality into a more pleasurable world of phantasy. The real world, which is avoided in this way by neurotics, is under the sway of human society and of the institutions collectively created by it. To turn away from reality is at the same time to withdraw from the community of man.[49]

Lévi-Strauss focuses on Freud's analogy between individual psyche and social formation to maintain the uniqueness and specificity of the incest taboo. As he writes:

> Freud's work is an example and a lesson. The moment the claim was made that certain extant features of the human mind could be explained by an historically certain and logically necessary event, it was permissible, and even prescribed, to attempt a scrupulous restoration

48. Sigmund Freud, *Totem and Taboo: Some Points of Agreement Between the Mental Lives of Savages and Neurotics*, trans. James Strachey (New York: Norton, 1989), 194.
49. Ibid., 93.

of the sequence. The failure of *Totem and Taboo*, far from being inherent to the author's proposed design, results rather from his hesitation to avail himself to the ultimate consequences implied in his premises. He ought to have seen that phenomena involving the most fundamental structure of the human mind could not have appeared once and for all. They are repeated in their entirety within each consciousness, and the relevant explanation falls within an order which transcends both historical successions and contemporary correlations.[50]

In other words, although Lévi-Strauss credits Freud for thinking the individual and the social together through this "social contract model," he criticizes him for remaining caught in historical explanations that Freud himself constantly put into question.[51] Freud's methodological "timidity," Lévi-Strauss continues, leads him to a "strange and double paradox":

> Freud successfully accounts, not for the beginning of civilization but for its present state; and setting out to explain the origin of a prohibition, he succeeds in explaining, certainly not why incest is consciously condemned, but how it happens to be unconsciously desired. It has been stated and restated that what makes *Totem and Taboo* unacceptable, as an interpretation of the prohibition of incest and its origins, is the gratuitousness of the hypothesis of the male horde and of primitive murder, a vicious circle deriving the social state from the events which presuppose it . . . The desire for the mother or the sister, the murder of the father and the sons' repentance, undoubtedly do not correspond to any fact or group of facts occupying a single place in history. But perhaps they symbolically express an ancient and lasting dream. The power of this dream, its power to mould men's thoughts unbeknown to them, arises precisely from the fact that the acts it evoked have never been committed, because culture has opposed them at all times and in all places.[52]

Thus, according to Lévi-Strauss, the main problem with *Totem and Taboo* (and with psychoanalysis more generally) is not the actual event that Freud focuses on (the killing of the father), but rather the fact that Freud still thinks this prohibition in historical terms. Freud's inability to abandon history is paradoxical, Lévi-Strauss tells

---

50. Lévi-Strauss, *The Elementary Structures of Kinship*, 490–491.
51. Freud, for example, calls his story "a hypothesis which may seem fantastic but which offers the advantage of establishing an unsuspected correlation between groups of phenomena that have hitherto been disconnected" (in Freud, *Totem and Taboo*, 175).
52. Lévi-Strauss, *The Elementary Structures of Kinship*, 491.

us, since in his other writings he has often suggested that "certain basic phenomena" such as anxiety and sublimation, "find their explanation in the permanent structure of the human mind, rather than in its history."[53] Hence, Lévi-Strauss concludes, Freud's "hesitations" in *Totem and Taboo* are revealing: "They show a social science-like psychoanalysis . . . still wavering between the tradition of an historical sociology . . . and a more modern and scientifically more solid attitude, which expects a knowledge of its future and past from an analysis of the present."[54] This "more modern and scientifically more solid attitude" will be structuralism.

Indeed, the last pages of *The Elementary Structures* can be read as a theoretical manifesto for Lévi-Strauss's new discipline of structural anthropology. Avoiding the methodological impasses of biology and history, of the natural and social sciences, structural anthropology would also avoid the political polarization of anthropology and ethnology that characterized the pre-war period. Its model would not be French sociology or American anthropology but rather, structural linguistics:

> Only one science has reached the point at which synchronic and diachronic explanation have merged . . . This social science is linguistics. When we consider its methods, and even more its object, we may ask ourselves whether the sociology of the family, as conceived of in this work, involves as different a reality as might be believed, and consequently whether it has not the same possibilities at its disposal.[55]

Lévi-Strauss's interest in linguistics dated from his years in New York, particularly from his friendship with Roman Jakobson who was also exiled at the École Libre des Hautes Études during the war. In addition to Jakobson, the works of Saussure, Nikolai Troubetzkoy, and Émile Beneveniste were all foundational for Lévi-Strauss's introduction to structural linguistic theory. Structural linguistics offered Lévi-Strauss an alternative to history and to historical sociology by providing a universal, logical, and relational model particularly well adapted to the study of "total facts." This model was not only descriptive in its nature: it was explanatory and could posit general rules.

The analogy between kinship and linguistics that Lévi-Strauss establishes at the end of his book has several crucial consequences.

53. Ibid.
54. Ibid., 492.
55. Ibid., 492–93.

First, if we return to the diagram mapping the logic of Lévi-Strauss's argument (what I have been calling his structuralist social contract), language can be added to the side of culture, as another effect of the incest prohibition, opposite the camp of nature. Language, kinship, culture, symbolic thought, sociality, and psychic adjustment are now structurally equivalent, whereas sounds (with no signifier attached to them), mating, nature, selfishness and isolation (like the bachelor), and psychic damage are on the other side. Another way to say this is that the structuralist social contract is also a linguistic contract: it assumes that signifiers and signified are attached to one another in a particular way.

Nature		Culture/Society
Universality		Norms, Regularity
Spontaneous	**Incest Prohibition**	Relative, Particular
Isolation, Mating		Kinship
Sounds	$\longrightarrow$	Language, Symbolic
Psychic Damage /		Thought
Psychosis		Psychic Adjustment

Consequently, being outside the social contract means not being able to "signify" to others. It is in this sense that we should understand Lévi-Strauss's assertions: "the relations between the sexes can be conceived as one of the modalities of a great 'communication function' which also includes language,"[56] and "language and exogamy represent two solutions to one and the same situation"[57]—the situation of social exchange. In opposition to the tower of Babel "when words were still the essential property of each particular group"—a synonym, we could say, of the state of nature—words have now "become common property" and as such, they function as vehicles of solidarity:

> If the incest prohibition and exogamy have an essentially positive function, if the reason for their existence is to establish a tie between men which the latter cannot do without if they are to raise themselves from a biological to a social organization, it must be recognized that linguists and sociologists do not merely apply the same methods but are studying the same thing. Indeed, from this point of view, 'exogamy and language . . . have fundamentally the same function—

56. Ibid., 494.
57. Ibid., 496.

communication and integration with others' . . . The incest prohibition is universal like language.[58]

Renouncing heterosexual exchange means renouncing kinship, integration, sociality, psychic cohesion, a common language, and culture.
Moreover, any "renouncement" is precluded by the fact that the state
of nature is hypothetical, foreclosed, not actually—historically or empirically—available to humans. Hence, the state of nature, as well as
the possibility of breaking the incest taboo, function as categorical
imperatives. It is in this sense that kinship can be said to be ethical
in Lévi-Strauss's work. The incest prohibition is not made necessary
by any empirical reality, nor does it translate an ideal type of moral
conduct, a manifestation of the general "good." Rather, it is ethical
because it is psychically *and* socially necessary.

Faced with the theoretical difficulty presented by his concepts
of nature and society, Lévi-Strauss contends that the incest taboo
is neither cultural nor social, but rather structural (like language),
universal, and in some way, inevitable—a forced choice. As Maurice
Merleau-Ponty has put it in his analysis of *The Elementary Structures*, exchange is presented as mechanical, as *"allant de soi"*: "The
subjects who live in a society are not necessarily conscious of the
principle of exchange that regulates them, just as the speaking subject
does not need in order to speak to go through the linguistic analysis of his language. Rather, the structure is practiced as if it were
obvious."[59] The structure of this social contract might not be obvious (and in fact, according to Lévi-Strauss, it is not), but its practice,
its performance, is. In that sense, Lévi-Strauss can argue that it is
not "symbolic thought" or culture that produces the prohibition of
incest. This would be a socio-historical explanation. Rather, the prohibition, and its correlation, exogamy and the family, are coextensive
with the symbolic: they are the "general condition of culture."[60]

My contention here is not that the politicians and scholars opposed to the PACS are reading Lévi-Strauss correctly or that Lévi-
Strauss is responsible for having elaborated, more than forty years
before the fact, the theoretical basis to prevent gay people from ex-
ercising certain rights in France. Rather, I have tried to show that

58. Ibid., 493.

59. Maurice Merleau-Ponty, "De Mauss à Claude Lévi-Strauss," in Merleau-Ponty,
Éloge de la philosophie et autres essais (Paris: Gallimard, 1967), 128.

60. Lévi-Strauss, *The Elementary Structures of Kinship*, 24.

The Elementary Structures of Kinship is an intrinsically political book, that this political dimension is grounded in sexual difference, and that it is constructed as symbolic: universal, transhistorical, and normative. Lévi-Strauss's structuralist social contract was appealing during the PACS debates precisely for these qualities, for seemingly depoliticizing what was, and will always be, a political discussion.

BORIS WISEMAN

Lévi-Strauss and the Archaeology of Perceptible Worlds

FIELD NOTES

The manuscript of the field notes from Claude Lévi-Strauss's second Brazilian expedition (1938–1939), housed at the Bibliothèque nationale de France, occupy a dozen or so small format notebooks.[1] They provide, along with what remains of his correspondence from that period, a unique glimpse into the practices and thought processes of an anthropologist often criticized for his relative lack of field experience, in particular by Anglo-American anthropologists. These field notes are an especially precious record, since the notes from his first expedition disappeared when his Paris flat was pillaged by German soldiers during World War II.[2] As Vincent Debaene reveals, Lévi-Strauss drew extensively on the notebooks, as well as on various published essays, when he wrote *Tristes tropiques*, assembling fragments in the manner of the "bricoleur."[3] It was also in these notebooks that Lévi-Strauss began work on two literary projects that he subsequently abandoned, a "vaguely Conradian" novel, as he described it to Didier Eribon, and a play, *The Apotheosis of Augustus*, which is mentioned in *Tristes tropiques* (Chapter XXXVII). Both projects, of which very little remains, seem to give expression to the ethnographer's self-doubt. The plot of the novel was supposed to be based on a true story about trav-

---

1. NAF 28150. I would like to thank Mrs. Monique Lévi-Strauss for allowing me to cite from Claude Lévi-Strauss's unpublished field notes. For a detailed presentation of these field notes, along with those kept by Lévi-Strauss during his 1950 journey to India and Pakistan, see Vincent Debaene, "Notice," in Claude Lévi-Strauss, *Œuvres* (Paris: Gallimard, 2008), 1675–1721 (see 1690–1694 for the relationship between the notebooks and *Tristes tropiques* and 1730 for a material description).
2. Lévi-Strauss *Œuvres*, 1691.
3. Debaene, "Notice," 1690.

YFS 123, *Rethinking Claude Lévi-Strauss (1908–2009)*, ed. Doran, © 2013 by Yale University.

elers who use a phonograph to trick an indigenous population into believing that their gods had returned to earth. The play, based on Corneille's tragedy *Cinna ou la Clémence d'Auguste*, is set in Ancient Rome. Its central character, Cinna, is himself a traveler recently returned from his long journeys to distant lands, disillusioned with himself and his ambitions. Lévi-Strauss later separated out the pages of his field notes relating to these literary projects and filed them separately, presumably with the intention of working on them. This was never to be the case.

Lévi-Strauss's fragile, messy, small-format notebooks, written in pencil, exude a strong smell of smoked paprika. One cannot help wondering if this smell has been preserved since the time of his travels.[4] If so, it would constitute the last remaining point of contact with the vanishing world he later described in *Tristes tropiques*. These notebooks contain a disparate mix of materials. Alongside the many vocabulary lists and kinship diagrams, the outlines of maps, the numerical data, one finds a variety of descriptive passages, snippets of analyses, as well as numerous drawings and musical notations. Daily jottings relating to customs or beliefs stand side by side with fragments of interpretations, summaries of stories that Lévi-Strauss had heard, descriptions of landscapes, and narratives of experiences he had had while travelling or fragments from his novel and play. Very little escapes the anthropologist's observant eye. He notes, in a few quick sentences, the position of a defecating man, and the precise gestures he uses to attend to his hygiene. He captures a crouched woman hanging on to a stick planted vertically in the ground, in the midst of childbirth, and the familiar gestures of her birth partner. The description of the weave of a basket is accompanied by a drawing that includes precise measurements. When he comes across an unfamiliar bird he notes its local name and characterizes its song—that of the Urutal, we find out, is made up of three descending notes. Lévi-Strauss pays particular attention to customary behavior, of course. In the Campos Novos notebook (dated "Second fortnight August 1938"), he recounts a dispute over a bow and arrow in which two men grab

4. I have since found out that the odor does indeed date back to the time of Lévi-Strauss's field expeditions. It comes from the creosote that he and other anthropologists put in their trunks to preserve the contents from humidity and insects (Debaene, personal communication). See also the "Notice" to the Pléiade edition of *Tristes tropiques*.

each other's penis sheaths in macho defiance. On another occasion, he details the various prohibitions surrounding the preparation of a particular kind of fish for ritual cooking: it must not be seen when the sun is high in the sky, only at dawn, and even then only at certain periodic intervals, and never by women.

The notebooks preserve the trace of something that is often omitted from the published ethnographic accounts: the process of grappling with the reconstruction of a lived experience. This is perhaps best illustrated not by something that he wrote, but by a series of drawings that can be found in the second of the three notebooks devoted to the Tupi-Kawahib. These almost identical drawings are renderings of the type of knot used by the Tupi to fasten a hammock to a fixed point. There is nothing remarkable about these sketches. The first is light and tentative. It betrays the draftsman's uncertain attempt at capturing the intricate series of loops by which the knot is tied. The second, a close replica of the first, is drawn in thicker, surer lines. It confirms the accuracy of the ethnographer's initial observations. The third and final drawing, perhaps done without recourse to the model (it is on another page and in a different style), fixes once and for all the type of knot and gives it a more realistic, rope-like appearance. These drawings of a knot could stand as a metaphor for the work of the field ethnographer. Each successive one more closely approximates the object it tries to grasp. Together, they reveal the repetitive and always unfinished labor of attempting to render reality accurately and to endow it with intelligible form.

The notebooks bring to light the vast descriptive enterprise that lies at the core of ethnography as well as the always ambiguous nature of such an endeavor. The ethnographer's ambition is to capture the many manifestations of a culture apprehended in terms of what makes it different or "other." The traveler, author, and Calvinist, Pastor Jean de Léry, writing nearly 400 years before Lévi-Strauss,[5] had already noted, in relation to his own encounters with the Tupinamba, the formidable difficulties inherent in such an undertaking: "During the year or so when I lived in that country, I took such care in observing all of them [the Tupinamba] that even now it seems to me that I have them before my eyes. [. . .] But their gestures and expressions are so completely different from ours, that it is difficult, I confess, to

5. Jean de Léry's *Histoire d'un voyage fait en la terre du Brésil* was first published in 1578.

represent them well by writing or by pictures."[6] Nevertheless, the ethnographer must attempt to transform description into a tool of inquiry, to harness it to the task of "recording" unfamiliar customs and institutions, exploiting all that the ethnographer's point of view has in common with that of the novelist: a certain exteriority toward the objects he or she describes and a close attention to particulars.

As a form of textual production, ethnography, despite its scientific aims, has therefore always remained close to literary writing, with which it has always entertained complex and ambivalent relations.[7] One may interpret the famous opening lines of Tristes tropqiues ("Travel and travelers are two things I loathe—and yet here I am, all set to tell the story of my expeditions")[8] as a way of positioning anthropological discourse in relation to other kinds of literary discourse, in particular the travel account. Literature has often been thought of in terms of a division between narration and description, in which the latter is usually considered to be the poor cousin of the former. The first sentence of Tristes tropiques locates the truth-value of anthropology textually, situating it on the descriptive side of this great divide. Its ironic debunking of travel accounts is also, more seriously, a way of saying that anthropology does not belong on the side of narration. It is only reluctantly that Lévi-Strauss himself ventures onto this terrain. Debaene makes a similar point.[9] The whole of Tristes tropiques, he argues, is constructed in opposition to the false teleology of narration, as exemplified by the famous "la marquise sortit à 5h," cited by André Breton in the Surrealist Manifesto. For Breton, the problem with narratives constructed on this model is that they confer a false and extrinsic necessity on the sequence of events they narrate simply by virtue of narrating them. No such necessity joins together the events that make up a life. It is revealing that Lévi-

6. de Léry, History of a Voyage to the Land of Brazil, trans. Janet Whatley (Los Angeles: University of California Press, 1990), 67.

7. For a book-length analysis of these relations see Debaene, L'adieu au voyage : l'ethnologie française entre science et literature (Paris: Gallimard, 2010). Debaene has focused on a French tradition, that of writing not one but two field accounts, a scientific account for an audience of specialists, followed by a second, more literary and personal work (e.g., Alfred Metraux's Easter Island, Marcel Griaule's Burners of Men, Lévi-Strauss's Tristes tropioques, etc.). His argument is in part that one account is not complete without the other.

8. Lévi-Strauss, Tristes tropiques, trans. John Russell (New York: Atheneum, 1970), 17.

9. In Lévi-Strauss, Œuvres, 1698–99, and L'adieu, 309.

Strauss quickly abandons his attempt to arrange his notebooks in diary form, as if his approach to the materials he was marshaling was inherently ill-suited to any kind of sequential ordering.[10]

This descriptive ethnography, which Lévi-Strauss sees as a first step toward the higher-order synthesis of anthropological understanding proper (it lacks the cross-cultural perspective of the latter), shares, in some of its aspects, the totalizing ambitions of realist literary description. The latter may be exemplified by Flaubert's famous description of Charles Bovary's cap:

> It was one of those head-gears of composite order, in which we can find traces of the bearskin, shako, billycock hat, sealskin cap, and cotton night-cap; one of those poor things, in fine, whose dumb ugliness has depths of expression, like an imbecile's face. Oval, stiffened with whalebone, it began with three round knobs; then came in succession lozenges of velvet and rabbit-skin separated by a red band; after that a sort of bag that ended in a cardboard polygon covered with complicated braiding, from which hung, at the end of a long thin cord, small twisted gold threads in the manner of a tassel. The cap was new; its peak shone.[11]

Flaubert seems to say everything that there is to say about the cap on Charles's head. A similar intention lies behind Lévi-Strauss's recording of the gestures (and sounds) of an oarsman, observed during a canoe trip along the Rio Pimeta Bueno.[12] His notations are of course not literary but functional, hence the difference in style and register compared to Flaubert's descriptive passage. "To push away," Lévi-Strauss notes,[13] "[one?] dip per stroke = plouf – plouf." "Setting off," he continues, "one dip followed by a beat to the side of the canoe followed by an empty return and a beat." He specifies: "empty return = paddle outside of the water and perpendicular to the canoe, turned sideways, with a twist on the exit allowing the paddle to dovetail with the horizontal position." With his customary attentiveness to

10. Lévi-Strauss kept a diary from June 6–16, 1938. See *Œuvres*, 1963.
11. Gustave Flaubert, *Madame Bovary*, trans. Eleanor Marx-Avering <http://www.gutenberg.org/catalog/world/readfile?fk_files=2755694 >, accessed June 15, 2012.
12. Box 124, Notebook 5.
13. My translation. It is not easy to make out what exactly Lévi-Strauss is attempting to describe in these notes, which were primarily a mnemonic. He uses the phrase "retour vide," which I take to designate a moment when the paddle rests parallel to the canoe, exerting no pressure on the water.

auditory experience, he captures the rhythm of this stroke in an ono-
matopoeic diagram:

$$
\left\{ \begin{array}{l} \text{tra} \\ \quad - \text{ tra } - \\ \text{plouf} \end{array} \right.
\qquad \text{tra} \quad
\left\{ \begin{array}{l} \text{tra} \\ \quad - \text{ tra} - \\ \text{plouf} \end{array} \right.
\qquad
\left\{ \begin{array}{l} \\ \\ \text{plouf} \end{array} \right.
$$

During the journey itself, yet another stroke is used. "Cruising
stoke," Lévi-Straus notes, "a dip, followed by an empty return, each
time followed by a beat to the side of the canoe," to which he adds
another diagram:

$$
\left\{ \begin{array}{l} \text{tra} \quad \text{tra} \\ \quad - \text{ tra } - \text{ tra } - \text{ tra } - \\ \text{plouf} \end{array} \right.
\qquad
\left\{ \begin{array}{l} \\ - \text{ tra } - \text{ tra}-\text{tra}- \\ \text{plouf} \end{array} \right.
$$

Finally, Lévi-Strauss notes the color of each face of the paddle: orange
and blue. One may say of both Flaubert's and Lévi-Strauss's descriptive passages what Lévi-Strauss says about classificatory systems,
namely that they aim to "exhaust" the real by means of a finite set
of classes. It is the very attentiveness to detail, the will to note down
even that which seems insignificant—a knot, a hand gesture—that
betrays the ambition to reconstruct a total world and to assign to each
of its components, however small, a place within it.

It was perhaps a description similar to that of the oarsman cited
above that Lévi-Strauss had in mind when, some twenty years later,
he inserted another description in *Tristes tropiques*, also taken from
his notebooks: that of a sunset. He prefaced it as follows:

> I felt that if I could find the right words to describe these ever chang-
> ing phenomena, if I could communicate to others the character of an
> event that was never twice the same, then I should have penetrated—
> or so I felt—to the inmost secrets of my profession: bizarre and pecu-
> liar as might be the experiences to which I should be subject in my
> career as an anthropologist, I could be sure of putting them, and their
> implications, at the disposal of the common reader.[14]

Both the description of the sunset and of the oarsman's gestures attempt to capture phenomena that are evanescent by nature—the fluid

14. Lévi-Strauss, *Tristes Tropiques*, 66.

gestures, on the one hand, the ever changing effects of light, on the other. These descriptions track a world of microscopic events that seem to defy linguistic expression, but that the anthropologist manages both to accurately record and to render in their essential articulations. The open ended, transient nature of the phenomenon is contained within a closed structure—a process with a beginning, middle and end. Yet, when the notebooks are examined more closely, the story they tell about the relationship of field work to the descriptive enterprise reveals itself to be more ambiguous and problematic than I have just suggested. It is these ambiguities and problems that are the most revealing of the intellectual project to come, for they bring to light the relationship between the early field notes and what would later become structural anthropology.

If, on the one hand, the notebooks manifest a totalizing ambition inherent in anthropology, they also clearly bear the signs of the failure of that ambition. What strikes the reader is the endless proliferation of descriptive styles and modes, as if each taken on its own is always insufficient in expressing the field experience. The result is a truly multisensory ethnography, one that captures experiences through language, through visual means and, by virtue of the numerous musical notations, through auditory experience. While most of the notebooks are peppered with staves of music that capture snippets heard here and there, the second "Tupi" notebook transcribes over some thirty or so uninterrupted pages the entire score of *The Farce of the Japim Bird*, a sort of Amerindian operetta that was sung over two nights by a Tupi chief (it is described in *Tristes tropiques*). It is among the most revealing moments of the notebooks precisely because it highlights what is so distinctive about them, namely their fluid espousal of experience. Through their endlessly shifting means of transcription, the notebooks mold themselves as closely as possible to the lived moment. The result is that each form of notation, each style of description, has the quality of something *tried out*. It is as if Lévi-Strauss was experimenting with the best means of capturing reality, the best way of approaching lived experience, which is also to say of grasping a multiplicity of perceptible worlds. It is this endless experimentation with languages that reveals to what extent the relationship between the observing individual and the reality he/she observes is problematic for the anthropologist.

The description of a sunset mentioned above captures the essence of the problem Lévi-Strauss confronted after his field work. It is a key text for any understanding of Lévi-Strauss's works, not least of all because it has accompanied their development, acquired different senses over time, and provided something like a mirror image of them.[15] The sunset presents the image of a phenomenon that is at once particularly complex and ever-changing, one that the anthropologist must nevertheless try to grasp. It is also a vanishing phenomenon (the entropic dissolution of the anthropologist's object of study is one of the guiding metaphors of structural anthropology). As has been recently argued, the gesture of inserting this page from the notebooks in the later work is paradoxical: it exhibits the earlier literary endeavor (the passage was supposed to constitute the opening pages of the novel that Lévi-Strauss never wrote), while signifying that it has been cast aside.[16] But what it also points toward—displays while casting aside—is the mode of description, the approach to the perceptible world, *against which* structural anthropology constituted itself.[17] The description of a sunset is far from being one of a kind. The notebooks display a recurrent interest in atmospheric phenomena and processes. Lévi-Strauss clearly has a penchant for the genre of the meteorological description, a sub-category of the landscape description. Some are more memorable than others. The evocation of rainfall over São Paulo, which would also find its way into *Tristes tropiques*, although not in the form of a citation, stands out as a high point. It begins: "[In São Paulo] in January, the rain does not 'arrive'; it emerges spontaneously from the dampness that pervades the city."[18] This evocation of rainfall condenses the exoticism of São Paulo into its peculiar rain cycles, giving an immediate, sensual expression to the feeling of *dépaysement*.

What are the features that characterize the genre of the meteorological description, as practiced by Lévi-Strauss? These descriptions are all, first of all, written at moments close to or simultaneous with the events or processes they describe. (The description of the sunset

15. See Lévi-Strauss and Boris Wiseman, "Le coucher de soleil," *Les temps modernes* 628 (2004): 2–18 (7–8).

16. Debaene, *L'adieu*, 322.

17. According to Debaene's reading, the description of the sunset, once cited, provides a model for "a possible and successful union of the perceptible and the intelligible" (Debaene, *L'adieu*, 309). From my point of view, such a "union" had not yet occurred at the time of the writing of *Tristes tropiques*, although its possibility is glimpsed later in this text, and the means by which it will be effected still remain to be found.

18. Lévi-Strauss, *Tristes tropiques*, 103.

was drawn, as it were, from life, on the deck of the ship on which Lévi-Strauss stood while observing it.) They are therefore firmly anchored in the experiences of an observer. In other words, they have a distinct first-person quality to them. The observer is, furthermore, essentially a passive onlooker, taking in the landscape, and therefore also free to inspect his own impressions or states of mind, which are brought to the fore, as is the case, for example, in this excerpt from the sunset description:

> A light swell had set her [the ship] rolling, and with each oscillation the heat had become more apparent, but the change of course was so small that one might have mistaken the change of direction for a slight increase in the ship's rolling. Nobody had paid any attention to it, for nothing is so much like a transfer in geometry as a passage on the high seas. There is no landscape to point up the transition from one latitude to the next.[19]

So much so that the illusions of subjectivity are often substituted for external reality. Unable to measure their progress against a changing landscape, the passengers on the boat feel immobile. The description captures well what some might call the form of an experience.

When Lévi-Strauss goes on to cite the description of the sunset in 1955, presenting it as a model of the kind of problem with which the anthropologist is faced, he does indeed change the meaning of the description, as Debaene suggests. What now comes to the fore is the analysis whereby the anthropologist attempts to bring to light and communicate to others the recurring "articulations" and "phases" of an event previously thought to be unique. The phenomenon of the sunset has now become a problematic threshold the anthropologist must cross in order to arrive at intelligibility. The author of *Tristes tropiques* now looks upon the descriptive confidence of his younger self with doubt and skepticism. Thus the description of a sunset cited in *Tristes tropiques*, and the many other meteorological processes that fascinate the Lévi-Strauss of the field notes, may now be seen for what they are: multiple allegories of the very motif of appearance.[20] It is no coincidence that the first illuminations cast by the setting sun in the passage cited in *Tristes tropiques* are compared to the sudden

19. Ibid., 68.
20. The conversion of a lived experience into allegory is a recurring feature of *Tristes tropiques*, as the well-known "writing lesson" illustrates.

illuminations that "instead of the traditional three knocks," indicate, in certain theaters, the beginning of the show. The spectacle of the sunset, we are told, is a "phantasmagoria." With this description, we are literally and metaphorically in the phenomenon, a phenomenon that Lévi-Strauss will have to exorcise before moving on to a different conception and approach to the perceptible world.[21]

What is missing from the description of the sunset for it to qualify as proto-structural is a synthesis of experience that Lévi-Strauss owes, in part at least, to Baudelaire.[22] It may be argued that no description can be structural in the strict sense of the term; only a certain type of analysis, one that requires at least two objects in a relationship of transformation, can be termed "structural." While this is true, Baudelaire's music criticism does indeed provide us with a sort of montage of a series of descriptions which, once put together, start to point the way toward such an analysis. Nothing resembles more the abstract world of transforming shapes and colors captured in a sunset over the Caribbean Sea than the descriptions of Wagner's music in Baudelaire's famous 1861 essay "Richard Wagner et *Tannhäuser* à Paris."[23] Baudelaire compares three separate evocations of the overture to Wagner's *Lohengrin*: the description of the overture in the 1860 program of the *Théatre-Italien*, where the piece was first performed in front of a French audience; an evocation of the same piece of music by the pianist, composer, and champion of Wagnerism, Franz Liszt;

21. Debaene is right to say that *Tristes tropiques* is at once "a farewell to phenomenology and to the mode of narration particular to it" (*L'adieu*, 309). The modalities of this "farewell" are what interest me here, as well as Lévi-Strauss's subsequent development.

22. Lévi-Strauss's familiarity with Baudelaire goes back at least to the 1940s. "Indian Cosmetics" *VVV* 1: 33–35 (1942), whose title alludes to "Éloge du maquillage" in Baudelaire's *Painter of Modern Life*, is steeped in Baudelairian conceptions of the relations between nature and artifice. Baudelaire undoubtedly influenced Lévi-Strauss's use of the nature/culture dichotomy. Lévi-Strauss grew up in a Paris that was still that of the post-Symbolists. References to Baudelaire and the Symbolists are no less present in the works of the Surrealists whom Lévi-Strauss frequented while in New York in the 1940's.

23. Debaene uncovers a different intertext. He focuses on the practice of self-citation and draws a parallel to a similar device in Proust's *Du côté de chez Swann* (the description of the bell towers at Martinville and Vieuxvicq is similarly presented by the narrator as a fragment written many years earlier, which is later inserted in the narrative in the form of a quotation). For Debaene, Lévi-Strauss's insertion of the description of the sunset is a way of marking the difference between his two, consecutive ways of seeing the journey: as Conradian quest and as Proustian reminiscence.

and Baudelaire's own "rêverie." Let us cite a few lines from Liszt's evocation:

> [Wagner] introduces us to the Holy Grail; we are made to see glimmering before our eyes the temple of incorruptible wood, with its sweet-smelling walls, its doors of *gold*, its joists of *asbestos*, its columns of *opal*, its partitions of *cymophane*, and its splendid porticoes, which may only be approached by those whose hearts are uplifted and whose hands pure. [. . .] He shows it first of all reflected in some *azure wave* or mirrored by some *iridescent cloud*. At the beginning it is a vast, *slumbering lake* of melody, a *vaporous, extending ether*, on which the holy picture may take form before our profane eyes . . . The horns and the bassoons join in to prepare for the entrance of the trumpets and the trombones which repeat the melody [. . .] *with a dazzling burst of color*, as if at this unique moment the holy edifice had *blazed forth* before our *blinded eyes*, in *all its radiant and luminous magnificence*. But the vivid sparkle which has been gradually raised to this *intensity of solar effulgence* dies away swiftly, like a *celestial glimmer*. [24]

The description of the sunset and the above evocation of Wagner's overture plunge us into worlds that cannot easily be grasped in structural terms and that challenge structuralism's modes of analysis. (Ravel's *Bolero*, analyzed at length in *L'homme nu*, provides the counter example of an eminently structural piece of music.) These are worlds of varying *intensities*, whose increases and decreases form *continuous* movements that seem impermeable to any kind of systematization. As Gilles Deleuze suggests in his analyses of German Expressionist cinema, which uses light as a "potent movement of intensity,"[25] variations in intensity cannot be localized. The structural imaginary, however, is essentially spatial. Even if it is possible to determine the points *between which* a change in intensity occurs, the change itself cannot be grasped, except by converting it into something else, into an extensive quantity, for example the *height* of mercury in a thermometer.[26] Opposition loses its sway over the analytic process: "Light and shadow [in German Expressionist cinema] no longer con-

---

24. Quoted in Charles Baudelaire, *The Painter of Modern Life and Other Essays*, trans. Jonathan Mayne (New York: Da Capo, 1964), 115 (original emphasis).

25. Gilles Deleuze, *Cinema 1: The Movement-Image*, trans. Hugh Tomlinson and Barbara Habberjam (Minneapolis: University of Minnesota Press, 1986), 49.

26. Deleuze, seminar of 17/11/81. "La voix de Gilles Deleuze en ligne" (<*http://www2.univ-paris8.fr/deleuze/*> accessed November 6, 2011).

stitute an alternative movement in extension and enter into an intense struggle which has several stages."[27]

Nevertheless, Wagner's overture and Baudelaire's meditations on it will provide Lévi-Strauss both with a model for understanding primitive mythology and with a theory of signification.[28] Baudelaire notices that, though unique, the three sets of impressions provoked by Wagner's overture share a number of common features. All three listeners describe a feeling of spiritual and physical beatitude, an impression of isolation, a sense of something infinitely vast and infinitely beautiful. All three accounts evoke the same vision of intense light and the sense of space extending as far as can be conceived.[29] In other words, music—or *true* music, to use Baudelaire's qualifier—suggests "analogous ideas in different brains."[30] (The phrase is cited by Lévi-Strauss in the "Overture" to the *Mythologiques*.) It does so, Lévi-Strauss will later suggest—by way of a late reply to Baudelaire, in a passage that explicitly connects his own theory of myth to Baudelaire's theory of music—because it mobilizes "shared mental structures."[31] It is this synthesis of experience that for Baudelaire, and for Lévi-Strauss after him, enables one to rescue music from the multiplicity of individual experiences it generates, and to confer upon it the ability to "translate ideas," as Baudelaire puts it. Approximately one hundred years later, Lévi-Strauss articulated a program for anthropology that seemed to abstract its general principle of analysis from the theory of musical intelligibility put forward by Baudelaire in his essay on Wagner. Indeed, the underlying aim of the structural method, Lévi-Strauss would often repeat, is to uncover the unchanging relationships between the elements of a transforming cultural system. What matters in the present context is that the analysis of these transformations (which allows the passage from one level of analysis to another) is the means of an archaeology. I am using the term "archaeology" here in a sense close to that which Michel Foucault gives it but extending its relevance. Lévi-Strauss's archaeology no longer designates solely the

27. Deleuze, *The Movement-Image*, 49.

28. The *Mythologiques*, ultimately, tell the story of an "intensive fall" of the kind that Deleuze associates with Expressionist cinema, that of the progressive decline of oppositional thinking and, ultimately, that of the death of mythical thought.

29. Baudelaire, Pléiade II, 785.

30. Ibid., 784.

31. Claude Lévi-Strauss, *The Raw and the Cooked*, trans. John and Doreen Weightman (London: Penguin, 1964), 26.

excavation of systems of *conceptual* possibilities underpinning discursive formations, but also that of a material context and a physical environment, which have their own history as well.

AFTER THE RETURN

It was gift theory, transformed in the light of Jakobsonian linguistics, that was to provide Lévi-Strauss with the means of developing this archaeological perspective into a broader intellectual project. Having fled Nazi Europe for New York, Lévi-Strauss found himself attending Jakobson's classes at the New School for Social Research while simultaneously working on his PhD dissertation on kinship at the New York Public Library. This fortuitous conjunction was to lead to a series of then daring cross-disciplinary connections, which opened new intellectual horizons, and not only for Lévi-Strauss and anthropology. He came to realize that kinship systems, considered from a formal point of view, presented striking similarities to the phonological systems that underpin natural languages. By taking up the models of structural linguistics and applying them to kinship, Lévi-Strauss was able to effect a passage from one level of observation to another and bring to light the small number of recurring patterns of exchange underlying the wealth of observed customs and kinship nomenclatures. He was later able to construct abstract models of a small number of "elementary" patterns of kinship exchange by using set theory, which he applied to his data with the help of the mathematician André Weil. In doing so, he confirmed the validity of an approach that favored a vertical exploration of phenomena, one to which Lévi-Strauss's subsequent works would essentially remain faithful. These later works explore its ramifications through the study of a series of interconnected problems: classification, mythical invention, social structure, plastic art, and so on. My aim here is not to retrace the stages in the development of Lévi-Strauss's thought, which has already been done, including by Lévi-Strauss, but to point out the underlying unity given to his project by this archaeological bias.

The preparatory notes for *La pensée sauvage* (1962) tell a story similar to that of his formative years in New York. These notes are written on a series of loose sheets, a mix of salvaged materials— letter-head paper, printouts of daily radio programs on France 2, the flip side of a flyer announcing the broadcasting of a play by Musset, even a metro ticket. The notes contain plans for various sections of

La pensée sauvage, numerous tables and diagrams, bibliographic references, and the first formulations of a number of key passages that would later be integrated, sometimes more or less unmodified, into the finished work. What comes to the fore when one examines these materials is the almost physical process of grappling with the empirical data. The proliferation of charts, diagrams, and quotations reveals the tremendous effort involved in pooling together a vast quantity of material culled from numerous sources, and the patient work of then excavating them. Sheet 6 in the folder entitled "The Logic of Totemic Classifications" and headed "Concrete Logic," reads as follows:

I. Multiplicity of axes = logic with several values. Relations can be =

a) contiguous = grass / termitarium (luapula) proximity
   resemblance = red ants / snakes (Nuer) = color
b) superficial = bee /python (Nuer) = concentric rings on body
   deep = bee / canoe-man (Australia) : 'makers'
c) perceptible = squirrel /cider (Ojibwa)
   intellectual = elephant / eagle (Mapula ?)
d) static = [crossed out]
   dynamic = rain rusting metal, metal killing animals.[32]

This sheet, with its four pairs of logical connectors, shows Lévi-Strauss trying to establish the dimensions (terms, operations) of a particular instance of "concrete logic" at work. If one compares the limited dimensions of the symbolic system laid bare here with the greater complexity of those analyzed in the four volumes of *Mythologiques,* it becomes apparent that the ethnographic materials provided by classificatory systems did not allow Lévi-Strauss to do justice to the new kind of logic that he had intuited—although the merit of his work on totemic classifications is to have isolated the distinctive operation made possible by the use of the species as a logical operator. This may be in part due to the fact that classificatory systems, especially totemic, are more directly tied to external empirical contents, such as demographic variations. Despite this, one can see how each table provides Lévi-Strauss with the samples that he worked on.

At the bottom of the same sheet Lévi-Strauss jotted down a four-term chart showing associations in Hanunoo color categories. This

32. My translation.

chart, like the diagram evoked above, is not something added to the manuscript at a later stage, by way of an illustration, but the means of an operation. Needless to say, I cannot share Adam Shatz's view that the diagrams of structural anthropology "now look like relics of some mid-twentieth-century technocratic fantasy."[33] They are the tools used to dismantle symbolic systems to try to determine the cognitive operations that these systems at once presuppose and allow. They are essential to what Lévi-Strauss sets out to do in *La pensée sauvage* and elsewhere; they are at the root of his archaeological approach to the perceptible. Along with the 3-D mobiles that Lévi-Strauss would later use to model mythical transformations, and the many versions of his "canonical equation," they reflect a constant endeavor: that of giving their proper dimensions to the mental operations charted by structural anthropology. Here too, as in the field notes, Lévi-Strauss seems to proceed experimentally, to borrow philosopher Claude Imbert's phrase (see below), seeking out in each case the language best suited to grasping his materials. The vast enterprise of the *Mythologiques* proceeds, similarly, by a series of excavations—in Lévi-Strauss's vocabulary: "levers en rosace" (they follow the contours of a rosette). The engagement with the ready-to-hand materials comes first, which is why Lévi-Strauss comments that the myths he analyzes will themselves dictate the order of his exposition. Here as elsewhere he remains confident that reality will serve as his guide.

The relevance of such an enterprise to the current anthropological debate is brought into focus by a chapter in a late work by Lévi-Strauss, *Look, Listen, Read* (1993), a book that offers a striking modern continuation of the salon genre of art criticism. The book contains, among many other things, a series of excursions into literary criticism that intertwine literary and anthropological concerns in revealing ways. One of them is devoted to Rimbaud's famous synaesthetic sonnet, "Voyelles" (1871). Beyond the immediate problem discussed in this chapter, that of colored audition, Lévi-Strauss's analysis provides a valuable model of how to integrate the findings of neuroscience into an anthropological understanding, a question of much concern today. Lévi-Strauss returns here to an hypothesis already put forward in *Tristes tropiques*, in 1955, namely, that the basis of colored audition is not to be found in one-to-one correlations between sounds

33. Adam Shatz, "Jottings, Scraps and Doodles," *London Review of Books*, November 3, 2011: 3.

and colors, but in an unconscious comparison between two sets of differences: those between the colors of the chromatic scale and those between the phonemes of a language. His argument is that the mind apprehends these sets of differences as similar and mounts them together, as it were. Thus, for the poet, if A is black and E white, it is because the opposition between A (the most highly chromatic of vowel sounds) and E (the least chromatic—it is frequently rendered as schwa or mute "e"), constitutes the maximal opposition possible within the French vowel system, just as black and white constitute the maximal opposition within the color spectrum. Lévi-Strauss goes on to argue that the other instances of colored audition evoked by Rimbaud similarly connect contrasting pairs of sounds and colors, and do so in a way that follows the neurophysiology of visual processes. Indeed, the experience of color is dependent on photoreceptors contained in the retina that process wavelengths into three independent channels. The first is sensitive to the opposition between light and dark, the second to that between red and green, and third to that between blue and yellow. Together, these three channels are responsible for generating the data that the brain processes as the experience of color. It is precisely these three oppositions that are functional in Rimbaud's poem. Rimbaud, in short, has matched pairs of vowel sounds with the opposing colors, which, neuroscience tells us, are constitutive of visual experience. He intuits the importance not only of the two chromatic codings of our "color space"[34] but also of another, more archaic or elemental coding, that of luminance. Lévi-Strauss is interested in the sonnet's "architecture"[35] and the cognitive basis of that architecture, which he tries to unravel by resorting to the neuroscience of color perception. Where his use of neuroscience differs from that of much reductionist neuro-aesthetics is in the very particular place he assigns to physiology and the brain. Herein lies the interest of Lévi-Strauss's interpretation. Paradoxically, the understanding of how we all pro-

34. Thomas D. Albright, "Color and the integration of motion signals," *Trends in Neuroscience* 14.7 (1991), 266–69. See figure 2, 268, for a diagram of color-space. The expression is to be understood in a literal sense. As Albright explains: "perceivable colors can be uniquely defined by their relative activation of the three channels. They can thus be described by single points in a three-dimensional color-space in which the three channels form the principal or 'cardinal' axes. [. . .] The azimuth and elevation of any point measured relative to the origin of this space identify the familiar attributes of hue and brightness" (ibid., 267).

35. Lévi-Strauss, *Look, Listen, Read*, trans. Brian C. J. Singer (New York: Basic Books, 1997), 135.

cess color is a way of grasping what is unique about Rimbaud's poetic relationship to color. For Rimbaud's "poetic verb accessible to all the senses"[36] favors one channel of color processing over the two others: "It would thus seem that Rimbaud's visual sensibility gave the advantage to luminance over chromatism."[37]

Rimbaud resembles, in this respect, the Japanese, who similarly privilege the opposition between black and white, at least in their color terminology, over chromatic differences. The synaesthesia of Rimbaud's sonnet is the result of the combination of two cognitive maps: the map of colors and of the sounds of the French language. The maps themselves are rooted in physiology and neurology as well as the contents given to those maps by a particular culture (the phonological oppositions that underpin French are different from those that underpin English, just as French color perception has a cultural dimension). However, Rimbaud found a way of assembling these maps in an unusual way and of using that assemblage as an element in his poetic innovation. Lévi-Strauss's argument retraces, retrospectively, the processes whereby the sonnet "Voyelles" came into being, uncovering successive levels of organization, and trying to determine how each one is related to the next. Neuroscience and physiology allow another step in the archaeological process; they provide the means of extending it to yet another level of organization. However, they do not provide a final cause for the poem but a set of parameters within which Rimbaud was constrained to work. Lévi-Strauss's exploration of neuroscience is tantamount to an exploration of possible worlds which, unlike Leibnitz's possible worlds, are not infinite, but are on the contrary limited fields. Rimbaud's poem actualizes one set of possible relations between sound and sense. In doing so, Rimbaud sets himself apart from earlier generations of poets, such as the Parnassians, who had largely ignored such relations, and from other synaesthetically aware poets, who were perhaps more chromatically minded than he was.

The story I take away from my reading of Lévi-Strauss's field notes and of how they fit into Lévi-Strauss's later works, in particular *Tristes tropiques*, is that of a series of experiments with multiple

36. "Verbe poétique accessible [. . .] à tous les sens" (Arthur Rimbaud, *Œuvres* [Paris: Classique Garnier, 1981, 228]). My translation).
37. Lévi-Strauss, *Look, Listen, Read*, 135.

languages. I am taking my cue, here, in part from Imbert's suggestive readings of Lévi-Strauss's work. Imbert sees Lévi-Strauss as a sort of successor to Cavaillès, whose mathematics broke with previous ways of thinking and of formalizing thought by instigating what he termed a "fundamental experiment of thought."[38] The expression is paradoxical and evokes the a posteriori logic brought to light in *La pensée sauvage*. Cavaillès's originality lay in the way he "tried out new ways of thinking."[39] It is experimentation of this kind that one finds in the field notes, which for this reason cannot be reduced to "jottings, scraps and doodles," except in the most superficial of readings.[40] The anthropologist's later works do not depart from this mode of anthropological inquiry; what differs is the complexity and sophistication of the languages Lévi-Strauss explores.

One might think of Lévi-Strauss's experiments by analogy with another kind of experimentation, the one described by Émile Zola in his naturalist manifesto, *Le roman experimental* (1881). Like the novelist, the anthropologist starts from observations and facts, and then conducts an experiment of sorts. Just as in Honoré de Balzac's *La Cousine Bette*, the baron Hulot is made to go through a series of trials and tribulations designed to reveal "the functioning of the mechanism of his passion,"[41] the anthropologist submits the data collected from various sources to a series of operations—his "trials and tribulations." These consist essentially in the arranging and rearranging of transformational groups, the trying out of combinatorial variations, a process that draws on various kinds of formalization as well as on a writing process, both inherent to the experiment. These processes reveal the functioning of mechanisms that are symbolic, cognitive, or sensory rather than "passionate." What replaces the twists and turns in the novelist's plot is the anthropologist's quest for a symbolic language and a syntax adequate to the reconstitution of experience.

38. For a discussion of this notion, see Claude Imbert, "An Interview with Claude Imbert," *Paragraph* 34/2 (2011): 158–66.
39. Ibid, 159. As Imbert points out, the phrase "fundamental experiment of thought" was subsequently reused by Merleau-Ponty and Foucault.
40. Adam Shatz, "Jottings, Scraps and Doodles." The phrase was first used to describe Lévi-Strauss's notebooks by Patrick Wilken's in *Claude Lévi-Strauss: The Poet in the Laboratory* (London: Bloomsbury, 2011).
41. Émile Zola, *Le roman expérimental* (Paris: Éditions du Sandre, 2003), 15 (my translation).

At another level, the story told by the field notes is that of the rejection of an approach to describing the real that is phenomenal, or perhaps phenomenological, which I take to be Lévi-Strauss's way of preparing the ground for his own distinctive structural approach. The latter locates the production of meaning in "stratigraphies," to borrow a term from field archaeology. It attains intelligibility at a level beyond or beneath the experiences of the perceiving subject: that of anonymous social structures, shared and collectively produced symbolic systems, mental operations that belong to everyone and no one. Immediately after his return from his second field trip in the winter of 1939, Lévi-Strauss started work on a novel whose opening pages were going to be the description of a sunset (discussed above), his model of the phenomenal description. The novel was already, at that point, a split-off part from the rest of his ethnographic work.[42]

TOUCANS AND ARARAS

There is, in fact, in the notebook entitled "Campos Novos," which covers the second half of August 1938, a brief passage, no more than a few lines long, that provides a striking early glimpse of the new and original approach to the phenomenon and to anthropological understanding that I have outlined here. It is worth citing, since it poses with particular acuity (perhaps because it captures an idea in the making) a key question for current anthropology, that of the nature of the human relationship to the sensorium. Lévi-Strauss notes:

> Little problem to be studied = toucan area, arara area. I get the impression that there is a geographical area of Amazonia defined by the presence of the toucan + [black?] feathers of the type belonging to the mutum[43] and a central area (but that probably extends to the Antilles) defined by the arara and the feathers of large birds (wading birds/predators).[44]

In the margin, Lévi-Strauss has drawn a rough map of South America and indicated the boundaries of the two zones, marking out the first with forward hatchings, the second with horizontal lines. The brief note goes on to speculate about the Manduca, who use arara feathers, but seem to attach only a secondary significance to them. Lévi-

42. This bifurcation is no doubt bound up with a choice between literature and science, which Vincent Debaene explores at length in *L'adieu au voyage*.
43. Otherwise known as the Red-knobbed Curassow or Red-billed Curassowand.
44. My translation.

Strauss immediately recognizes that the geographical distribution of feather types has technological implications. Each type of feather allows certain kinds of artifacts to be made while excluding others. Toucan feathers, for example, can be used only for relatively small artifacts, while arara feathers permit more monumental constructions. In other words, the feathers lend a style to the material culture developed by the populations using them. Lévi-Strauss interrupts his fertile line of thought without pursuing the more radical shift in understanding it calls for. The implications of this passage start to emerge when one revisits it in the light of Lévi-Strauss's later works. Lévi-Strauss is in effect imagining here—or inviting us to imagine — a map whose distribution of space depends on a pair of birds and the types of feathers they possess. This map orders the world according to a small number of contrasting qualitative differences apprehended directly in nature, those between the small, black feathers of the toucan and mutum and the larger, brighter feathers of the arara. These differences, similar to those that would later form the basis of a series of styles of Northwest coast masks (see *The Way of the Masks*), have been extracted from the natural world—taken away from the phenomenon, as it were—and recycled for another purpose, that of figuring the limits not of a physical territory but of an imagined community—an inhabitable cultural space. In the process, the sensorium has acquired new dimensions and new depth. It has started to resonate culturally.

This simple map goes to the core of the program of structural anthropology. It draws in dotted lines the place of a future logic of perceptible qualities, a concept that would be put forward in 1962 in the *La pensée sauvage*. It points in the direction of a creative mode of thought rooted in the exploration of the qualitative dimensions of things and of a form of symbolism that uses natural species because they are "good to think with." Imbert has amply developed the philosophical (cognitive, aesthetic) implications of this qualitative mode of thought, in particular in her *Lévi-Strauss, le passage du nord-ouest*.[45]

*   *   *

Differences apprehended in nature have already become, in the brief passage from the notebooks cited above, the means of articulating

45. Imbert, *Lévi-Strauss, le passage du nord-ouest* (Paris: L'Herne, 2008).

other kinds of differences that are, on this occasion, spatial, and which will later be social, moral, metaphysical, and so on. Whether or not Lévi-Strauss's intuition about toucans and araras is verified empirically is less significant than the progress made by his hypothesis. In this brief note-to-self, Lévi-Strauss has grasped something of the importance of the qualitative dimensions of experience for indigenous world-making. "Qualia clusters," as Imbert calls them, peeled away from the things to which they once adhered, have acquired sufficient autonomy to serve as the supports of something else. Lévi-Strauss's ruminations—which were jotted down shortly before the outbreak of World War II, when modern French anthropology, still in its infancy, was seeking out its modes of inquiry and understanding—place the "savages" he encountered in a space very different from the scalar and geometric space of the cartographer. And very different from the notion of space implicit in the ethnography of the day. It is the "qualitative space" later evoked in *Tristes tropiques* ("space has values peculiar to itself, just as sounds and scents have their colors and feelings their weight").[46] It proceeds not from the projection of the world of experience onto a two-dimensional surface, as does the cartographic imagination, but from a preexisting distribution of colors and forms (we are close, here, to Jacques Rancière's "partage du sensible"—his distribution of the perceptible world). None of this is expressed in the passage from the notebooks cited above, but one can easily see how Lévi-Strauss's "little problem to be studied" could be developed into a more complex anthropological model of the kind that underpins key later works, such as *La pensée sauvage* and the *Mythologiques*, a model in which qualitative differences apprehended in the perceptible world are used as the basis for a form of world-making (or mapmaking). Although speculative and schematic, the passage is a first step toward a structural understanding of the human relationship to the sensorium.

46. Lévi-Strauss, *Tristes tropiques*, 126.

Contributors

JONATHAN CULLER is Class of 1916 Professor of English and Comparative Literature at Cornell University, and a member of the American Academy of Arts and Sciences. His *Structuralist Poetics: Structuralism, Linguistics, and the Study of Literature* (1975) was awarded the MLA's James Russell Lowell Prize and has been widely translated. His other books include: *Flaubert: The Uses of Uncertainty* (1974, 1985), *Ferdinand de Saussure* (1976, 1986), *The Pursuit of Signs: Semiotics, Literature, Deconstruction* (1981), *On Deconstruction: Theory and Criticism after Structuralism* (1982), *Roland Barthes* (1983), *Literary Theory: A Very Short Introduction* (1997), *Roland Barthes: A Very Short Introduction* (2001), and *The Literary in Theory* (2006). His current book project is entitled *Theory of the Lyric*.

VINCENT DEBAENE is Associate Professor of French at Columbia University. He is the author of *L'adieu au voyage* (2010) and, with Frédéric Keck, of the intellectual biography *Claude Lévi-Strauss. L'Homme au regard éloigné* (2009). He edited and supervised the critical edition of the works of Lévi-Strauss for the Bibliothèque de la Pléiade series (2008). Principal teaching and research interests include French anthropology, twentieth-century French literature, literary theory, intellectual history, and the points of contact between scientific discourses and literature. His current book project is a study of the engagement of early Francophone writers and intellectuals with anthropological knowledge during the colonial period.

ROBERT DORAN is James P. Wilmot Assistant Professor of French and Comparative Literature at the University of Rochester. He also taught for three years at Middlebury College as Visiting Assistant Professor of French. He specializes in nineteenth-century French literature, aesthetic theory, and continental philosophy, and has edited three books: *Mimesis and Theory: Essays on Literature and Criticism, 1953–2005*, by René Girard (2008), *The Fiction of Narrative: Essays on History, Literature, and Theory, 1957–2007*, by Hayden White (2010), and *Philosophy of History After Hayden White* (2013). He is also the editor of a special issue of

YFS 123, *Rethinking Claude Lévi-Strauss (1908–2009)*, ed. Doran, © 2013 by Yale University.

SubStance, "Cultural Theory after 9/11: Terror, Religion, Media" (2008). His book manuscript, *The Theory of the Sublime from Longinus to Kant*, is under review.

MARCEL HÉNAFF is a philosopher and an anthropologist who teaches in the political science and literature departments at the University of California, San Diego. Three of his major books have been translated into English: *Sade, the Invention of the Libertine Body* (1999), *Claude Lévi-Strauss and the Making of Structural Anthropology* (1998), and *The Price of Truth: Gift, Money, and Philosophy* (2010), which won the Grand Prize of Philosophy from the Académie Française. His recent work includes: *Lévi-Strauss. Le passeur de sens* (2008), *La ville qui vient* (2008), and *Le don des philosophes. Repenser la réciprocité* (2012).

ELEANOR KAUFMAN is Professor of Comparative Literature, English, and French and Francophone Studies at UCLA. She is the author of *The Delirium of Praise: Bataille, Blanchot, Deleuze, Foucault, Klossowski* (2001), *Deleuze, the Dark Precursor: Dialectic, Structure, Being* (2012), and *At Odds with Badiou: Politics, Dialectics, and Religion from Sartre and Deleuze to Lacan and Agamben* (forthcoming). She is the co-editor of *Deleuze and Guattari: New Mappings in Politics, Philosophy, and Culture* (1998). Her current book project is entitled *The Jewry of the Plain*, which is simultaneously an exploration of the archives, museums, and cemeteries that commemorate late nineteenth-century Jewish settlements in remote regions of the American West and a meditation on the work of Jacques Derrida.

FRANÇOISE LIONNET is Professor of French and Francophone Studies and Comparative Literature, and Director of African Studies at UCLA. Her most recent publications include *The Creolization of Theory* (2011), and a two-volume project on the Indian Ocean: *Writing Women and Critical Dialogues: Subjectivity, Gender and Irony* and *The Known and the Uncertain: Creole Cosmopolitics of the Indian Ocean*, both published in Mauritius in 2012. She is also the author of *Autobiographical Voices: Race, Gender, Self-Portraiture* (1989, 1991) and *Postcolonial Representations: Women, Literature, Identity* (1995).

THOMAS PAVEL is Gordon J. Laing Distinguished Service Professor in Romance Languages and Literature, Comparative Literature, and the Committee on Social Thought at the University of Chicago, and a member of the American Academy of Arts and Sciences. His *Fictional Worlds* (1986), *Le mirage linguistique* (1988), and *La pensée du roman* (2003) have been translated into several languages. He has also published *The Poetics of Plot: The Case of English Renaissance Drama* (1985), *L'art de l'éloignement: Essai sur l'imagination classique* (1996), *Comment écouter la littérature* (2006), and, with Claude Bremond, *De Barthes à Balzac: Fictions d'un critique et critiques d'une fiction* (1998). The English version of *La pensée du roman*, a history of the novel, is forthcoming from Princeton University Press in 2013.

JEAN-MICHEL RABATÉ is Professor of English and Comparative Literature and Vartan Gregorian Professor in the Humanities at the University of

Pennsylvania, and a member of the American Academy of Arts and Sciences. He is a managing editor of the *Journal of Modern Literature* and one of the founders and curators of the Slought Foundation in Philadelphia. He has authored or edited more than thirty books on modernism, psychoanalysis, contemporary art, and philosophy. His recent books include *Lacan literario: La experiencia de la letra* (2007), *1913: The Cradle of modernism* (2007), *Given: 1 Art 2 Crime: Modernity, Murder, and Mass Culture* (2007), and *The Ethics of the Lie* (2008). Currently, he is editing an anthology on modernism and literary theory, and completing a book on Beckett.

CAMILLE ROBCIS is Assistant Professor of European Intellectual History at Cornell University. She is the author of the forthcoming book *The Law of Kinship: Anthropology, Psychoanalysis, and the Family in France*. Her current book project explores the history of institutional psychotherapy after World War II, in France and abroad. Her other publications include: "How the Symbolic Became French: Kinship and Republicanism in the PACS Debates" (*Discourse*, 2004) and "French Sexual Politics from Human Rights to the Anthropological Function of the Law" (*French Historical Studies*, 2010).

CAROLINE VIAL is a Ph.D. candidate in comparative literary studies at Northwestern University. She holds a B.A. in philosophy and Italian from Middlebury College and an M.A. in Comparative Literature from the Sorbonne Nouvelle-Paris III and is currently spending a year at the École Normale Supérieure, rue d'Ulm in Paris. Her research focuses on the aesthetics and politics of decadence in the French novel and cinema of the late nineteenth and early twentieth centuries. She has published translations in *SubStance*, *Revue Théologique des Bernardins*, and *Éditions du Cerf* (forthcoming).

BORIS WISEMAN is Associate Professor of French and Francophone Studies at the University of Copenhagen. His research focuses on modern French thought and culture, from the nineteenth century to the present, and is centrally concerned with various forms of interdisciplinary connections. He is the author of *Lévi-Strauss, Anthropology and Aesthetics* (2007) and the editor of the *Cambridge Companion to Lévi-Strauss* (2009). He has recently co-edited the anthology *Chiasmus and Culture* (forthcoming) and a special issue of the journal *Paragraph* (2011) on the philosopher Claude Imbert. His current work is focused on the visualization of movement in nineteenth-century France.

Yale French Studies is the oldest English-language journal in the United States devoted to French and Francophone literature and culture. Each volume is conceived and organized by a guest editor or editors around a particular theme or author. Interdisciplinary approaches are particularly welcome, as are contributions from scholars and writers from around the world. Recent volumes have been devoted to a wide variety of subjects, among them: Levinas; Perec; Paulhan; Haiti; Belgium; Crime Fiction; Surrealism; Material Culture in Medieval and Renaissance France; and French Education.

Yale French Studies is published twice yearly by Yale University Press (yalebooks.com) and may be accessed on JSTOR (jstor.org).

For information on how to submit a proposal for a volume of *Yale French Studies*, visit yale.edu/french and click "Yale French Studies."